D1304255

VIKING FUND PUBLICATIONS IN ANTHROPOLOGY
edited by COLIN TURNBULL

Number Forty-Eight

THE WAHI WANYATURU
Economics in an African Society

The Wahi Wanyaturu

Economics in an African Society

by HAROLD K. SCHNEIDER

ALDINE PUBLISHING COMPANY / *Chicago*

Copyright © 1970 by

WENNER-GREN FOUNDATION
FOR ANTHROPOLOGICAL RESEARCH, INC.

First published 1970 by

ALDINE PUBLISHING COMPANY
529 South Wabash Avenue
Chicago, Illinois 60605

Library of Congress Catalog Card Number 70–102764
SBN 202–01074–1

Printed in the United States of America

PREFACE

T HIS book results from fifteen months of field work in two villages of the Wahi subtribe of the Wanyaturu in 1959 and 1960, while I lived adjacent to one and a mile from the other and was in close contact with the people almost every day. The experience was made possible by a grant for scientific research from the National Science Foundation, to whom grateful acknowledgment is made.

Much of the material in the book has been published elsewhere in different forms. Most of Chapter 5, on the market system, appeared in *Economic Transition in Africa*, edited by M. J. Herskovits and M. Harwitz; the essays, entitled "Economics in East African Aboriginal Society," were combined with some comparative material on other African societies possessing livestock. Portions of Chapter 2 and part of Chapter 3 appeared in *Africa* in July 1966 under the title "Turu Ecology: Habitat, Mode of Production and Society." Chapter 7 is substantially the same as an article called "People as Wealth in Turu Society," published in the *Southwestern Journal of Anthropology* in 1969.

Since the research was completed, Tanganyika has become Tanzania, reflecting other revolutionary changes, and most of the Europeans have left. Some of my African friends have died, and the fate of others is unknown because of the difficulties of maintaining communication. Conditions in Unyaturu have changed, and this book is therefore a measure of the Turu at the dawn of independence.

Field work is a highly personal as well as a scientific experience. To accomplish it one must depend on the cooperation of many people who only vaguely understand the aims and methods for whom true payment can only be to see the results of their aid published. This book is dedicated to these friends, African and European, some of whom have waited patiently for too many years to see the results of their help. I hope that it is of interest and relevance to them.

Among the Wanyaturu whose help I want especially to acknowledge are Lisu Musandi (whose name, like those that follow in this preface, I spell, for simplicity, in the English orthography), Petero Musandi, the rest of the sons of Musandai and Mwantui, the son of Lisu (who, I am told, was tragically killed several years ago by other young men of his village, just as he himself had previously murdered his father). In many ways these men, who were so kind to me, symbolize the violence that is so much a part of Turu life. I am honored to record also the help of Mujuu Lasika; Bula, or Mwajuma, daughter of Nyambi; Sakume Mos; Diu Munyankonde; Jumaine Mughwai; and Ihonde Chima.

Other than these people of the villages of Utatuu-Mumbi and Sunja, I owe thanks to former Chief Senge; Omari Munchori, one-time Secretary of the Turu Council; and last and most, Simon Idabu, presently of Community Development, who was my interpreter and assistant while I was in Singida District.

Among the Europeans who helped me I owe a debt to Philip Gulliver, who directed me to the Turu while he was government sociologist in Tanganyika; Ian Norton, who was district commissioner during the first part of my stay in Singida; Peter Johnston, who was provincial commissioner of the Central Province; David Owen-Pawson and Cyril Rolfe of the veterinary department, who were of special help because the research so importantly concerned itself with livestock; the Medical Missionaries of Mary at Makiungu, led by Sister Christina Hanley, who treated the wounds of my family and me, and notably Sister Mary Sybil Magan, who translated from the French and shared with me a handwritten volume called *The Rimi or Turu*, composed around 1915 by the White Fathers of St. Leo's Mission, Makiungu; the Reverend Howard Olson of the Augustana Lutheran Mission of Ihanja, whose invaluable unpublished works on Turu linguistics and proverbs were made available to me; and Mr. James LeBechee of the agricultural department of Singida. Lastly, I thank Miss Marguerite Jellicoe, who has worked with the Turu off and on for many years and whose anthropological interests have led her to learn much about the Turu that she has shared with me.

I thank also my wife, Carol, who accompanied me to the field, who endured the discomforts of sometimes living in a tent while caring for a small child, and who made many essential contributions to the work, including seeing that I was fed on schedule and kept healthy as well. Gratitude must also be expressed to my colleagues at Lawrence—William Schutte, John Bucklew, and James Dana—for help in preparing the manuscript.

Acknowledgments are of little interest to readers of a monograph. I hope mine will be endured so that I may permanently record my gratitude to the people I have named.

A NOTE ON ORTHOGRAPHY

THE orthography here used to represent the Turu language was developed by the Reverend Howard Olson. It is based on the International Phonetic Association alphabet, which Olson has had to alter slightly for his purposes. The main alteration is in the method of writing the upper back and front vowels and in the forms of certain consonants. For convenience, I have retained the more usual notations. These vowels are therefore written /I,i,U,u/ as in hit, heat, put, boot. Those consonants of which special note must be taken are the bilateral fricative /f/, the unvoiced and voiced uvular fricatives /x/ and /γ/ respectively, and the naso-velar /η/. I have written /č/ as /c/ wherever it occurs.

As might be expected, the spelling of certain place and proper names has been standardized by long government use, even though such use is phonetically unsystematic. Where this is so, as in *Unyanganyi* (which is properly *unyiηanyi*) or *Unyaturu* (which is properly *UnyatUrU*), I have used whichever form is proper to the context. In such unsystematic spelling, the upper vowels are indiscriminately written as *i* or *u*, while the consonants are written /γ/ as gh, the /x/ as kh, and the /η/ as ng.

The Turu language has only two tones, but no attempt has been made to indicate them in the book. Other than that, as in other Bantu languages, noun roots may vary their meaning by altering the prefixes. The Turu language has these important prefixes:

- *a*   Plural of living things (e.g. *a-rImi*, the people of Rimi).
- *mU*   Singular of living things (e.g. *mU-rImi*, a Rimi person).
- *kI*   The language (e.g. *kI-rImi*, the language of Rimi; the equivalent form in the writing of Swahili is *Kiswahili*).
- *U*   The country (e.g. *U-rImi* or *UnyatUrU*, the country of the Rimi or Nyaturu) or the process (e.g. *Uriha*, the loaning system, compared to *mUriha*, a person who has made a loan).

The forms Airwana, Mwirwana, Wilwana, or Vahi, Mwahi, Wahi are variants of the first, second, and fourth of the above, respectively.

For convenience I have taken to referring to the Nyaturu or Wanyaturu as Turu. Though this word has no meaning among the Turu, it has gained wide acceptance in Singida among English-speakers.

Finally, one class of nouns, which includes *mbUγa* (marsh) and *ηombe* (cattle), does not differentiate singular and plural by means of prefixes. The intended number, however, can be readily understood from the context.

CONTENTS

LIST OF PLATES AND MAPS

PLATES

MAPS

1. THE COMPETITIVE APPROACH
TO AFRICAN SOCIETY

Now I shall say why I think that individualism will outlive both the capitalist system and the present image of communal thinking, which the Communists take to be inherent in collectivism . . . I believe that the rejection of individualism and the emphasis of communal thinking as an ethical principle is most appropriate in the condition of poverty and danger.

ANATOLE RAPOPORT
Fights Games and Debates
(1961, 351)

IN 1959 in Tanzania, while I was studying the people of a village of the subtribe of Wahi in the country of the Turu (Unyaturu), I was startled one day by the refusal of a group of brothers to help their ancient mother cultivate her field. The old lady, Nyankambi (the mother of Nkambi, her first son), was so agitated by the danger of permanent damage to her crops that she prevailed upon me to carry to a mill five miles away a load of grain she wanted ground. With the flour she planned to make some beer with which to pay her sons and others to help her cultivate her field. This incident and others of the same type raised questions in my mind about the theory I was working with—a theory based on the assumption of cooperation and mutual aid among the members of the family and the larger community. Brothers of all degrees sometimes refused to loan livestock or even small amounts of grain to each other. Co-wives within the same homestead frequently refused to help each other. Increasing knowledge of the life of the Turu made it clear to me that these conflicts were not merely an effect of a fifty-year contact with European culture but were almost certainly an aspect of the original culture itself—one, however, that may have been accentuated by our individualistic traits.

Anthropology in general, and social anthropology in particular, for a very long time have tended to stress what Williams (1960, 478–479) calls a communalistic view of society at the expense of an equally valid conflict or competitive approach. It is perhaps for this reason that a true economic anthropology has not developed; because economics when defined as the study of the allocation of scarce means among alternative ends—a definition approved by the more spohisticated economic anthropologists, such as Burling (1962, 810–813)—is essentially the study of a competitive process. In Africa, on the other hand, it is usual for anthropologists to de-emphasize selfish motives among indigenous people by overemphasizing their communalism. Even communalistic theorists rec-

1

ognize that competition can exist in these societies, but they represent competition as subordinated by social processes to the goal of persistence of the society.

A communalistic theory is clearly stated in a contemporary article by W. O. Jones (1961, 13–14), who feels that extra-economic sanctions lead Africans to actions considered desirable by the community. In Africa, he asserts, the over-all patterns of economics resembles that of a family in which all share more or less equally in consumption. In such a situation, Jones feels, it is difficult for an individual to accumulate property in excess of that held by each of his fellows, with the result that accumulation of wealth tends to be achieved only be the leaders, who hold it for the total community.

Jones' views carry a good deal of weight among anthropologists, although he is not one himself. Among anthropologists interpretation of bridewealth or land tenure often seems based on assessments of the nature of African life similar to those used by Jones. Bridewealth is usually seen as passed from one group to another to achieve the effect of stabilization of group relations. Land is considered to be owned by the group and private property is seen as lacking. In both cases the idea is implicit that the conditions exist because they are necessary for the preservation of the group.

In the account of Turu economics that follows I have attempted to approach life in this African society from an alternative point of view, which stresses a competitive dimension hitherto obscured. Beginning most notably with Raymond Firth, this way of viewing society has become increasingly common, although its benefits have not been generally appreciated. In his *Elements of Social Organization* (1951), Firth made a distinction between *structure* and *organization* by pointing out that social anthropology had traditionally paid attention to structure, the conservative (or what I have called the communalistic) principle in society. To quote him (Firth 1951, 40):

> Members of a society look for a reliable guide to action, and the structure of the society gives this—through its family and kinship system, class relations, occupational distinctions, and so on. At the same time there must be room for variance and for the exploration of variance. This is found in the social organization, the systematic ordering of social relations by acts of choice and decision. . . . In the aspect of social structure is to be found the continuity principle of society; in the aspect of organization is to be found the variation or change principle by allowing evaluation of situations and entry of individual choice.

While Firth initiated in social anthropology the essential idea necessary to a competitive approach to society—namely that individuals make choices in terms of goals—he has not developed the idea far beyond this point.

Various scholars have subsequently moved in the direction of Firth and beyond him, but it will suffice here to mention only a few. One is Leach, who in his *Political Systems of Highland Burma* (Leach 1954, 8) focuses attention on decision making by utilizing the assumption that individual decisions are directed to the maximization of power. Leach notes that such a view is in conflict with the communalistic structural-functional approach because it does not assume that society seeks equilibrium. If one chooses to see individuals as competitive, one is driven away from this sometimes teleological idea so central to structural-functional theory.

More recently Lucy Mair has taken a stand in favor of decision making. Discussing change in "small-scale" societies, she concludes (Mair 1965, 34):

> I have tried, with examples of people's conduct in different contexts to argue that the social changes we are witnessing today (in small-scale societies) are effected by social forces that have been in operation in all societies in all times—the manipulation of whatever areas of free choice there may be by people who are able to calculate where their advantage lies.

Pospisil (1963, 18–31) has utilized an aggressive market orientation in describing the Kapauku Papuans, to whom he ascribes an "individualistic money economy." Barth (1959; 1964) has used game theory to analyze the lineage system of the Swat Pathans and a market model to explain why the Bassari nomads settle in towns.

It is one thing to speak of employing a competitive, decision-making point of view and another to specify its type, since there is no one such point of view. Firth's is rather general, barely broaching the subject and not interfering severely with the communalistic orientation that marks his generation of British structural-functionalist anthropologists. Leach and Mair point their analyses at the competition for power rather than in the direction of traditional formal economics, which concentrates on material means and services even though claiming for its economic actors a desire to optimize utility in general. Pospisil's description of the Papuans is almost a parody of the economists' view of our own economy. As he says, the Kapauku economy "combines, strangely enough, one of the world's most primitive technologies with a rather sophisticated and complex economic system. The latter in its main features resembles a simplified version of capitalism" (Pospisil 1963, 18). Barth's analysis of the Bassari takes a similar line, emphasizing that Bassari continually choose to invest where the best marginal return is to be had, with the result that, as they reach a certain level of livestock ownership, they shift to investment in land and settle in towns.

It is plain, therefore, that the particular type of decision-making theory one intends to use must be spelled out. Is it to be a market model or a game model? Is it to focus on power or on material means or perhaps on both? The rest of this chapter is devoted to clarifying the way of viewing Turu society that underlies the analysis to follow.

The main orientation in my thinking parallels Pospisil. I have endeavored, without engaging in parody, to see Turu economy in the same way economists look at our own economy—as a system of decision making with respect to the utilization of scarce means to alternative ends focusing on material means and services. There are certain drawbacks to such an approach, one of which is not the one most usually put forth, that it cannot be done or should not be done. I have done it, and the justification for so doing is how well it helps us understand the facts, particularly certain facts, such as the role of cattle, that are otherwise poorly understood. There is no one way to see people or to analyze behavior. The only justification for denying any approach is its lack of fruitfulness for the understanding of the phenomenon it seeks to explain. Gray's remark that anthropologists have not chosen to view marriage in Africa as economic because, if it were so, it wouldn't be nice (Gray 1960, 55), may be applied to the analysis of the whole of indigenous African economies. Anthropologists have acted as if one should not seek individualistic money and market systems in traditional African societies because it would be scandalous if they existed.

The main drawback is that this approach leaves out almost the whole of what Belshaw (1968, 30) very aptly refers to as social transaction except insofar as this is implied. Increasingly such investigators as Blau and Homans have made clear the existence in the sphere of social relations of an economy in which, for example, people trade deference for valuable information. It seems to me that this economy is one with the economy of material means and services. It should therefore be possible and potentially valuable to study an economy like that of the Turu as a single system of material, service, and social transactions. When I studied the Turu I focused, as economists in our own society do, on only the first two of these areas because of the ease and convenience of the approach. This is not to say that the method I employed is therefore untenable. No theory is complete, and every theory gives only partial answers. If the method helps to understand facts about the Turu that a traditional, communalistic approach cannot explain, the theory is adequate despite its incompleteness. But the value inherent in the other approach is now so apparent that one must feel the need to include it.

To employ the traditional, formal economic approach one must also augment it. Traditional economics is insensitive to the constraints, normative, cultural, and ecological, that condition the play of the market. Anthropologists like myself are particularly aware of the existence of these constraints, so that I have had to modify the formal approach to introduce them and thereby to make more understandable the way Turu make decisions in the market.

A formal approach to traditional African economics, in my view, should ultimately include mathematical and statistical analysis, after the fashion of sophisticated, formal economics and along the lines indicated by Massell (1963), who in fact did a marginal analysis of the data included in Table 5.2. As it is, I have had to be content with merely indicating the possible explanation for various actions, in terms of a decision-making model that assumes that each Turu is attempting to maximize his own utility. Furthermore, I have done so more implicitly than explicitly, by the manner in which I describe events.

A synopsis of the contents of this book will help to indicate the way in which I have employed economic modes of thought. Chapters 2 through 4 concern themselves with establishing the constraints within which Turu economy operates. In Chapter 2 the technological kit available to Turu and the habitat within which it must be employed are indicated in order to delimit the conditions of production. Chapters 3 and 4 are devoted to the social constraints—the system of norms and statuses within which the individual must work to achieve his aggrandizing ends. Chapters 5 through 7 are given over to detailing the system of economizing, the market. The main features are indicated in Chapter 5, which shows individual males to seek an optimum mix of investments in land, women, and cattle in order to aggrandize cattle as the store par excellence of wealth. Chapters 6 and 7 are, in a sense, merely modifiers of Chapter 5 in that 6 attempts to show lineages as cooperatives, rather than as corporate groups, thus displaying the individual as free to control his own resources to a greater extent than is usually represented in accounts of African lineages. Chapter 7 indicates the way ownership of persons is conceived, thus underpinning the implicit notion of Chapter 5 that women constitute a labor market. Chapter 8 is added for the sake of completeness. It is my feeling that the status of women as sisters and wives is tenuous in Turu society, making for a continual instability in the system of production and economizing. Various rituals and other means, detailed in this chapter, have been devised to cope with this chronic problem. The last chapter attempts to assess the changes that have occurred in Turu society since first contact and to indicate, to some degree, the theoretical meaning of the general lack of change.

In connection with the latter, it should be made clear that in one respect this study closely resembles traditional communalistic views of African societies in the assumed static quality of the system. However, stasis is not attributed to the society as a real state but is theoretically assumed for the purposes of analysis. That is, in order to explain the actions of the economic actors, we must show decisions made in terms of certain constant conditions that enable the actors to be rational. To some extent, therefore, actors see the situation as static, as does the analyst for purposes of analysis.

Allowing for the theoretical need to emphasize the stable, it is also apparent that the system has been remarkably stable by almost any measure, as is shown in Chapter 9. The reason for this, I think, is that Europeans have made no concerted attempts to upset Turu society, and the Turu, despite much agitation for change—especially among the young men—have been able to find no good economic basis for it. No startlingly productive and valuable cash crops, like the coffee of the Chaga, have been discovered to fit this habitat, and no minerals have been found to engender quick wealth, as is the case in certain neighboring areas of Unyaturu. Paradoxically, however, a theory of change can be built on the static theory.

An extreme relativistic point of view, which marks much anthropological thinking, seems to suggest that change is impossible except by the intervention of some outside force or by internal and accidental invention, because a society is a system sui generis. In actual fact people's wants—certainly those of the Turu —outstrip the power of their socio-cultural system to satisfy them. Such wants, of course are general—the desire for power and control, for example—rather than specific, such as the desire for some material object that has never been brought to the acquaintance of the people, although desire for such things appears quickly enough once the acquaintance is made. Thus people like the Turu seem sometimes to act as if they have been waiting for certain new opportunities to appear, so quickly are they accepted, regardless of the past history and system of wants of the acceptors. All over Africa, for example, the alacrity with which people incorporate livestock into their economies when given the opportunity is startling. But a system of wants, its devotees realize, also requires some realistic methods of attainment. Turu will not abandon traditional modes to chase after new opportunities unless they know the rules of the game in which these new wants may be satisfied. A wise man does not enter a poker game, no matter how large the possible winnings may be, if he does not understand the rules and strategies of the game. Hence stasis in Turu society is partly a function of the lack of new goals and partly a function of the lack of understanding of how economically to pursue new goals.

The surprise I felt by the actions of the brothers mentioned at the beginning of this chapter, who showed an apparent lack of respect for their mother, dissipated when I stopped trying to interpret Turu life in terms of a communalistic model and began to accept the reality of the competitive dimension of Turu life. In this case the incident was easily explainable. In Turu society each woman is responsible for her own fields and the prosperity of her own house, although she is aided by her husband. All of Nyankambi's sons were married and all had wives demanding help with their crops. The men were thus pulled reluctantly from their mother, from whom they had little further to gain, to their wives, with whom their interests were allied. The exception was the youngest son, who stood to inherit his mother's fields and residual property and who did help her somewhat. Therefore, while the sons respected their mother and even spoke of her as the owner of their lands because they originally had been obtained from her holdings, and while they may even have felt guilty about not heeding her call for help, they were inevitably drawn in the direction of their main interests. The old woman, in turn, attempted to counter this attitude with a strategy that was costly but necessary—making beer to pay the men of the village to come as a group and spend a small amount of time each to cultivate her field. Interestingly, however, we should note that she combined this traditional strategy with a new one—prevailing upon me to haul her grain to town, where a mill could grind it.

2. PEOPLE, HABITAT,
PRODUCTION TECHNIQUES

Moon, Creator, create all things, girl and boy babies and animals in the
forest, all in twos. Make the mpusi *gourd to have a handle. Create for us*
the diviner and witch smeller, the blacksmith and the potter with strong
hands. . . . Make the bulrush millet, the pumpkin and the dabwa *gourd for*
the bride. Millet come early this year; you were a little late last year. Bring
us coolness and sweet water that we may rest, O you Pleiades.

EXCERPT FROM TURU PRAYER TO THE SUN

O N THE basis of language and certain cultural traits, the Turu (WanyatUrU,
pl.; MUnyatUru, sing.; or, traditionally, ArImi, pl.; MurImi, sing.)
belong to the great Bantu-speaking group of African societies. Until the
latter half of the nineteenth century they had no direct contact with the world
outside Tanzania, and within Tanzania there seems to have been only sporadic
but increasing direct contact with neighboring indigenous societies, such as
Sandawe, Gogo, Barabaig, Iramba and Nyamwezi, with whom the Turu traded
and quarreled. Relations with the Sandawe seem to have been fairly intense, as
shown by frequent exchanges of persons and some intermarriage, and Masai
cattle raiders appear to have been the Turu's most fearsome enemies. However,
isolation was being broken down prior to the appearance of Europeans, as is
shown by the two alternative names Turu use for themselves, of which the name
WanyatUrU (The People of NyatUrU) has been replacing the more traditional
ArImi (The People of RImi), reflecting increasing use of the coastal Swahili
trade language, in which the *wa-* plural prefix for living things is typical, in
contrast to the *a-* normal to KInyatUrU (the original language of the ArImi).

The gradual Arab penetration of the interior of Tanzania, beginning in the
early part of the nineteenth century, and the creation of trade routes across the
east-west axis of the country, led by the 1870's to occasional contacts between
Turu and Arabs as the latter hesitantly probed into UnyatUrU. This incursion
was severely inhibited by the natural barriers of the dense Itigi thicket on the
south between the Turu and the main caravan route, the Wembere River and
forests on the west that separate UnyatUrU from the secondary trade route
from Tabora to Mwanza on Lake Victoria, and the forests on the east and north-
west. The Arabs had barely begun to breech these barriers when they were
pushed aside by European colonialists. Stanley was the first known European to
enter Turu country, which he did in 1874 and again in 1889. In both instances
he seems merely to have been taking a shortcut from Mwanza on Lake Victoria
to the main east-west trade route at Dodoma. In 1893 the German explorers

Stuhlmann and Baumann entered the country, after which there was an increasing series of European contacts. By 1894 the Germans had firm possession of Tanzania's interior and established a military post at Kilimatinde just south of the Itigi thicket; from here they sent out pacifying forces to UnyatUrU as well as other places. They also set up some sort of system of headmen in areas not under direct control; von Luschan, who passed through Wahi during the 1890's, aided in the "election" of such a one, who was to represent the country to any Europeans who passed through.[1] Eventually, in 1908, unrest in UnyatUrU led to the establishment of a secondary military post at what is now the town of Singida. From this date the Turu have been under direct administration of a central government in an area labeled Singida.[2] While it is clear from the record that the Turu were very aggressive toward foreigners in those early days, within the country they tend to be very friendly to strangers, an attitude now transferred to Europeans. Entry to any Turu village is typically facilitated, as von Luschan found, by the very cordial attitude of the people.

Contacts with the world outside Tanzania before European administration were mainly through trade for beads, cloth, iron goods, and a few less common items. The Gogo, straddling the caravan route to the south, extracted tribute from passing caravans and traded some of these goods into UnyatUrU. The Nyamwezi to the southwest seem to have become deeply involved in the Arab slave trade and while they refrained from sending raiders into UnyatUrU to capture slaves—partly because of the legendary hostility of the Turu—they did send agents during famine years to buy mainly children in exchange for grain. The Turu remember this history well, and some ascribe the actions of their forebears to their desire to save the children from starvation. Today they like to tell stories of how the Nyamwezi were cheated in many of these transactions.

The first commander of the German post at Singida was Eberhard von Sick, whose remarkable account of Turu culture presents us with an ethnographic baseline against which to measure present change. Among other things, von Sick records a census he made in 1911 showing the population to be 107,444 people, 173,514 cattle, and 123,446 sheep and goats. Since that time the population had increased until in 1957 it reached 195,000 people, of whom 176,000 lived con-

1. The most extensive early account of the Turu is Eberhard von Sick, "Die Waniaturu (Walimi), " Baessler-Archiv. (Vol. V, 1916), pp. 1–61. Except in one or two instances, it has not seemed necessary to encumber the book with footnotes to this and various other early sources because these sources are brief. They are: F. von Luschan, "Beiträge zur Ethnographie des abflusslosen Gebiet in Deutsch-Ost-Afrika," pp. 368–376, in C. W. Werther, Die Mittleren Hochländer des Nördlichen Deutsch-Ostafrika (Berlin, 1898); Oscar Baumann, Durch Massailand zur Nilquelle (Berlin, 1894), pp. 110–111, 188–195, 238; Otto Reche, Zur Ethnographie des abflusslosen Gebiets (Hamburg, 1914), pp. 31–68, 120–128; F. Stuhlmann, Mit Emin Pascha ins Herz von Afrika (1894); Henry M. Stanley, In Darkest Africa, Vol. II (New York, 1891), pp. 445–446; and White Fathers, The Rimi or Turu (unpublished manuscript translated from the French by Sister Mary Sybil Magan, c. 1915).

2. See Map 2.1 of Singida of the German occupation. Under the British the area was called Singida District, but the present independent African government calls it Singida Area. Throughout the book I will, for convenience, continue to refer to it as Singida District, but I shall call the country by its new name, Tanzania, unless the context requires the older form, Tanganyika.

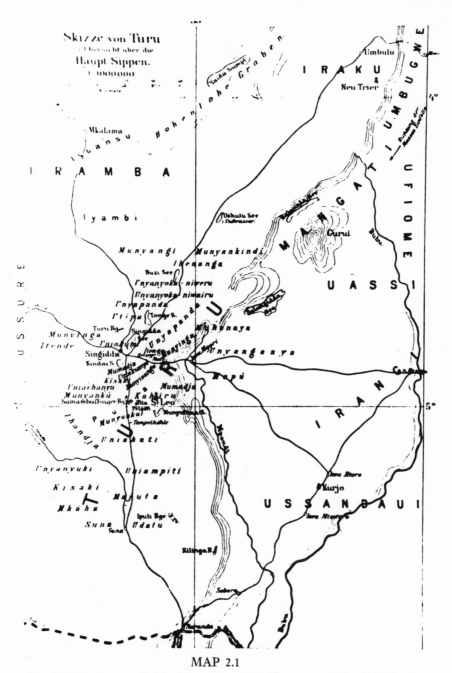

MAP 2.1

Singida During von Sick's time, about 1910 (from von Sick 1916, 3).

tiguously in the indigenous homeland consisting of Singida District, southern Iramba District to the north, and northern Manyoni District to the south of Singida.[3] The remainder of the Turu are or were scattered over Tanzania, working on plantations, as domestic servants, or in various menial jobs. These expatriates are to be found principally at Nzega, Mbulu, Arusha, and Moshi. Today the Turu are the twelfth-largest tribe in Tanzania.

By 1959 the livestock population, according to district records, had increased to 207,474 cattle and 276,626 goats and sheep, making UnyatUrU one of the richest livestock areas in the country. This increase in population—both human and livestock—without serious disruption of traditional modes of life, has been managed by a gradual expansion of settlement into formerly unused forest lands (see Map 2.2).

Among the various subtribal areas of UnyatUrU the proportion of livestock to people varies. The Turu equate goats and sheep with cattle in a ratio of three goats or sheep to a bull or steer (ox) and five to a cow. If we strike an average of four goats or sheep to one head of cattle, we find that they are equivalent to about 69,000 more cattle, or about 1.5 additional cattle per adult man (counting one quarter of the population as adult men, adulthood being set at the age when a man was considered old enough to be taxed under British rule—about sixteen to eighteen). On this basis, the adjusted ratio of cattle units to adult men is about 6.2. Taking account only of cattle, the wealthiest area had 5.9 head per adult man in 1957. The poorest area was Unyanganyi, with about 3.13 head, while the Wahi area stood between these, with 5.4 head. However, Wahi had the greatest proportion of goats and sheep.

THE MAIN GROUPINGS

The Turu consist of three subdivisions, which may be called three subtribes, among which exists a feeling of unity, expressed in the myth that all are descended from MUnyatUrU or MUrImi.

The largest subtribe is that of the Airwana in Wilwana, containing 53 per cent of the people, which extends from the town of Singida in a northeasterly direction. The second largest subtribe is the Vahi in Wahi, extending from just south of the town of Singida to the south and east. The smallest subtribe is that of the Anyiŋanyi, containing the remaining 10 per cent. Evidence suggests that the Anyiŋanyi originally were Airwana who migrated into Unyiŋanyi in well-spaced groups. Subsequently they developed a composite form of subculture because of some mixture with Vahi. This book has little to say about Wilwana and Unyiŋanyi, since it is based on study of people in the two major clans of AnyahatI (the People of NyahatI) and AkahiU (the People of KahiU) of Wahi, where intensive village studies were carried out in one village of each of these groups.

3. Census figures are from East African Statistical Department, *Tanganyika Population Census, 1957* (Nairobi, 1958).

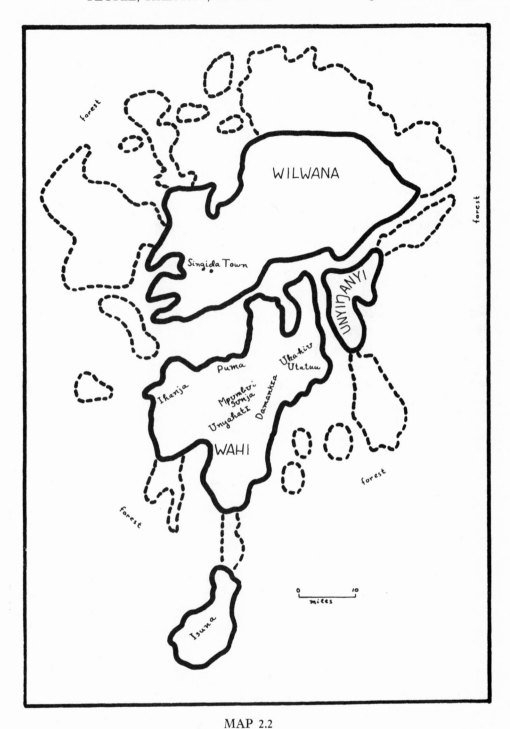

MAP 2.2
Unyaturu Area of Settlement PreContact and Present
Showing-places mentioned in the text and the three subtribes (in capital
letters)

Turu clans will be considered in detail subsequently, but it should be noted here that each of the subtribes consist of a large number of clans varying enormously in size, from no more than the inhabitants of a single village or even less up to such aggregates as that of the AnyahatI of Wahi, whose clans contain five levels of lineage and dozens of villages. Because of this discrepancy, the number of clans of any of the subtribes is not precisely known by any Turu, although a fairly accurate estimate of the number of Wilwana and Wahi can be made, giving the former nineteen and the latter twenty-six. In Wahi, except for the two great clans of AnyahatI and AkahiU, other clans tend to be small and to occur in clusters in the areas of Isuna, Ihanja, and Puma (see Map 2.2). Turu expansion has been fostered by the large amount of forest land surrounding them and has traditionally proceeded by sloughing off individuals who then pioneer new settlements in the forests, to which others then come. These settlements gradually form into villages consisting of a single lineage each if we count only the men and ignore the women who go out from their home villages in marriage.[4] These lineages then profess alliance to pre-existing clans or form new ones. The villages tend to turn inward and become differentiated culturally from each other, a process that is in conformity with the large amount of autonomy that exists in the relations of Turu lineages with each other. Some clans have expanded hugely and many small clans have been created as a result.

Each of the major subdivisions of the tribe have cleared distinct sections of the forest. The subtribes in Wilwana and Unyiŋanyi are contained within single pockets, cut off from other areas, within which movement is easy. However, the Wahi area has several pockets containing the major sub-Wahi groupings, such as the clans of NyahatI and KahiU.

THE HABITAT

UnyatUrU possesses at least one feature that has proven crucial in shaping the Turu way of life: the marshes (mbUγa) that dot the land everywhere. Over the whole tribal area three subhabitats can be distinguished, corresponding to the three subtribes, suggesting that an important reason for the main subtribal divisions is varying ecological adaptations. The habitat of the Anyiŋanyi) is at an altitude of about 4,500 feet, where the climate is hotter and less healthy than in the rest of Turuland, as is indicated by the frequency of baobab trees. The greater amount of livestock disease is a factor helping to make this the poorest area in terms of number of livestock. Above Unyiŋanyi, in the Rift Valley on the Turu fault block (averaging about 5,500 feet in height), the Vahi live at the highest point of the three subtribes. The Airwana live in the Singida Depression at an average altitude of about 5,000 feet.

The variety of flora is very great because of variations in altitude, though the

---

4. This is a useful distinction, since women are not as a rule jurally considered adults. If the distinction is not made, lineages will be thought of as dispersed, a concept that is contrary to Turu common sense and analytically confusing.

plants are all of a type that can exist in the sandy, poorly watered soil character-izing most of the districts. Almost all the flora is put to use in one way or another. Miombo (*mUfumbu*) is a common tree whose bark is used to make grain storage bins; albizzia (*mUsUnguUa* and *mUfoγoo*) is used to make handles for tools; euphorbia matabelense (*mUtUfotUfo*) is favored for fencing because it regenerates from cuttings and exudes a milky sap that on contact causes a skin reaction, thus discouraging intruders; acacia in its many forms is good for fire-wood and building materials. The manyara (*mUnyaa* or Euphorbia tirucalli) is desired as a marker of the gates of homesteads, becoming a permanent marker of the grave after the death of the owner and removal of his house. One semi-domesticated tree, called *mUlade*, provides fruit to flavor beer. Even the baobab (*mwandU*) is utilized for its fruit, to make ropes from its bark, and as a meeting place for the settlement of serious disputes, so that these meetings and payment of fines have come to be called by the same name as the tree—*mwandU*. Examples of other trees familiar to the Turu are bulge-stemmed palm, com-bretums, commiphoras, pod ebony, kaffir boom, wild fig, German sausage, san-seviera, sclerucarya, and terminalias. Of Burtt's (1936) list of East African flora, fifty-three are known to the Turu, who also recognize many types of trees and shrubs that Burtt does not record. The extensive knowledge and use of their shrubs and trees contrasts with their emphasis on livestock.

The surface of UnyatUrU is undulating, with few sharp rises other than those along the fault block, the sides of the Singida Depression, and the Rift Valley wall. Low hills and rides are common, and granite outcroppings, espe-cially at Puma, are sometimes heroic in appearance. The dessicated nature of the soil indicates the geological antiquity of the surface, which has been rejuve-nated in geologically recent times only by faulting here and there and by the creation of the Rift Valley. The Turu recognize several varieties of soil; their classification agrees with that of Eades and Reeve (1938, 8–9) in their geological survey of 1938. Most of the arable area is called *iseke* and *itoγoo* by Turu; the former is a white sandy soil and the latter gray and sandy. In various scattered areas, and particularly in northern Wilwana, the predominant soil is *nkuhI*, which is red and known to be more fertile than the others.

The Germans termed this area a "drainless region" because of the internal drainage that creates the many swamps or marshes and the two great saline Lakes, Singida and Kindai at Singida Town. These marshes, which are composed of calcareous black clay, vary greatly in size from small patches that lose their water quickly in the dry season to giant expanses, especially in the Singida Depression, where the Lakes Kindai and Singida hold surface water most of the time. Since, few depressions are so deep that they will hold more than a little surface water, however, it is possible to use swamp vegetation for reserve grazing. Combined with the fact that the swamps provide a permanent water supply, this unusual condition makes possible a sedentary life for these herding people.

The importance of the marshes derives from the pattern of rainfall. From June to September there is no appreciable rainfall, while most of the rain falls from December through March. For eight months of the year, therefore, there is no significant rain. The rain that does fall is erratic both in the amount that descends each year and in the time of year when it begins and when it peaks. The twenty-year average to 1952 was 25 inches per year, peaking anywhere from December to March. When the significant amount appears late in the agricultural season, production suffers even though the average rainfall for the year is good. Turu are adept at replanting their fields in those years when early rains are not followed by others that will encourage the growth of the young crops. This replanting is facilitated by the relatively simple method of planting seeds that can be employed in the sandy soil.

It is an incidental but prominent aspect of the climate that a steady and fairly strong wind blows across the area from the east throughout most of the year. This brings the temperature down in the winter months in some places to as low as 40 degrees at night and requires shelters that are able to provide warmth and break the wind. Homesteads are therefore invariably backed to the east. During the harvest the wind is utilized in the winnowing processes to blow the chaff from the threshed seeds.

THE ECOLOGICAL COMPLEX

It is questionable whether this habitat could maintain nearly the number of people it now supports if the more usual African method of slash-and-burn agriculture alone were utilized. This procedure would require a greater dispersion of population and less intense utilization of land; however, Taeuber (1949, 30) in her study of the population of Tanganyika shows UnyatUrU to be one of the most densely populated areas. By my own rough calculations, giving UnyatUrU an area of about 1,750 square miles, the density is about 100 persons per square mile. Though concentration of population is made possible where the fertile red *nkuhl* soil exists, over most of the country the pattern of settlement is related to a technology developed to take advantage of the unique conditions. The villages in the older areas of UnyatUrU have cultivated on the same soil continuously without rotation for a very long time. When Baumann passed through UnyatUrU in the 1890's, he described it as already a very old settled area. The village of Utatuu (see Map 2.3), which will receive extensive attention later, has probably been fixed at its present site for over 100 years, and it is not by any means the oldest village in UnyatUrU. Villages often move or are rearranged but seldom because of land exhaustion. One way of ascertaining this fact is that it is possible to relate to the genealogy of a village the trees left to mark the sites of an ancestral home and of graves. When a man dies, a worn-out grindstone is placed on his grave, and the tree is left standing by the entrance to his corral while the house is torn down. In the village of Utatuu trees associated with ancestors up to five generations back can be found. Since there seems to be a general decline in importance of even older ancestors, lack of more ancient trees is not a sign that the village is not older. In the whole complex of

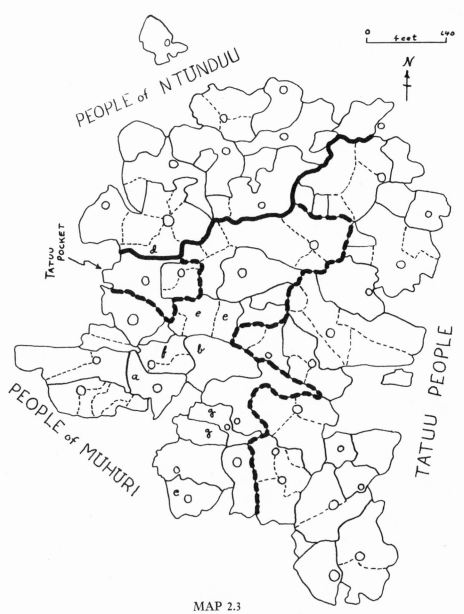

MAP 2.3

Villages of Utatuu and Mumbii

Heavy solid line indicates division between villages of Utatuu and Mumbii.
Broken heavy line indicates division between the affiliated lineages of
Muhuri and Tatuu. Circles indicate homesteads, lines homestead boundaries,
and broken lines internal boundaries of homesteads.

Utatuu, with about forty homesteads, at least fifty-six such ancestral trees are scattered.

The technological feature upon which Turu depend is systematic manuring of the arable land each year. In consequence it is necessary to keep the animals penned for long periods, to collect the droppings, and to graze them close to home. In Wahi the livestock are kept in the corral as late as 11:00 A.M. and never leave before about 10:00 A.M. They return before sundown, at about 6:00 P.M., making possible only about seven or eight hours of grazing per day. The animals are grazed on the open lands around the village or in the nearby forests until the grass is gone. Then they are turned loose in the marshes, which will normally support them throughout the winter except during the occasional periods of severe drought. The forests are important ecological elements; few Turu villages are very far from them. Not only do they provide supplementary grazing, but their products are necessary for fuel and building materials, medicine, tools, and the like. In a few cases they even supply sufficient grazing to make marshes unnecessary.

The typical Turu village (Plate 2.1) consists of a hill or high place on which the village (*itUmbi*, "high place" or "village") rests; it is comprised of the homesteads and fields (*mlγunda*, pl; *mUγunda*, sing.) under cultivation around them. Surrounding the village is open grassland (*ikuja*, sing; *makuja*, pl.) into which cultivation can expand and where grazing can be obtained for small stock and other animals during part of the year. The marsh lies in a depression alongside

PLATE 2.1
Typical Turu Village in Wahi, Showing Standing Crop of Finger Millet,
Various Sized Homesteads, and Ancestral Trees

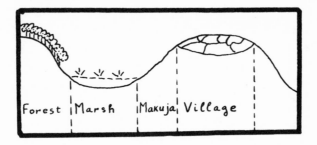

FIGURE 2.1
Cross section of ecological pattern of Turu village.

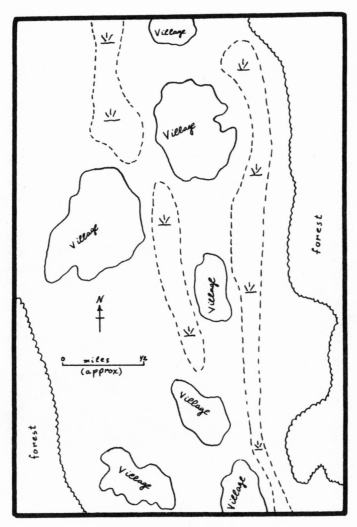

FIGURE 2.2
Air view of ecological pattern, Mpumbui area of Nyahati clan in Wahi.

the village, and the forest (*ihaka*, sing.; *mahaka*, pl.) lies beyond (see Figures 2.1 and 2.2).

Von Luschan in his trip through Wahi estimated the size of villages as from three to eight homesteads. While the meaning of such an estimate depends somewhat on what is meant by a village, we may presume he meant the clearly bounded settlements, such as seen in Map 2.3, which I call a village. If this is true, his estimate was wrong. No doubt three homesteads may operate in isolation under certain circumstances, but more typical is the village in Map 2.4, which has fifteen homesteads, and that in Map 2.3, which actually consists of what may be called, for reasons later explained, two villages; the southern containing thirty-one homesteads and the northern, ten. These are much more typically the sizes of Turu villages.

The only buildings erected by the Turu are what I will refer to as homesteads; all are basically of the same pattern, with some minor variations between Wahi and Wilwana. The form is illustrated in the two diagrams in Figure 2.3. The total homestead complex (*xaya*) consists of the houses of the women (*nyUmba*) and the corral (*mUsae*), surrounded by a fence (*ikita*) of high shrubs that contains a gate (*mUfita*). Large animals are penned within the corral, which is also the burial place of those who die while residing in the homestead. An individual house is divided into two chambers—the sitting room (*mwango*), with its opening to the outside (*kInyamwango*), and the inner room, called *mbee*. In this back room are the bedroom as well as the storage bins (*kIu*) for grain (Plate 6.1). These circular bins are raised off the floor on low platforms and are lined with ant-hill mud (*irongo*), which has the consistency of plaster. This mud is also used to seal the whole interior of the house and to cover the roof.

The homestead shown in diagram A of Figure 2.3 is that of a newly established couple, the husband living with his wife in her house. Normally a second house, duplicating the first but smaller (as in diagram B), called an *ikumbu*, is built for the husband's daytime residence and to domicile sons when they leave the mother's house. Newly built houses follow this pattern. If a man has very many wives, the homestead may eventually become a complete circle because each new wife acquires her own house, storage facilities, and fields on which to produce her grain.

Turu think of a homestead as composed of nesting segments. The word *mUfita*, designating literally the main outer gate of the homestead, may also refer to the whole family unit, while the word *mwango* refers also to segments within the *mUfita*—units of women and their children. Chapter 3 will show that this concept can be used on a broader basis to designate levels of lineage.

Certain variations on the basic homestead pattern may include a fence (*iγafIηgo*) before the houses, to prevent large animals from damaging the eaves and walls. Sometimes the corral consists of such a fence, built concentrically to the outer fence to make a gangway from the outer gate all around the corral. The advantage of this latter method is that during the rains it provides a passage on high ground away from the muddy manure. In the case of old, established

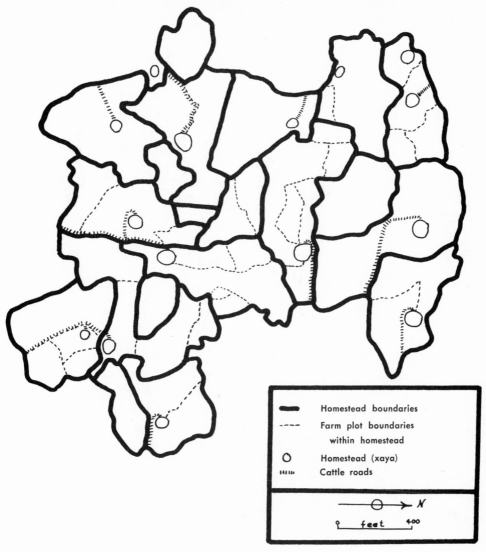

MAP 2.4
Village of Sunja

homesteads a fence may be built around the back, to shield the houses from intruders and from the wind. In Wilwana the men's houses are built in the corral before the outer gate to guard the livestock from night raiders.

Except in the few cases where a homestead commands land in two different places, it is built in the farm plot. The position on the plot is unpredictable, although one common pattern is for a son to build his own homestead at the farthest point from the father's house, on the plot given him by his father from his mother's holdings.

The farm plots are strictly bounded from the other houses in the same home-

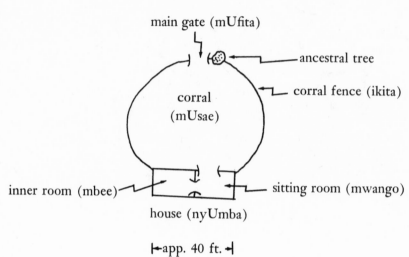

DIAGRAM A

main gate (mUfita)

ancestral tree

corral fence (ikita)

corral
(mUsae)

inner room (mbee)

sitting room (mwango)

house (nyUmba)

⊢app. 40 ft. ⊣

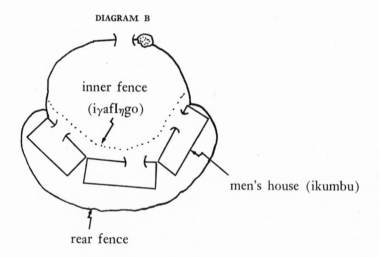

DIAGRAM B

inner fence
(iɣafIŋgo)

men's house (ikumbu)

rear fence

FIGURE 2.3
Pattern of Homesteads

PLATE 2.2

Turu Homestead, Showing Corral, Corral Inner Fence, and Houses. These houses, built by Membe of Nyongongo, are of exceptionally fine quality and are greatly admired by those Turu who know of them.

stead and between different homesteads. Paths that connect all the homesteads of a village usually follow the boundary lines; these paths are sometimes used as boundary lines, although boundaries are normally of mounded earth or consist of fences that also enclose the livestock or cattle roads (*ifanda*, sing.). Gates are placed in fences to permit access to the paths and to cross them. A strong tendency exists to keep homesteads of the same village close together, both for protection and for general convenience. Villages thus tend to become oval or round, while all the farmsteads are contiguous. Sometimes a village is surrounded by a fence to protect the crops from cattle grazing in the open fields outside, but each section of this fence is individually erected by the person whose fields are threatened. During the dry season fencing is not important, and people and cattle are allowed to cut across the fields by the most convenient path.

HORTICULTURAL PRODUCTION

Time is measured by various means, the most important of which are the phases of the moon (*mweri*), seen as coincident with the menstrual cycle and therefore used to measure the length of pregnancy. (The moon is associated with the Creator, *Matunda*.) The annual appearance of the Pleiades (*kIlmla*) signals the onset of the rains. The agricultural year consists of two major parts: *kItikU*, the season of rain and cultivation; and *cwI*, the dry season. Since these two phases occur irregularly, Turu have no regular months or weeks as we know them. The divisions of the cultivation season are, however, indicated by the condition of crops in a given area as follows:

iu na ŋombe   Planting begins as vegetation begins to turn green and cattle are fattening on the new grass.

mUkinda   Millet is about one-half foot high, which is time for the first cultivation. This occurs about one month after planting.

mUnkUkUta   Millet is about one and a half to two feet high: time for the second cultivation, about two months after planting.

mUnti   Heads beginning to appear on the millet, signaling the success of the planting and the readiness of pumpkins to be eaten; about three months after planting.

mUmbII   Millet heads have fully appeared and are in flower.

mUhatU   First eating of new grain is now possible, although the heads are still immature.

mUxandatofe   Grain is ready for harvest; about six months after planting.

mUnye   Post-harvest period, when the stover stands or lies in the fields and the cattle are turned in to eat it and the grass.

MUnye is about eight months after planting and subsequent to a month of threshing; horticultural activities thus occupy much of the year. The work is not continually demanding, however, planting and cultivation and harvesting and threshing being the most energy-consuming. During the dry season there is little to do in the fields, although in the latter part, in September and October, people begin to rake the field stover into piles; in the evening, after the wind abates, these piles are burned. The resulting ash fertilizes portions of the field that do not receive manure. During this time people concerned with expansion of production also clear small portions of the forest, piling the cut wood on the plots to dry throughout the dry season in preparation for firing before the agricultural season begins. As the rains approach, the tempo of activity increases. Women make more frequent excursions to the forest to bring back fuel, which is piled around their homesteads against the time when they will be too busy in the fields to go to the forest. There is a speeding up of stover burning; the first desultory removal of decayed manure from the corrals to the fields also begins, although this activity is not seriously undertaken until after planting.

Turu are known for planting before the rains begin, in October, although they may replant after the onset of the rains if the first planting is unsuccessful. Planting is done with the wooden *mUfambajo*, an oar-shaped paddle or, these days, with the short-handled iron-headed hoe called *iɣembe*. The oar is thrust into the sand and twisted to make a small excavation into which a pinch of ten to twenty seeds is dropped. This hole is then covered by pushing the earth over it with the foot. Excavations are made about two feet apart throughout the planting area. Though this is not an especially laborious task, it must be followed by the distribution of manure over as much of the area as can be reached before the first cultivation. The manure is dug out from under the undecayed top layer in the corral (Plate 2.3), each woman taking what is on

PLATE 2.3
Household Head Demonstrating the Depth of Manure in Corral

her side of an invisible line extending from between hers and the next woman's house to the main outer gate. The manure is placed in troughs small enough to carry on the head and is dumped in separate piles between the already planted seeds until all is used up. Because the amount of available manure is seldom sufficient to cover an entire field, the tendency is for the area closest to the outer gate to be manured first and for the further reaches of the field to be omitted. Some people rotate the placing of manure on different portions of the field; others pick a favored area small enough to be efficiently handled, which gets first attention in all respects, including the depositing of manure. Over a long period of time all areas of a house's fields tend to get manure, thus building up the fertility of the soil and making the land more valuable than untreated soil.

When first cultivation begins, all the manure must be spread; the weeds and manure between the young plants are then scraped up with the hoe and mounded around the base of the plants to fertilize them. This is the first occasion for extensive cooperative labor; since cultivation may not be put off for very long without permanent damage to the crops, cultivation work parties are to be seen everywhere. The second cultivation is the last. Thereafter the plants will be thick enough to discourage the growth of weeds and high enough to be un-affected by them. At this time plants in the more luxuriant areas are dug up and replanted in the thin parts of the field. The young shoots are pushed into mounded earth and the tops of the leaves are removed. Again, work parties are common because this chore must be done quickly.

The long period after second cultivation is a time of waiting. There is little to do but keep birds and other pests out of the crops and wait for the harvest. Just before the harvest the night *ilanda* dances are held, and circumcision is supposed to take place. Also during this time the heads of weak plants, whose seeds will drop out if they are allowed to dry, are collected, dried, and pounded in a wooden mortar, as a substitute for the regular threshing procedure. When the harvest begins, the heads of the healthy plants are cut off with a special curved knife, and simultaneously the stover is trampled to allow access to the crop yet to be cut.

By far the most important crops are *Uvee*, or bulrush millet (Plate 2.4);

PLATE 2.4
Bulrush Millet

laŋgilaŋga, a larger-seed feather-topped millet; and *mafemba*, another large-seed millet, the head of which is like a tight fist. In some places *laŋgilaŋga* is favored by the soil, but throughout most of Wahi, bulrush millet is the chief grain crop. Maize (*mUntama*) is a new crop, which is used widely only in a few places, and finger millet (*UkUhi*) is an uncommon but traditional crop. Other traditional crops of importance include tobacco (*matumbatU*), gourds (*masuki*), cow peas (*mahaage*), cassava (*mUhogo*), and *mamamai* and *mahukuma*—kinds of squash or pumpkin. Up until 1960 there was not much change in the kinds of crops of importance to Turu since Bauman's time in 1894, when he described sorghum and eleusine as the "only" crops.

During harvest a special rack about chest high must be built on which to place the heads of *laŋgilaŋga, mafemba,* and *UkUhi* to preserve the seeds that come loose as the heads dry. Since the seeds of all important millet hold firmly in place, the crop is merely piled on the ground near the threshing area, sometimes topped with a leaf of the euphorbia, which is thought to be potent for warding off the evil eye. When the harvest is completed, the threshing place (*kIhawa*) is prepared. It consists of a bowl-shaped area cut out of the side of a white ant hill, surfaced with water manure that subsequently dries. This provides a clear, smooth surface on which none of the tiny threshed seeds will be lost. Each morning a pile of millet is placed on the surface of this threshing area; after the biggest heads with the biggest seeds are removed, to be threshed separately for the following year's planting, the pile is beaten, with a long willow switch to the rhythm of sharp exhalations of breath. In contrast to observed habits in many other areas of Africa, this is the only instance in the Turu agricultural process where workers consciously act rhythmically. In the afternoon the threshed pile of grain and chaff is put into troughs and shaken over the head to allow the chaff to blow to the west as the clean seeds fall directly to the ground (see Plate 2.5). These seeds are then gathered up and

PLATE 2.5
Winnowing Bulrush Millet

stored in bins in the houses. About 160 pounds, or four *debes*,[5] of bulrush millet can be prepared this way each day. Large producers may need a month to thresh their crops by this slow process. Since millet is very resistant to rotting and insects, it can be stored for about three years if necessary. It is placed at the top and bottom of the bins to protect the fragile seeds of the other plants sandwiched in between. The bin's hole is then sealed with ant-hill mud, and the season is over.

The sustaining force for production of crops is women. Men frequently do nothing to aid the women in their households, although usually they will give some help with planting, cultivating, harvesting, and threshing. The winnowing is almost entirely in the hands of the women, as is the planting. On the other hand, cooperative work parties are made up principally of men, who are the ones with sufficient freedom to engage in them. These are called up mainly for cultivation, harvesting, and threshing. Without the labor of women there could be little production of crops, for few men would be willing or able to persist with the labors necessary throughout the season. One rare widower who was observed doing the job alone grew only about 150 pounds of grain, far short of what any woman could obtain. Even when devotedly assisting in the horticultural process, men seldom work past noon, while women may work for the whole day. On the other hand, women view the production of this food as their prerogative; while they may grumble about the amount of energy they expend in comparison with the men, they also know that their control of crops gives them their chief power.

DOMESTIC ACTIVITIES

Domestic labors also are carried on almost entirely by women. There are certain tasks which must be performed almost every day. Most important and time-consuming is the preparation of food. The staple food is *uɣal*, a very stiff porridge made of millet flour. Each woman has in her house an *igwe ra usiera*— a granite grinding platform, with a worn depression made by constant sharpening and wearing by the grindingstone (*nsio*). Compatible with the sedentary life, the grinding platform is large and heavy and therefore practically immobile. Usually it is mounted in the bedroom of the tightly closed house, where a woman grinds each day's ration of grain during the darkness of night or by the small amount of light cast by a small hole in the wall. The labor that grinding requires makes flour a valuable commodity; it is, therefore, frequently used for a gift, being presented to the recipient in a *dahwa*, or decorated gourd. Women rise very early in the morning, long before daylight, to grind the flour for the day, sometimes returning to bed afterward. Each woman gives the cooked pot of porridge to her husband at the 10:00 A.M. meal (*malljanga*),

---

5. A *debe* is a four-imperial-gallon tin. *Debes* are used everywhere to measure and transport grain and other goods.

before the livestock go out, and again in the evening around 6:00 P.M., when the livestock return. Dried pieces of porridge are made available to the children in the earlier part of the morning, saved from the previous evening's meal. Porridge is never served alone if any relish is available, as it usually is. Skimmed milk (*maya*) is taken if there is any. Other than that, the usual vegetable relishes (called *nyonyi*) are *maxonda*, made from a green succulent plant that grows in the fields around the village, and *marimbe*, which is like *maxonda* but less favored, although it can be stored for the dry season and replaces *maxonda*. This relish, when cooked, is deep green in color and of the consistency of egg yolk. The balls of porridge, made by kneading the *uɣal* after removing it from the pot, are dipped in the relish and popped into the mouth. Gathering these plants—almost a daily labor during the rains—is accomplished in half an hour or so. If chicken or some other form of meat relish (*matuli*) or any other form of relish is available, this main relish may be dispensed with. Usually cooking is done by boiling. When men cook meat, as at ceremonial slaughter of livestock, it is roasted on open coals. The male head of the house and other males present, including boys who have moved from mother's house, are served first. When they have finished, the wife removes the pot of porridge and side dishes to her house, where she eats with her daughters and with other women who may be visiting.

Cleaning the houses is another daily task that is carried out before the morning meal. The sitting room, where the small stock have been kept during the night, must be swept out, as must the domicile of the boys. The walkway around the corral must also be swept.

When the first meal of the day is finished and the homestead and the utensils have been cleaned, the work of the day away from the house may begin. If the husband is on call to herd, he leaves; otherwise he may lounge around the man's house, attending to whatever affairs concern him. Similarly, the woman may leave the house to attend to her affairs; before the evening she will find time to pick a supply of relish, to draw water, and most importantly, to go to the forest for a supply of firewood, which she does in the company of her friends. The women pass over the hills to the forest in single file and return much later with the heavy loads of wood on their heads. Women may also find time to visit with their sweethearts while in the forest, a favorite trysting spot. Male children are sent out to herd the small animals but also find time to play, since grazing is obtained at the edge of the village. Girls are more confined; they accompany their mothers in most tasks or remain at the house attending to domestic duties.

Besides these tasks and other less significant ones—such as milking the cows, churning the milk, and preparing ghee (*ikuta*)—a very important but intermittent duty of women is the preparation of beer (*ntul*). This process requires a number of days. The grain must be soaked and allowed to sprout before it is dried to make the mash. It is then roughly ground. After this, dried porridge (*maxoxo*) is cooked, sometimes mixed with honey to make the most favored beer, and then allowed to sour. Next the mash is placed in hot water, stirred, and put aside to cool. Finally the *maxoxo* is added, and the mixture is allowed to ferment over night. The process may take ten or twelve days. Women who make good beer and do so frequently are exceptional and highly desired as wives.

The agricultural productive arrangements are such as to throw the greatest burden on the women, making it possible for men to choose to a large extent how active they will be. The industrious man is admired; the poor man is uncritically branded as lazy, indicating the strong negative attitude some Turu have toward inactivity, even though poverty is not due simply to laziness. Men perform the chief labors in house building, fence building, hafting of tools, clearing of new farm lands (which is infrequent), harvesting, and such tasks as preparing tobacco. They spend much time together drinking beer. They are not inactive in a real sense, however. Even when they are not engaged in physically enervating tasks like those of the women, the managerial problems of operating a successful homestead are worrisome. Men are constantly on their way from one place to another or in conference about one matter or another, making the typical woman's attitude that men are a leisure class as unjustified as the general opinion among the men that women are weak.

LIVESTOCK PRODUCTION

Almost all Turu homesteads have livestock, the exceptions being so insignificant as to require no attention. Care of these animals is the other great productive activity of each household. There are two methods of classifying livestock: one in terms of sex and age and the other in terms of color and pattern of markings, the latter being the most commonly used. The age-sex classification is as follows:

ŋombe, the generic plural and singular for cattle
ŋombe, or *nxema a ŋombe*, any female animal
ndama, a young female who has ceased sucking but has not yet borne a calf
baisa, a bearing cow who has had one calf
mboɣoma, a cow who has two or more calves, up to six
ixombi, a cow who has had seven or more calves; that is, a cow who is at the terminus of production
njaɣamba, bull
mUjaɣamba, a young bull
mUjikU, fully grown steer, about 300 to 400 pounds
nxama, an exceptionally large steer

The distinction between bulls and steers is not absolute, the terms for bulls sometimes also being used to mean steers. However, it usually can be understood that the terms have the above referents.

As with cattle, there is a generic term for sheep—*nxoo*—which applies to both sexes. The specific term for a male is *nkambakU*. Correspondingly, *mbUri* is the general term for goats, while a castrated goat is *mpahi* and the uncastrated mature male is *ŋgUata*.

Unlike some other East African herding societies, especially the Nilotic peoples,[6] the Turu have only a small number of names for cattle based on color and pattern; all can be listed here:

Male	Female	Description
kidUmu	Umu	brown and black
kidea	area	off-white to light brown
kitu	titi	black
kisamu	samu	mottled white, black, and brown
killIkIni	lIkIni	brown and white
kidaγula	γula	spotted
kinyisi	nyisi	gray
kiseneku	seneku	black; white tip of tail
kidabwasi	bwasi	black and white spotted
kidoγwani	doγwani	dark brown
kidamuri	muri	"dirty" brown
kidamaa	maa	black body with white face
kidaγofou	γofou	mottled "like a hyena"
kidampondo	mpondo	"green [sic] like manure"
kidabai or	baγadi or	very mottled mixture of all colors
kibaγani	baγanti	white
kisyUli	syUli	

While there may be other colors and patterns in Wahi, this list includes all names normally used. Goats and sheep are not given names, but they can be described by referring to some natural event; for example, one type of goat is sometimes described as a "crying goat" because of black tearlike dots under the eyes. Similarly, a cow name can be modified if necessary to make particular distinctions.

Turu do not normally speak of their cattle either in terms of age-sex or total numbers but in terms of these color patterns. They cannot give a reason for this custom. In my experience few Turu can say without giving the matter some thought how many cattle they possess, but they can say immediately how many they have in each of these name categories—I suspect partly because of the belief that there is a correlation between breeding potential and color pattern, so that some colors are disliked (although the preferences vary from place to place). Those colors or patterns occurring most frequently in the herds are thought to be best, the frequency arguing to the Turu greater fertility (the logic of this reasoning is clear if disputable). Such animals are spoken of as "having a herd." When animals are castrated or contracted for bridewealth, this situation may be an important factor. At one village in Ukahiu principles of selection for castration were designed to remove from breeding not only the calves of *baisa* and *ixombi* cows—those that are the first- and last-born of cows—but all colors except *kitu*, *kidaγula*, and *kinyisi*. These, according to the men, "look like males." In contrast, at a village in the clan of AnyahatI the

6. By Nilotic I mean both the Nilotes of Sudan and Uganda, but also the so-called Nilo-Hamitic people of Kenya and Uganda, such as Turkana, Pokot, and Masai.

kitu, kidaγofou, kidampondo, and *kidaγula* were thought to "have a herd." Of course such rules are not absolute; a man who has no lucky animals will use others for breeding.

Although livestock are assigned and are said to belong to the houses of the various women in a homestead (a subject whose complexities will be taken up below), livestock management is in the hands of the men. Because of the cooperative herding groups, the work is not as demanding as women's labors but is no less important. There is a seasonal rhythm to herding, as there is for agriculture. During the rains it is possible to obtain grazing in the open fields around the village and other such areas as well as in the forest (Plate 2.6). However, herders

PLATE 2.6
Cattle Grazing in Mangu Marsh and in Makuja Between the Marsh and
the Village

must decide where to take the cattle and which of the various varieties of grass to seek. Grasses are known to have different effects on the cows, some making them fat, others causing them to give more milk, and so on. Persons owning marsh land form the cores of cooperative herding groups to which others attach themselves by giving labor as herders in repayment for grass. To be relieved of much of the herding duties is a mark of high status, indicating possession of grazing land and animals. The composition of these groups varies frequently as members join or leave, seeking advantages in varied arrangements, or are asked to leave or join in accordance with their diligence or laziness. The groups also vary seasonally because some join during the rainy season for the benefit of shared herding duties and are asked to leave during the dry season because of a shortage of marsh grazing for the core herds. Those without grazing must scrounge in the forest, beg or buy temporary grazing in the dry season, or even drive their cattle into known tsetse-fly areas, hoping their cattle will not catch sleeping sickness. Small boys and girls are kept busy each day herding small animals in the open fields around the village.

The men speak of herding as hard but satisfying work; they feel pride in managing the herd and pleasure in contemplating all the riches it represents. Nevertheless, they do not seem to be very alert herders. When walking cross-country or watching the animals graze, the men seem to lose contact with their surroundings, their reveries resulting in loss of many animals, who stray into the forest. Such animals, if they are not found by nightfall, are usually lost to predators—leopards, hyenas, lions, and the like. Even though the men profess to like herding, it is a boring task because it consists mostly of standing and sitting, as one would expect with the pastures so close to the village. Eagerness to avoid much herding contrasts with professed enjoyment of it.

As was explained earlier, livestock are penned most of the time. The large ones are forced to sleep in the mud and water of the corral during the rains (Plate 2.7). This procedure is not thought to hurt them for various reasons, such as that it encourages the animals' appetites. Whatever other reasons there may be, the custom also achieves the conservation of manure. The small animals—calves, sheep, and goats—for their protection are put in the sitting room of the house because they are least able to cope with predators who sometimes enter

PLATE 2.7
Cattle Penned in Flooded Corral during Rainy Season

the corrals at night. That predators are a serious problem is clear from a survey conducted by the veterinary department in 1948 in Wilwana where, among ten homesteads in eleven months, leopards killed eighteen goats and sheep as well as the dog; hyenas caught eight goats and sheep, two calves, and two dogs; wildcats ate twenty-seven chickens; hawks caught thirty-seven chicks; and snakes killed three chickens. Of course, some of these animals were taken in the forest, where they had strayed, but most were killed in the homestead. Lions are not generally a serious menace to livestock, although they typically kill full-grown cattle. The great fear of lions, as Chapter 8 will show, has other bases.

Cattle diseases are another serious threat to the herds. Rinderpest was the most feared until it came under control, but East Coast fever and blackleg are still menaces, as are trypanosomiasis, contacted from tsetse flies, and certain other diseases. The veterinary-department survey listed thirty-two cattle dead of disease during the year, and such a proportion is not unusual. Death from starvation is also said to be a problem in serious drought years, although Turu animals are remarkably durable, as generally seems to be the case in East Africa. A recent estimate by Deshler (1963, 55) indicates that during extreme famine in the cattle areas of Africa only about 10 to 20 per cent of the animals will die.

When animals die of starvation or disease, they are eaten whenever possible. Although not a regular chore, the slaughter of animals goes on steadily, adding to the meat available from other causes of death, and sickly animals are slaughtered if the owners consider that they will not recover. Old cows who have stopped bearing and others producing deformed or inferior calves are also slaughtered, although the former are often dispatched with ceremony, milk being given them in the horn of a previous well-bearing cow, to bring luck to their offspring. Steers used to be slaughtered for feasts in this same ceremonious way, but by 1960 almost all these animals were taken to the government markets for sale. Nowadays cattle are seldom slaughtered merely for the joy of a feast. Sheep and goats are occasionally slaughtered for food as well as for sacrifices. Although the decision to do away with them is not taken lightly, any more than is the killing of cattle, they are killed more frequently. Animals formerly were killed by strangling them and stuffing the nose and mouth, but today the Moslem system is followed by most people; the animal's throat is cut, and the blood is allowed to run off. In former times, as is generally true throughout East Africa, blood was collected to drink just as it was taken from the living animals.

While milk production is not unimportant, it is viewed more casually by the Turu than it is by most East African pastoralists. Many people do not have milk-producing cows and do not seem to miss this commodity unless they have children, for whom it is a desired food. In such a case they must beg, borrow, or buy it from others. It is used as a relish with meals and is consumed as skimmed or sour milk or processed with cottage cheese, or ghee, which is used for cooking. Characteristically, the zebu cattle of the Turu will not drop their milk except in the presence of their calves. The calf is therefore given first access, after which it is tied to the corral fence with a leather strap while the rest of the milk is taken off. Milking is done by the women in the morning, before the cows are let out, and at night, when they return. Goats and sheep are almost never milked. Milk production is best during the first part of the rainy season, but even then it is poor. I could gain no firm idea of how much milk is produced because the Turu are so disinterested in the subject, but von Sick estimated that at the most cows give only about a quart to a quart and a half a day.

Livestock are branded by clipping the ear in a design chosen by the homestead head. The principle for marking varies in Wahi. In some places each individual brands his cattle and small animals with a private brand, in other places the brand may pertain to a whole lineage, in which case the small animals may have private brands. This distinction has importance for our later discussion of owner-ship of livestock. For now it may be said that the brands are important identify-ing marks. Unlike some other East African people, Turu do not claim to know each cow individually, and confusion about ownership therefore often results when animals are stolen or go astray. The brand helps allay this confusion. When a cow is bought already branded, the owner does not attempt to alter the brand unless he has inclinations that way, for any brand will serve this purpose of identification.

Branding the animals, arranging for castration during the middle of the dry season, taking turns herding, driving off predators, seeking proper grazing, at-tempting cures for some of the diseases, loaning out, borrowing and selling and buying livestock, are all activities in the livestock-keeping system that fall to men. Girls and women may help out with herding duties in emergencies, for they are not tabooed from association with livestock, but the division of labor be-tween men and women in respect to pastoral and horticultural duties is almost complete.

3. KINSHIP AND LINEAGE

It is hard to travel alone.
Turu Proverb

THIS chapter is devoted to a brief overview of the main normative elements in Turu life. It is within the context of these norms that Turu play their social game. The term *norm* should be taken in the broad sense to mean, not only the specific rules governing behavior and the system by which violation is adjudicated, but also the modes of thought and views of the universe that delimit their believers in their attempt to establish courses of action. A person's fear that an ancestor will harm him if he follows a certain strategy is restrictive just as is the law in the more specific sense.

THE KINSHIP AND LINEAGE SYSTEM

A kinship terminological system may be thought of as assigning status to individuals; in a society like that of the Turu, where it performs this function very broadly, it must therefore be seen as a chief element in the normative system. Turu terminology seems unusually contradictory. The way Turu classify kin corresponds only partly to the realities of interaction, contrary to Radcliffe-Brown's (1952) axiom that people who are called by the same term may be thought of as having some important similarity in their relation to the one who names them. The most curious anomaly is that although Murdock classifies the terminology as Hawaiian (Murdock 1967, 174)—that is, as generational—on the basis of terms used for *female* cousins, it is Omaha—that is, emphasizing the unity of lineage groups rather than generation—in "intent" and on the basis of terms used for *male* cousins. As Figure 3.1 shows,[1] all female cousins, cross and parallel, matrilateral and patrilateral, are referred to as *mUuna* (*-una* with the singular *mU-* prefix), a term that is also used for brother and certain other male cousins, such as patrilateral parallel cousins (FBS). However, when the term is

---

1. For the sake of completeness, following are other important kinship terms:
muxemwa: W, WZ
muxwa: WF, WFZ
moram: WB
mwana: WZS & D, WBS & D
mUjUkUU: WBSS and D, WBDS and D, MBSD, ZSD, BDS and D
yiu: MFZD
kUkU: MFZS

34

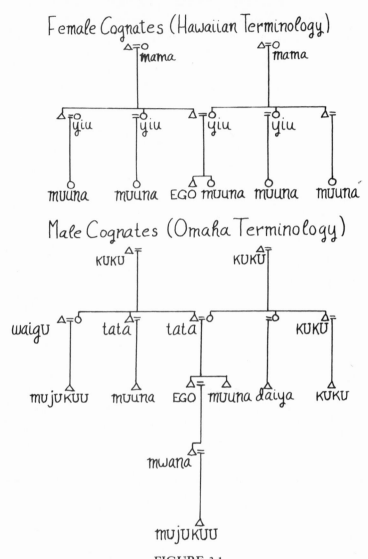

FIGURE 3.1
Diagram of Kinship Terminology for Female and Male Cognates

used for women, the context indicates that a woman is meant (as it does with two other important terms presently to be discussed: *mwana* and *mUjUkUU*).

Not only female cousins are generationally arranged, but so are women of the first ascending generation, except for the wife of mother's brother. The term *yiu*, which is used for mother, is also used for FBW, FZ, and MZ. Finally, the term *mUjUkUU* is applied to the daughters of *mUuna*, with the exception of those in Ego's patrilineage who, like his own daughter, are designated *mwana*.

This strong cognatic bias extends to some degree to men also. It is usual for a male informant to qualify the primary terms for male cousins by saying that mother's brother's son *(kUkU)*, father's sister's son *(mUjUkUU;* alternately *mwifwa* wherever this term is used), and mother's sister's son *(daiya)* are "really" *mUuna*, or "brother," thus suggesting a generational emphasis for them as well. And although mother's brother *(kUkU)* and father's sister's husband *(waigU)* are terminologically distinguished from father, informants speak of *waigU* as "really my *tata*, [father]," and mother's sister's husband is actually called *tata*. Mother's brother is always kept distinct from *tata* by both sexes, but he is seen as having a role similar to that of the father. One elder of my acquaintance, conscious of the dilemma involved in the fact that his mother's brother's son was at the same time classed with mother's brother and thought of as a sibling, said he preferred to avoid the problem by calling this person by his personal name.

The existence of these conflicting modes of classifying relatives gives rise to certain marriage problems. For example, while there is no prohibition against a man's marriage to his mother's brother's daughter—it is even relatively common and spoken of as "taking your mother back"—there is suspicion that such a union with a "sibling" may have adverse effects on the offspring because of a possible violation of the incest taboo. A special rite of *itlma* or "cutting" of the relationship is held, and a special bridewealth assessment is made for the rite. In most marriages a "cow of relatedness" *(ŋombe a nduɣU)* is paid, to overcome the chance that the relationship of bride and groom is "too close." Another strange reflex of the terminology is that a man may marry his child *(mwana)*. If his wife does not produce children, he has the right to demand a "sororal" replacement of her from her father or brothers. A legitimate and usual candidate for this position is wife's brother's daughter, who is "child" to Ego.

The reason for this strong cognatic emphasis in the Turu system is not clear, although it seems related to the tight hold a brother retains over his sister, and to some extent over her children, throughout her marriage. Ego speaks of mother's sister as being just like his mother, and he refers to his matrilateral parallel cousins as "siblings." He considers the people of a lineage into which MZ marries as a wife-talking lineage and so classifies them in the same way as the people into which his FZ or his own sister marries. Even so, he realizes that in truth the people of MZ lineage are different in important ways, particularly with respect to the fact that he does not share cattle with them, and he therefore refers to his MZ's as *daiya*, a term he alternates with *mUuna*, because they are outside the cattle-sharing cooperative, which is Ego's patrilineage.

Allowing for this cognatic or generational bias in dealing with women, it is therefore plain that the society is more accurately describable as a segmentary one, in which the emphasis among men is on the distinctness of unilineal descent groups and for which the Omaha method of classifying kin is apt. In Ego's patrilineage the first and second ascending and the first and second descending generations are all differentiated from each other and from Ego's generation. *Tata* (father and his brothers, real and classificatory), and *kUkU* (the fathers of *tata*) are set off from *mwana* (sons of *tata*) and *mUjUkUU* (sons of *mwana*). Persons of Ego's generation are *mUuna*. Of course *mUjUkUU* and *kUkU*, in contrast to these other terms, are not generational terms, since they are also used for second ascending and all previous generations respectively. Furthermore, *mUjUkUU* is applied to most members of wife-taking lineages to Ego's, and kUkU to mother's brother and other men of all wife-giving to Ego's.

In fact, the term *kUkU* generally conjures up in the mind of a Turu a wide range of foreign lineages, those from which the women of his lineage came. And the term *mUjUkUU* brings to mind an array of wife-taking groups. Yet these terms must be seen as operating at two levels—the one just described and a more personal one. Each Ego has certain men, mother's brothers and grandfathers, whom he thinks of as his specific *kUkUs*, just as he sees his relation to his actual father in far more personal and practical terms than to other fathers. At this level the terms lose some of their lineage particularity and serve rather to describe to Ego concentric circles of competition and cooperation. Ego is flanked on the one side by his father, who resists passing birthright cattle on to him, and on the other side by his son, who is trying to take cattle from him. A step beyond each of these persons are others who are similarly tormenting those who are tormenting Ego. The paternal grandfather and mother's brother are respectively trying to keep from giving cattle and are trying to get more cattle from father, while the paternal grandson and daughter's husband are conducting themselves in a similar manner with respect to Ego's son. With these people, who compete with the person with whom Ego competes, Ego carries on relations of friendliness, equality, or privileged familiarity.

To summarize the discussion of kinship terminology, two elements of the Turu system stand out as central to terminology as well as to other features of the society that will be subsequently discussed. One is the strong emergence of patrilineally defined corporate groups, which are responsible for the Omaha type of terminology. The other is the relationship between a man and his wife's brother, which is a continuing and competitive one throughout the marriage. The cognatic bias of the system seems to derive from this relation, since the wife's brother maintains perpetual ownership of his sister and to some extent claims ownership of her children. Turu men, who are the main players in the social game, favor a segmentary lineage system and see as a serious problem the lack of normative clarity in control of their wives and children.

Turning now to a consideration of the lineage system, Turu conceive of it ideally in terms of the classical nesting pattern of segmentary systems (Fortes 1953, 25ff) such that a number of low-level lineages, each with an apical founding ancestor, are a single lineage at the next-higher level. In order to add precision to this discussion, the more common terms for designating different levels of lineage—such as minimal lineage, maximal lineage, and the like—will not be used. Rather, the levels will be labeled with Roman numerals beginning with the lowest level and working up:

Level I consists of a group of adult brothers.

Level II consists of a group of Level I lineages all purportedly descended from a common ancestor. This unit is encompassed by a broken line in the diagram of Figure 3.2 to indicate that it is also the village of a spatially isolated complex of

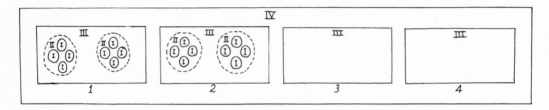

FIGURE 3.2

Model of Turu Lineages. Showing the different levels of segmentation in nesting pattern (Levels I to IV only). Broken lines around Level II indicate that this Level is coincident with the village. The number of units in both Levels I and II is greater than shown. The numbers 1 through 4 attached to the Level II lineages refer to the system of opposition of lineages such that 1 and 4, representing descendants of the first and last sons of the founder of Level IV, ally in opposition to numbers 2 and 3, who are descendants of the middle sons of the founder.

homesteads. Contained in this village is one Level II lineage. The depth of a Level II lineage—that is, the number of generations between the present adult group and the founding ancestor—is about five.

Level III consists of a number of Level II village lineages. This may consist of more than the two indicated in our diagram for the sake of simplicity. The actual number varies, with some containing as many as thirteen. While the Level III segments balance off structurally, so that there seem to be four in each Level IV, they do not necessarily balance in actual numbers of people or villages. The depth of this Level III lineage is about ten generations.

Level IV is coincident with the clan of the People of Kahiu, the second-largest clan in the Wahi subtribe. It is composed of four Level III lineages, located in the areas of Wijue, NyakUlu, γumpI and Weeya. All the people of these lineages are said to be descendants of Senge, who is said to have been directly descended from the founder of the clan, MukahiU. In comparison, the largest clan in Wahi subtribe is that of the People of NyahatI, which has two Level IV lineages, making the clan coincident with a fifth level of lineage—one level higher than KahiU. The eastern section at DamankIa is one Level IV and the western section at MpUmbUi is another. All these people claim descent from the founder of the clan, MunyahatI.

We could, if we wished, carry this division further by designating the subtribe and tribe as higher levels of lineage. In these the ancestor founding the segment would, as in the case of the clans, be designated by the name of the segment with a first person singular prefix, *Mu-*. For example, the founder of the Turu would be MUnyatUrU or MUrImi; the founder of Wahi would be Mwahi.

The Turu have no terms absolutely designating the different levels of lineage, although there are relative terms. For example, *irika* indicates that the persons or segments referred to are at the same level. More importantly, they use the terms *mUfita* and *mwango* (or sometimes *kinyamwango*), which we previously saw means "corral gate" and "sitting room," to designate different levels. Any segment from the highest down to Level II can be called "gate," while in the context the next level down is *mwango*.

The positions of the various lineages in relation to each other correlate with the relations of the founding ancestors. To the Turu the relations of the ancestors determine the relations of the lineages, but in fact the genealogical charts may be adjusted to take account of relations established on strategic grounds. While knowledge of genealogies is necessary to any competent adult, he needs to know only those relevant to his own interest, so that while a man usually knows in detail the genealogy of his own Level II village lineage, he does not necessarily know those of other Level II lineages. At higher levels he knows the genealogy of his clan and how the various Level III lineages fit into the larger system, but he knows little about the internal composition of other Level III lineages of his clan. He may know something about other clans, but he is unlikely to know more than their founding ancestors. The relations of clan ancestors to each other is especially vague; it seems to be taken as sufficient to assert that in some general sense they all descended from the founder of the subtribe. This attitude, I think, reflects the decreasing importance to individuals of lineages higher than Level II.

Reference has been made to clans and lineages without differentiating them. While it is usual to think of lineages as segments of a clan, to some extent in Turu society they take on the appearance of conflicting principles of organization. It has been suggested that *mbeyu* means "clan" among the Turu, but I found no confirmation of this among the people with whom I worked. When asked his "gate," a Turu will often respond with the name of his clan—"MukahiU" or "MunyahatI"—rather than any lower segment. A more definite way of determining his clan, however, is to ask the question, "umUnyafe?" ("Where do you come from; where do you divide?"). Von Sick described Turu clans as totemic, but in this he was mistaken. The main distinguishing feature of a clan, in addition to the fact that it has a name and a "sneeze phrase" that is uttered by a member whenever he sneezes, is that it is the unit for determining exogamy, marriage between members of the same clan generally being tabooed. Historically clans and lineages have regularly been augmented by incorporation of individual foreigners from the tribes of Nyamwezi, Sandawe, and so on, but, strangely, their foreign origin seems never to be forgotten. As a result, some Turu maintain that they are at the same time foreigners yet members of the clan of which their lineage has become a "naturalized" segment. In more than one case such "foreign" lineages claim membership in a Turu clan while practicing intermarriage with most of the lineages of which the clan is composed.

The practice of fusing "foreigners" into pre-existing clans and lineages is so widespread in Wahi that we can distinguish three different grades of incorporation:

1. In some place we find lineages claiming descent from founders who came from other tribes—Nyamwezi, Gogo, and the like—but which are separate from other Turu clans and are therefore clans in themselves.

2. There are lineages claiming descent from foreigners, whether from other tribes or other Turu clans, that are viewed, however, as legitimate component lineages of the clans with which they claim affiliation. They do not intermarry with other members of their new clan.

3. There are lineages in the same class as number 2 that, however, may intermarry with some of the lineages of their new clan if those lineages are not the ones with which they are directly affiliated.

These different degrees of incorporation suggest the possibility of a fourth: lineages of foreign extraction that are fully integrated with the clans into which they have moved. Such may occur, but there are reasons to doubt it. The genealogical charters of most of the foreign lineages are of considerable depth, yet the foreign extraction of the founders is not forgotten. It is even claimed by some that the largest clan in Wahi, the People of NyahatI, is of Gogo origin. Turu seem to remember aggressively each other's immigrant status.

In examining Turu clans and lineages, much confusion may result from a lack of understanding of just how this fusing process works. In one place in Wahi I was repeatedly told that a lineage on the next hill was composed of Airwana, giving the impression that those people had just recently migrated en masse from Wilwana, the northern subtribe. Upon inspection it was discovered that the people were in no way different from others in Wahi, that they were all descended from a single foreign immigrant, and that this founder of the lineage had migrated from Wilwana many years and generations before. It is true in almost all the cases of lineages of foreign extraction that only one foreigner was the reputed original founding ancestor.

It can be recognized as only a variant of the fusing process that to the people living outside the Puma (mpUma) area of Wahi, the collection of small clans residing there is thought of as a single clan, AnyapUma. The actual clans are seen as component lineages of this supposed clan. This attitude supports the view that presently it is the segmentary lineage system, with its various levels of balanced segments, that is functional and that the clan principle is to a large extent overridden by it or made to conform to it. In order to achieve such a balanced lineage structure, small clans are brought together, lineages of foreign extraction are incorporated, and in a number of cases lineages descended from females are viewed as legitimate units in a predominately patrilineal structure. Where this occurs, it is usually because a woman gave birth to a son whose father was unknown. Such a son is raised by his mother's father or brothers but is not accepted as a legitimate heir. If a lineage grows out of him, it may become a separate segment in the lineage structure. Since it is considered shameful to be descended from a woman, it is difficult to know how often this event occurs: when discussing other lineages, Turu frequently attempt to malign them by attributing this anomalous origin to them.

To summarize, the Turu system can be seen as under immense pressure to reconstitute as a system emphasizing the segmentary lineage principle. The great variability in the size of clans, which works against this aim, is on the one hand overcome by setting up in opposition to each other lineages of the same clan in the large clans. On the other hand there is an attempt to reconstitute small clans into larger ones (as at Puma) to achieve a structure comparable to the large clans. About the only function still served by clans is to regulate marriage through the rule of exogamy, and even this is sometimes violated in some clans where some of the lineages are of foreign origin. One might expect that the ultimate demise of the clan principle will occur when the marriage law becomes one of lineage rather than of clan exogamy.

As is usually the case in Africa, the strength of reciprocal obligations of members of lineages vary with the degree of distance of relation. This situation is reflected in terminology. Beginning with the group of brothers and sisters at the Level I lineage, kin terms classify generations such that father's brothers are all fathers *(tata)*, their wives are all mothers *(yiu)*, all children of fathers and mothers are siblings *(mUuna)*, and so forth. At Level II, the village, the same terminology again is employed as if all the members of the village were of the same family, the decision about which term to use for any person being based upon the number of generations he is removed from the common ancestor of the lineage in comparison with the speaker. To the speaker, all men of his Level II lineage who are two ascending degrees or more from him are *kUkU;* all of the first ascending generation are father *(tata);* all of the same generation, *mUuna* or "sibling" (actually *mUunane,* "my sibling," since the term is seldom used except with the possessive pronoun); all of the first descending generation are *mwana* ("child"), and all of the second descending generation and beyond are *mUjUkUU* or *mwifwa,* which are alternate terms. As long as any person is recognized by the speaker as being a descendant of the founding ancestor of his village, such terms apply regardless of the distance of relationship, which could be up to about fifth cousin. It follows, of course, that the women are similarly designated. All wives or sisters of *kUkU* are mama; all wives of father are *yiu;* all wives of siblings are *mUxemane* (literally, "my woman"); all sisters of male siblings are also siblings; and all females of descending generations, like siblings, are designated by the same terms as those used for males.

The extension of these lineal terms to collaterals does not occur consistently outside Level II lineages. The members of the Level II lineages of MUhUri openly debate the propriety of this usage, some feeling that members of other Level II lineages of their larger Level III lineage should be called by lineal terms, while others dispute this argument. At UnyahatI, in a similar situation, the question was not debated and the terms were uniformly extended. Whatever difference of opinion there may be at this level, outside of it there is no further extension of lineal terms, and members of the same clan in different Level III lineages think of each other merely as $ndU\gamma U$, "relatives."

It should be noted that the degree of relatedness of people in the same Level II lineage is variable and the extent of cooperation in the village itself is therefore variable. It is possible in a village for two lines to exist that have no closer connection than the common ancestor. It is my impression that in such cases there is a sharp drop of interaction between the sections. Whether the genealogical distance promotes the social distance or the reverse is an open question.

If whole lineages, even up to Level II, are classed terminologically as if all their members belonged to the same line, it follows that there is a wide matrilateral extension of affinal terms. All the members of the generation of a parent-in-law (*mUxwane*, "my parent-in-law") are also parents-in-law, at least within the Level II lineage, of the direct affinal relatives. A sibling-in-law (*mUramwane*) is any classificatory sibling of wife, and parents-in-law to a person's sibling are parents-in-law to him also. As a result, almost every Turu has a very large number of parents-in-law, siblings-in-law, and so forth.

There is no prescriptive rule of marriage among Turu. It is sometimes said that in precontact days certain Level II and III lineages were preferred to members of certain other lineages and that a son was directed by his father to find a bride among people of those groups. Even today mothers tend to try to find brides for their sons in the areas from which they came, with the result that certain Level II and III lineages of different clans exchange women with a high degree of frequency. However, the choice of a bride and the area from which she is to come was, and is even more today, left largely up to the youth, whose choice is then merely verified or vetoed by his father. Analysis of the source of brides shows a strong tendency for different wives of the same man to come from different clans. Other than this, it is prohibited, as noted earlier, to marry the direct mother's brother's daughter or father's sister's son, but it is possible to marry any other person of mother's or father's sister's lineage, although there is a vague uneasiness about the practice.

Because of the wide lateral extension of lineal terminology and the lack of a prescriptive rule of marriage, any two Turu from the same subtribe can, given a little time, discover a relationship between themselves showing them to be father-in-law and son-in-law, or more usually mother's brother (*kUkU*) and sister's son (*mUjUkUU*). These relationships are stabilized as a result of a previous affinal tie between the two lineages. Such relationships, which are actually distant although terminologically immediate, are not important. They are treated as curiosities, although they are given some serious recognition in the usual compulsory "cow of relationship" paid in the bridewealth. Turu are adept in adjusting norms to facts in cases of terminological anomalies so that, for example, if a marriage should occur with a mother's brother's daughter, the new relationship of father-in-law and son-in-law takes precedence over the older one. The conflict inherent in such a marriage, however, leads brothers to joke with the one who is involved in such a switch, because they continue to be on free-and-easy terms with mother's brother, while their brother must now treat him with great formality and circumspection.

The poor correlation between the cooperation normatively prescribed by the kinship classifying system and the degree of cooperation that actually occurs as distance of relationship varies (discussed in Chapter 6) requires individuals continually to assess how they will behave toward kin. No one expects indulgence from a distant classificatory mother's brother, even though that is spoken of as a norm and even though such a person is acceptable to play the role of mother's brother in certain rituals where it is required. Neither does anyone expect cooperation of the same intensity and quality from a distant lineal sibling as from one who is a codescendant of the same father. Classificatory siblings will assert that the wives of each are the wives of all, but a more serious view of adultery is taken when committed by a sibling outside the Level I lineage of the woman's husband. It is common for Turu to disclaim responsibility for terminologically immediate kin with the phrase "They are too far from me."

CORPORATENESS OF THE LINEAGE

The system of classifying kin serves the essential purpose of defining property rights rather than authority. This fact is not so clear in the immediate family, where the father wears one cap as controller of the wealth of the family and another as the governmental authority over his sons. It is clear when we survey relations of people at higher lineal levels, where property rights are distinct from authority.

It is a fundamental notion that the land, livestock, and people of a lineage belong to the ancestor who founded the village and to his lineal descendents, who share these rights jointly. This idea, of course, implies that at some point there is a distinction between one's own ancestors and those of other people who are lineally related to one at a higher level. In one sense the distinction is not made, and Turu are driven to the logical conclusion that the whole of Turuland belongs to all Turu because all descend from a common ancestor. Such a belief is not an empty one; there is evidence that WanyatUrU did on occasion band together to fight invading foreign tribes. It was once my good fortune to listen to one of the government-appointed chiefs defend his right to the nonexistent position of paramount chief of the whole tribe on the basis of his evidence that he was the rightful leader of his clan and that his clan was the only one purely descended from MUrImi. To him all other Turu were descendants of foreigners who have been fused to existing Turu lineages. As the legitimate senior descendant, he saw all the land as given in trust from the founder to him.

In fact, the most significant corporate groups are Level II village lineages and the Level I lineage of full siblings and father. Joint ceremonies, particularly to make rain, are sometimes held by members of the same Level III lineage, but cooperation among the segments of this lineage is low. In former days Level III was a jural community, whose segments banded together to fight other Level III lineages with whom they had disputes (including Level III lineages of their own clan). This function has disappeared with pacification of the country, although this unit to some extent still acts as a jural community. A good indication of the nature of relations between village lineages in the same Level III lineage is seen in the way diviners (*ayanga*, pl.; *mUyanga*, sing.) are used. It is felt that one should not take his problems to a diviner that "knows" him, because such a man is liable not to "tell the truth." What is meant is that such a man has intimate connections with his client and might give a biased prescription based on involvement in the disputes of the village. Therefore, no one ever utilizes a diviner of his own village. However, for some purposes a person may go to a diviner in another village of the same Level III lineage, with the implication that such a person does not really "know" the client.

Within a Level II lineage village inhabitants tend to brand their cattle with the same brand and to view the land as belonging to all of them, although the senior descendant of the founder is thought of as in some sense guardian of the joint rights. In discussions of land transactions any member of a village may speak of an exchange that was performed by some long dead ancestor as if he himself had accomplished it. In the mind of a member of a village the lineage is immortal and unchanging. His ancestors are not dead but continue to live spiritually in the village. They are thought to be located under the ground at the sites of their former homes and are reincarnated in the statuses of living persons who are named after them.

Each male has two names, one taken from some notable event that occurred at the time of his birth, such as a beer party, which might suggest the name NtuI (beer). The other name is that of an ancestor. Ancestors, it is felt, desire to "be called again" by their descendants. It is usual for a father to give to his child, whether male or female, the name of a recently dead ancestor of his lineage whose sex corresponds with that of the child. The paternal grandfather or grandmother is the first choice, although if the father is dead at the time of the birth of a son, the son will almost always be named after him. The only exception is that children are occasionally named after living but very old persons. Combined with the norm that two children of the same immediate family are not to be named after the same ancestor, the effect is to recreate partially the lineage by recalling the names of a wide range of ancestors. Turu do not see this practice as actual reincarnation but only as perpetuation of the social personality of the ancestor insofar as it is embodied in his name. While this naming system is to some extent a unifying device for the Level II lineage, it is significant that the names given to children tend to be confined to ancestors particular to their Level I lineage, with the result that the combination of names in different extended families in the village tend to be different. The one element that works against this outcome is the belief that if a child becomes sick when still an infant, some ancestor who has not been "called" is causing the sickness. This ancestor will be identified by a diviner and the child will be given its name, with the result that children sometimes receive the names of fairly distant lineal ancestors. Despite the tendency for a certain combination of names to be exclusive to Level I, names are mostly drawn from the same pool of remote ancestors of those of other families of the village and tribe, so that certain names appear throughout the tribal area.

Verifying the conclusion that ancestral names represent the resurrection of the status of dead persons, rather than the actual persons, names are not abandoned because their holders were witches or in other respects undesirable. Up to the time a child reaches the age of initiation, parents and other adults do not address him by his personal name but by the kinship term that the parent or other adult used for the ancestor for whom the child is named. Kinship terms are not otherwise ordinarily used as terms of address. If a boy is named after his father, his mother will address him as "my husband," and if after his grandfather his father will call him "my father." Playfully, and to a certain extent seriously, the parent will also treat the child the way the norms of interaction dictate that category of kinsman be treated. A mother who calls her child "husband" may play at being formal with him. An effect of this custom is to teach the child the kinship and genealogical system that will be so important to him, at the same time giving him and his parents a strong sense of security because of the continuity of the lineage represented in this play.

While the system of naming is a device for "immortalizing" the lineage, the source of the names makes it clear that the struggle for dominance between lineages which we saw before occurs here also. Figure 3.3 diagrams the source of names for all the children of Musandai, a man who produced through one wife an unusually large family. It can be seen that five of the names come from the maternal side, including that of the first son, and six from the paternal side (counting No. 7, who was named after No. 4 subsequent to No. 4's death). Naming the first child after a maternal relative is common, because the wife usually goes home to have the first child and can give it a name before the husband can assert his preference. Interestingly, in this example every one of the direct maternal family up to two generations back from the mother is recalled. On the other hand, No. 3 has five children, of whom only one, a girl, is named after a maternal kinsman, the mother-in-law. In another case two widowed co-wives have named almost all children born subsequent to the death of their husband after maternal kin. Among the Turu all children born to a man's legitimate wife are his even after his death and after they have been taken in by his heir.

Ancestral sacrificial rites are held within the village and principally concern property (Plate 3.1). Typically the ancestors (arUngu, pl.; mUngu, "God," a contraction of mUrUngu, is said to be "the same" as the ancestors) are believed to be the cause of prosperity or the lack of it. They can give children and bestow livestock or kill them and cause drought. An angry ancestor is assuaged with a sacrificial steer or goat, whose heart or "spirit" (moyo) goes to the ancestor; so does either the hide, which provides him with a mat on which to sleep, or milk.

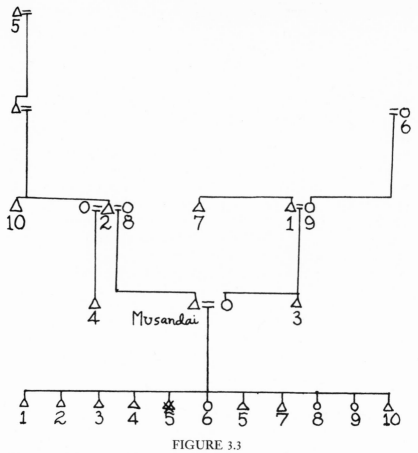

FIGURE 3.3

Diagram of Ancestral Names of the Children of MUsandai. Showing for MUsandai's eleven children the ancestor from whom each got his or her ancestral name. Child Number 5's name was taken by the next son when 5 died.

Cows are not sacrificed. To represent a cow, a steer is killed along with a sheep, the steer being surrogate for the cow and the sheep for a suckling calf, which always accompanies a cow who is giving milk. Ancestral rites are always initiated by an individual who has been advised by a diviner that one of his ancestors is responsible for his misfortune, but all members of the village are expected to attend the rite, as are all women of the family of the initiator who are living elsewhere and a sister's son (*mUjUkUU* or *mwifwa*) of the deceased. The latter is of special importance because it is believed that the ancestor, who is *kUkU* or mother's brother to this person, cannot refuse him anything. The *mUkUU* or chief descendant of the founder of the lineage must give a special blessing, and prayers are said at the grave by the people present, after which the grave is blessed with honey, as are all proximate graves. The graves of ancestors, like the homes of living people, tend to correlate in degrees of proximity with the degree

PLATE 3.1

Ancestral Sacrifice. Men are grouped at left in the old house site of the
ancestor and women at right in the old house of the wife of the ancestor.
The steer is being butchered at the site of the ancestor's grave in the old
corral.

of relationship, so that blessing graves near that of the ancestor, who is the
subject of the sacrifice, is an appeal to those ancestors who would probably also
be concerned about the troubles of the applicant, a concern that declines with
distance.

While the type of ancestral rite involving the whole village is the most usual,
a group of full brothers alone on occasion sacrifices to their father, using a sheep.
On the other hand, a Level III lineage may hold a rain-making rite that seems to
differ from the village rite in that it is not initiated by one person but by a group,
making this more truly a community rite of intensification than the ancestral
sacrifice. It is significant that, when the whole community is endangered, a
Level III group coalesces as the group of solidarity. In addition to these variant
forms of sacrifices, it is also said that a *kUkU* may hold a sacrifice at the grave
of his *mwifwa* or sister's son whom he may have offended, and a woman may
make sacrifice to her mother if she has private troubles, although the men of her
family and her husband's family manage the affair.

Questions of property are almost always settled by reference to ancestors and
degree of kinship unless a witnessed sale has been involved. A man's defense of
his right to a certain portion of land is by reference to his relation with the
ancestral possessor of the land, who is usually his father, the one who would
have given it to him. Implicit is the notion that land can never be fully alienated
to a person outside the lineage. When rain-making ceremonies are held, they

must be led by a descendant of the person who pioneered in opening the land, even though his people no longer live on it. A man's claim to some of another man's cattle is verified by lineal relationship. If he is a son of that man, he has the right to some of his cattle. Normatively the rights to land and other goods are held by the senior descendant of the lineage; in turn, segments of it are held by senior members of the sublineages, and so forth. Of course such rights do not consist of actual control, except in the general sense that men feel they should not, if possible, sell the land of their ancestors or withhold its use from other members of the lineage. Before such rights are alienated, it is felt that the senior should be consulted because he "knows" in a mystical way what is right simply by virtue of being senior. This is not changed by the feeling a man may have that the senior is, in fact, a fool whose practical advice is useless. Asking advice is a ritual act, a verification of the unity of the group.

The unity of the lineage is seen also in rights in persons composing it. When a member of a lineage injures or kills a member of another, all persons of his lineage are held responsible for paying compensation; when a member of the lineage seeks to marry, all are responsible for seeing that the necessary livestock are forthcoming. In these circumstances Turu say, "We are one." They may also say that the wife of one is the wife of all his male siblings of all degrees. In their view, if one is killed, all are killed a little bit, and if one kills, all kill.

The unity of the lineage is also expressed in its name and in the name of the place where it is located. Members of a Level I lineage are called by the name of the founder—"The Sons of MUhUri," for example—but there is no particular name for their place of residence within the village. The people of a single lineage village at Level II are also named after their founder. "The People of MUhUri." Their place of residence, the village, also has a name, however. The actual People of MUhUri in UkahiU live in the village called Utatuu; the People of NtUnduu nearby live in MUmbII; the People of MUnyankonde in UnyahatI live in SUnja. Level III lineages—collections of villages—are also called after the name of the founder—"The People of Kilongo"—but it is more usual to describe them by reference to the name of the territory, in this case Wijue. At higher levels, beginning with the clan, a social unit's territory is designated by prefixing the territory prefix U- to the name of the unit—the clan of KahiU, for example, resides in Ukahiu, the NyatUrU in UnyatUrU.

Not enough data are available to give precise figures about the average population of villages; in any case such figures would not be as significant as the number of homesteads, each of which is a basic economic complex. Villages tend to be composed, as previously noted, of from ten to twenty homesteads, with total populations of 100 to 150. Reckoning from the generation of the largest active group of adults, the villages are four to seven generations in genealogical depth in my limited sample. As also indicated previously, Level I lineages extend only to the generation above the father, and the Level III lineage to about ten generations. Up to this level the genealogies seem to approximate the truth, but beyond that they are almost purely mythical, since they are utilized as charters to rationalize the association of Level III lineages in the system of balance of segments. Even within Level III the genealogical charter is subject to frequent adjustments to fit circumstances. If a man calls another one "brother" or "father," it will usually not be because he has genealogically calculated his relation to that man—although he could—but because he can deduce the proper term from what his own father called that man. Any extensive discussion of a genealogy will quickly bring to light disagreements among men about the exact ordering of ancestors within it, with the consequence that it is possible to observe informants inventing and rearranging the elements to fit their already firmly formed conceptions of relationships to contemporaries.

We may conclude this discussion of lineages by admitting that the singling out of the Level II lineage, the village, as the most crucial corporate segment is partly a matter of intuition. No lineage level is in fact so strongly unified that the individuals in it are completely subjugated to it. The Level I lineage is certainly the strongest in intensity of corporateness; but selection of Level II as the main unit seems to fit Turu views. Frequently Level I consists of no more than one son. Insofar as the village is a necessary cooperative unit, it would not be efficiently replaced by Level I in most cases because of the chance that there would be insufficient brothers to constitute a viable economic complex. Functionally Level II is efficient. On the other side, Level III is too large for cooperative purposes.

An illustration of this categorization occurred one day when a young man, who was drunk and therefore in an aggressive mood, bitterly assailed me for allegedly recording the name of his village as Utatuu. He was of the MUhUri lineage allied with the Tatuu lineage; between the two, however, there is antagonism. He resented the slight to his lineage that is implied by this name which has, nevertheless, been generally accepted as the proper one for his village.

SEGMENTATION

The communalistic view of African societies emphasizes the corporate lineage at the expense of individuality. In Turu society the lineage is important as a coalition aiding the individual in the economic game, even though it also restricts him. It is important, however, to recognize that there are other norms that segment individuals rather than aggregating them and that are represented in classifying terms other than kin ones.

There are two sets of such segmenting terms. The first divides the group of full brothers into two, the senior segment consisting of the eldest brother (*mUkUU*) and the youngest brother (*mUtInampafo*). Brothers born between these two are *va mUxatI*, or "of the middle." Land, livestock, and sisters—the basic capital items for the establishment of a successful homestead—pass chiefly from the mother, under the guidance of the father, to the senior segment, while the brothers of the middle receive only a pittance. Technically all wealth passes to the eldest son, who must share it with the youngest. Next these two share with the middle brothers, the eldest with those from the center up and the youngest with those from the center down. Middle brothers commonly resent being given so little, and they are likely to be the ones who leave their native villages to pioneer new villages in hopes of achieving better lives. They are also likely to be the ones to remove themselves to the homes of their mother's brothers for whatever benefit this may give, and they are likely to be the ones sent to be raised at the home of mother's brother if there is no use for them at their natal home.

This splitting of middle from senior brothers is represented in the structure of relations of lineages in the two large clans of AkahiU and AnyahatI. In AkahiU as a whole, and in the two main segments of AnyahatI, each of which is structurally equal in size to the whole of the Akahiu, there are four Level III lineages. Figure 3.2 of the model of segmentation may represent any of these, for in these Level IV lineages, two of the Level III lineages (1 and 4) are said to be descended from the senior sons of the founder and the other two (2 and 3) from the middle sons. This arrangement at the top of the structure, therefore, duplicates that at the bottom, where the senior brothers cooperate and are allied in opposition to the middle with respect to property.

It is certainly one of the most interesting rules of the Turu game that the senior and most junior sons are so heavily favored, but the reason seems plain enough. This technique conserves capital and gives the Level I lineage as a whole a better chance of competing with other lineages for position and power. The same principle used at the top of the structure has a different function—the achievement of alliances that will be effective in preserving the interests of the different segments.

The other set of segmentary terms distinguishes each man from others on the basis of the heifer given him by his father at the time he completes the circumcision rites. Subsequently the father and son address each other by a reciprocal name based on the name of that cow. If the cow is a black heifer, a Titi, they call each other Wa-titi. It is worth examining other reciprocal names which use the *wa-* prefix in this way in order to understand its significance. Two men who like each other and who do not belong to the same village lineage may formally exchange wealth and address each other as *waiγembe* (from *iγembe*, "hoe"). The name stems from the days when the hoe was a more valuable item than it is now. Whenever one person gives another something of value, a reciprocal name based on the object may arise. In response to his request, I once hauled a granite grinding stone to the home of a Turu friend, who from then on called me *waigwe* (*igwe*, "stone"). The name would not emerge from the giving of insignificant favors, as is illustrated by the joke carried on between myself and an old man who was always requesting cigarettes; we called each other *wa-sigara* (from the Kiswahili for "cigarette"). The prefix appears also with certain kin terms, such as that used between brothers-in-law, who call each other *wa-mwana, mwana* being a child, referring in this case to exchange of the bride. Parents-in-law call each other *wa-UkUU* (from *UkUU*, "relative") referring to the fact that they have been involved in exchange of a kinsman, the bride. Men of the same village refer to each other as *witu*, probably a contraction derived from *-itu*, the first-person plural pronoun, and the *wa-* prefix, indicating in a general sense the reciprocal relations that exist among them. The significance of the *wa-* prefix, then, seems to be that it is an indicator of a special relationship of reciprocity between two parties based on the initial object exchanged, and the reciprocal name sets the person off from others.

When an adult man addresses his full brother, he may, in lieu of the personal name, use the reciprocal cow name that the person and his father use for each other. Each time a man addresses his brother, he is in effect reasserting the special relationship the brother has with their common father, as opposed to the one the speaker has. That this interpretation is proper may be seen when we examine the use of cow names outside the family. When a Turu addresses an adult male relation by a reciprocal cow name, he uses the one employed by the common ancestor of himself and the addressee which that ancestor applied to the one of his sons who gave rise to the line of the addressee.

This can be understood by reference to the diagram in Figure 3.4. If No. 1 addresses No. 3, he calls him WalIkIni, after the cow given No. 6 by No. 4. In contrast, when No. 1 addresses No. 2, he calls him Wamaa, after the cow given No. 2 by No. 7. No. 3 would call No. 1 and No. 2 by the name of the cow given to No. 5 by No. 4. It follows that Ego will address *all* the men of a neighboring Level II lineage by the same cow name derived from the cow given by the founder of the Level III lineage to the founder of Level II of that neighboring village. Within his own village Ego will distinguish whole groups of men

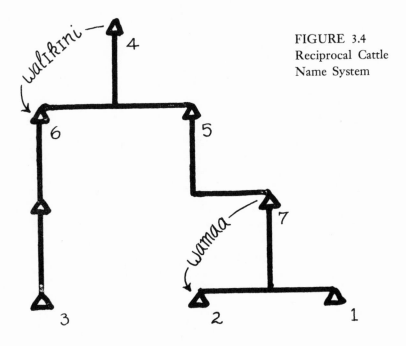

FIGURE 3.4
Reciprocal Cattle
Name System

who are distantly related to him with the same term. In certain circumstances, if the village consists of two large groups, each descended from a different son of the founder, any man will find himself addressing a large portion of the men of his village by the same cow name.

In contrast to the recognition of lineal individuality, the actual process of segmentation is never normative and seems to occur in at least two different ways. As a village grows, the remoteness of some segments from others becomes more and more emphasized by reciprocal cow names, and the difficulty of activating reciprocity between the remotely related people increases. Finally, a conceptual line may be drawn between the parts in the minds of the people. As one man put it, one tends to refer to a remote unit of the village as "The Sons of CIma," or whoever their ancestor is, and segmentation is complete when this changes to "The People of CIma," signifying a new Level II lineage. Another common process is migration by middle sons, or other disaffected elements from a village, who set themselves up in a new area where land is available. If the clearing and settlement of such a new place—normally in the forest—is successful, relatives from the village follow and others may also appear.

If the creation of new villages as it occurs today follows the traditional pattern, at the beginning the village is a collection of indifferently related people, but as it becomes successfully established, either the stronger lineage group forces others out or genealogies are revised to bring unity. Hence, the genealogical homogeneity of the village increases with time. While the tendency is never to completely eradicate remembrance of genealogical diversity, homogeneity is accomplished, as we saw at the beginning of this chapter, by the inclusion of foreign groups as if they were members of the lineage of the founder and, therefore, members of his clan. For some years one group of villages of UkahiU have been sending off such shoots to the southeast, giving rise to a whole new series of villages that are in various stages of achievement of homogeneity but that are identified as belonging to the clan of AkahiU.

The importance of the process of segmentation for the thesis of this book is that it shows that the concept of corporateness as it is sometimes understood must be modified to allow flexibility to members of corporate groups. If the groups were corporate in the absolute sense, the system could not operate. The segmentation and fusion essential to operating lineages are based on individuality. The *waiɣembe* relationship illustrates an ad hoc arrangement, cutting across all others, that does not even depend on relationship. The ideology of corporateness is a setting for cooperation that is essential to individual enterprise. As we have seen, however, the ideology that one must cooperate with his "brother" diminishes with distance and is mitigated by the segmentary process both as it is institutionalized and in its ad hoc form. This topic will receive more explicit attention in Chapter 6.

4. RELATIONS OF AUTHORITY

Adulthood carries authority.
TURU PROVERB

RELATIONS of authority—as opposed to property relations, which have concerned us up to this point—constitute an essential part of the normative system. We are handicapped severely in learning about this aspect of life by the strong intrusion of Western governmental and legal institutions into Turu life. Until 1960 the exercise of authority and the application of sanctions were in part usurped by the colonial government, which appointed courts and chiefs and their assistants. Formerly Turu had no chiefs (nor any now; since independence the position has been abolished) or any institutionalized focal position of authority except that of the father in the family. Von Sick described the indigenous government as consisting of "the old people," who were actually the heads of homesteads, regulating affairs in each village. Reche found no chiefs and noted that Stanley had not either. Baumann also found no chiefs. Reche noted that the elders had no power to enforce decisions, though they had the ability to protect their status. This old system still operates in some respects and can be described in a general way by utilizing information from people who know how it worked in precontact days and by including early accounts of the Turu by such people as von Sick in addition to observing some of the remaining practices.

AGE CLASSES

Within the family authority is correlated with control of property. This is not so above Level I, however. In the village there are three general classes of people distinguished by age and social condition: precircumcision youths, who are *mUηInya;* adult men and women, the women (*axema,* pl.; *mUxema,* sing.) being always subordinate to men (*aγosia,* pl.; *mUγosia, sing.*); and the important men (*anyampaa,* pl.; *mUnyampaa,* sing.) and important women (*axaikUU,* pl.; *mUxaikUU,* sing.), both of whom are usually elderly. The latter terms are used as polite expressions of respect for any elderly people and any adult persons of importance. This is particularly so of the male term *mUnyampaa.* However, the head of a homestead will be thus addressed by members of his homestead regardless of his age, and a young man of wealth and leadership in a village may be called this by all. The elder brother also is addressed as *mUnyampaa* by the other brothers when he succeeds to the father's position.

Succession to the position of adult occurs for boys after circumcision and for girls after cliterodectomy, allowing for the fact that girls never become adults in the legal sense that men do. The rites for boys and girls are held together every year at any homestead in which there are youths requiring initiation and whose head is willing to bear the cost. Not more than one homestead in a village is likely to take on the task in one year. If others in a village have children to be initiated, they participate with the children of the first man, to whom a fee is paid. These rites draw the largest crowds of any ceremonial occasion and may include boys and girls from widely scattered places. The boys stay together at the circumcision site for only a few days, after which they disperse to their homes. The status change effected by the rite, therefore, is with respect to a social group broader than the village. All men are graded by the particular year in which they undergo the circumcision such that all are senior to those circumcised in subsequent years and junior to those circumcised in previous years. In a hypothetical village of twenty adults it is possible for twenty sets to exist, although usually there are several men who are circumcised in the same year. It is the creation of these grades of seniority in the village that is the chief function of the men's rite, although it also encourages tribal unity by the participation of people drawn from a wide area.

This grading system cuts across kinship categories outside the family at Level II. The age set of full brothers will correlate exactly with their order of birth and therefore with their order of seniority, with the exception of the youngest brother, who is allied to the oldest. Between lineages of Level II it is possible, and it frequently happens that the classificatory father of a man is his age-set junior. The result of this grading may be seen in seating customs. Squatting, or hunkering, is the most inferior form of seating. Going up from that in order of prestige, a person may hunker using a piece of wood under the heels to take the strain off the leg muscles, or sit on a log, a small stool, a large stool, and finally, a chair, which in modern times has become the most prestigeful form of resting. When men are gathered in discussion and there are not enough stools, chairs, and the like, to go around, they will arrange themselves in order of seniority and will rearrange themselves every time a new person arrives so that the senior person will always have the more prestigeful form of resting equipment. It would be an insult to a senior for a junior not to offer him his seat. Now, if there are two half-brothers, and if the one born of the second wife of their father was circumcised before the son of the first, the son of the second is given the better seat even though junior in the kinship seniority system.

To understand notions of disrespect for authority, it must be specified that some acts of aggression are with respect to property and some with respect to social status. It is difficult in practice to separate these two, but such is precisely the basis of the authority system. Disputes over property usually seem to resolve themselves into authority-status conflicts. In order for a person to attack another, he must have the authority. In order for authority to be maintained, a junior must be prevented from attacking senior status. As the system operates, it is possible for a junior to attack a senior with impunity if the attack has to do with violation of his property by the senior, while in another circumstance where there is no conflict over property, the attack is subject to sanction by *njUγUda*. In such attacks words are weapons of aggression of even greater force than actual physical violence, although both tend to occur together. When a man is accused by the elders of being a criminal trouble maker, they will say to him, "You have words [*nxani*]," meaning evil words. It is thought that the soul or vital force of a person (*moyo*, "heart," in a living person and *mwimimi* when he is dead) can be attacked by that of another, the metaphysical attack being manifested in overt acts of hostility, particularly in evil words reflecting the hostile condition of the aggressor's own spirit. In any event, such verbal hostility is condemned when physical aggression may not necessarily be considered wrong. Turu speak of verbal or physical attacks on the status of persons when these are not related to property conflicts as attacks "without reason." Property conflicts are a matter for negotiation and argument, but the norms relating to attacks on the persons of seniors are strict and severely sanctioned.

Generally speaking, then, adult men canot attack their seniors, but they can attack juniors with impunity. The term *ntusio* refers to a man born next to another; such adjacent brothers are regarded as equal, regardless of age-set rank. In all other cases children are totally subject to authority. In compensation, however, they can never be accused of attacks on persons of authority, since they are not yet persons. Within the family the wife is ideally thoroughly subject to the authority of her husband but is also not subject to sanction for aggression against him. If she is a shrew, he can simply divorce her; if she is especially evil, he may accuse her of being a witch. Among men in a village, wives and sisters are subordinate to all the men and ideally can be verbally or even physically attacked by them without fear of sanction, although men may, of course, come into conflict with each other on this score, one objecting to another's treatment of his wife; in addition they may have to answer to the wife's brother if the attack is severe. Mothers can be sanctioned for attacks on their infant children, and older sons can be sanctioned for attacks on their mothers, whether real or classificatory. Finally, between alternate generations, who are regarded as equivalent to brothers, attacks on personal status are not recognized. These people joke with each other, and joking consists in part of playful insults. Although women are, socially speaking, quasipersons and without authority in relations with men (except in the status of mother), among adult women there is a subsystem of authority based on status. In its operation the younger women can be sanctioned for attacks on the seniors the *axaikUU*.

NJUγUDA

There is one powerful limitation on the behavior of men with respect to women: they are severely enjoined not to interfere with the secret rites of the women, by threat of the invocation of *njUγUda*. A man who sneaks into the rooms of a girl in menstruation seclusion, or who intrudes on the rites of *imaa*,[1] is regarded as violating women's prerogatives and is subject to a more severe form of this sanction than he is for attacks on seniors. The reason for this seems to be that these rites are fundamental to achievement of profitable relations between women and their husbands and are therefore crucial to the whole system. It is significant that on days when the rites are held, the persons of women are sacred, and wives cannot be beaten by their husbands. This is but the most prominent example of a whole series of instances where sacred things are protected from violation by this form of sanction. The person of a *mUhUngu* (a circumcision or clitoridectomy initiate) is also protected from attack during the period of the rites, and a person's actions may even be sanctioned for removing the gravestone from a grave.

NjUγUda is essentially a public shaming of the victim, who also pays a fine. Examples of offenders subject to *njUγUda* are:

An adult man who has been caught with a *mUnyambee*, a girl in seclusion subsequent to the onset of menstruation.
A man who reveals secrets of the women's rites.
A man who grossly insults his mother-in-law.
A man who beats his mother.
Young women who abuse a senior woman of a neighboring Level II lineage.
A man who beats his father.
A man who abuses all the members of a village.
A man who insults his mother by making uncomplimentary references to her private parts, forcibly reveals them and is suspected of incestuous relations with her.

The case of the man who abused all the members of a village seems to have been interpreted by the Turu as an attack on order in some more general sense than is usually conceived.

NjUγUda in its most violent form seems to occur when men violate women's secret rites. In such an event the women, backed by the men in authority, rend their clothing, cover their faces with soot as a symbol of uncleanness, abuse the accused in the most vile language, and violate his property by pounding on the walls of his house, breaking utensils, and taking one of his cattle to be killed by unceremoniously chopping it up before his eyes. The effect of these acts on a man is such as to sometimes induce suicide. The subject is not himself bodily attacked.

NjUγUda is not always so violent, however. Feeling must run high before an

---

1. Rites of *imaa* are discussed in Chapter 8.

accusation is made, and the matter may be discussed by the elders to decide if an offense has been committed. The penalty may be no more than a sheep or goat slaughtered by those angered enough by the offense to want to commit aggression against the accused. In such a case the aggression takes the milder form of simply eating the animal. A fine is also levied against the defendant and given to the offended party. The fine never seems to exceed a *mUjikU*, a young steer, or alternately three goats or sheep. In most cases where it is called for, *njUγUda* does not occur, the accused settling the matter privately by slaughtering animals for the offended person and giving him presents. The sanction in every case is so productive of tension in the community as to be avoided at all costs.

A form of sanction similar to *njUγUda* is *ηangU*, although some men claim it is not identical and others consider it a small form of *njUγUda*. The reason it is not viewed as true *njUγUda* is because it is not meant to cause severe shame, and the brunt is not borne by the accused alone; *ηangU* results when a woman or mother commits a verbal or physical act of aggression against a child when the child is seen as a social reincarnation of a person to whom the woman is inferior. For example, if her son is named after her dead husband, and if she should drop a hot coal on the infant while she is smoking a pipe, another woman of her village may accuse her of having injured "my husband" (that is, she would be of the same generation as the accused, and the accused's husband would therefore also be her classificatory husband). Having made the accusation public, the women cooperate by collecting grain, which they grind and make into beer to drink together. Since a woman would not be subjected to *njUγUda* for injuring her actual husband, this rite has to do with relations between men and women in the village into which the women are married. This is especially true with the methods women use to maintain peaceful relations with their husbands, with whom there is normally latent conflict. Dropping a coal on the child, or uttering abuse, is an overt sign of mystical aggression and must be cleansed. Women are thought to harbor feelings of aggression toward their children, as they do toward the men of the lineage into which they have married, and the older women, who have over time integrated themselves more fully into the village, resent such feelings in the younger women. This rite seems to counteract these feelings, producing a reduction of deviant tendencies in young wives. Since *ηangU* usually occurs only in connection with injury to infants, it follows that infants are present in most cases only in the homes of young wives.

The threat of *njUγUda* works differently at different levels of lineage. At other higher levels the sanctioned relations become more diffuse, correlating with the increasing looseness of social ties. In the relations of members of different Level II lineages, *njUγUda* is said to occur only in cases of abuse of grossly senior by grossly junior persons. In the case concerning the old woman abused by young women, if the aggression had been by women of more adult status, probably nothing would have happened. Similarly, adult men of different villages probably would be free to utter abuse against each other with impunity.

There is one important qualification to what has been said about abuse. Not only violation of senior status is abhorred by Turu. Any abusive language that is "without reason" is avoided; it is always a sign of aggression against the other person's essence (*moyo*) and is always bad. It is a matter of degree and setting that is referred to when it is said that a senior can abuse a junior, even though Turu conceive the normative system in the rigid terms described. If a senior is very crude when insulting a junior, he may himself suffer sanction. This is but recognition that all people are social persons and that aggression against the status of another person, even if inferior, is detrimental to the social game. We see this in relations of people of different Level III lineages. Though these have no jural relations and engage in feud, members of the different groups recognize kinship with each other and in some sense they therefore respect each other as persons and members of the same society. If a person of one of these lineages insults a person of another, the action will probably result in a feud, eventuating in the payment of compensation by members of the lineage of the person at fault to the offended person. One older man described this as a kind of *njUγUda*, in which case it is *njUγUda* between equals. Furthermore, in one case where the plaintiff was accused by the defendants of committing beastiality with cattle, the plaintiff was a male and the defendants women.

The accused, not the lineage, is solely responsible for his act in cases of *njUγUda*, as is to be expected in disputes having to do with relations of status and authority, since the group acts as a corporation only with respect to relations of property, while authority relations have to do with internal ordering of the corporation.

SYSTEM OF ADJUDICATION

The Turu system of adjudication, backed by *njUγUda*, works as follows. When disputes arise over property, it is normal for older men to be called in or to intrude themselves. This is true both within the jural community of the Level III lineage and between feuding Level III lineages where the elders from both sides, who favor peace and tranquility, debate the affair and attempt to work out a settlement between the younger men, who are more willing to fight. "Witnessing" a dispute about property is normal in any conflict where no actual witnesses are present. A large number of such disputes begin in the pastures, where there are no people other than the disputants. The offended party will take a piece of clothing, usually the sandals, from the accused to present as evidence of the conflict as soon as he can collect an elder or some elders to hear him. In lieu of this, the witnessing evidence will be a crease in the skull of the accused inflicted by the stick or *ηeηgo* (a combination axe and machete) of the offended party. His purpose in thus attacking the accused is not necessarily to injure him badly, for that would put him under sanction. A *caro* is then held to discuss the dispute, and the elders, with the help of the *arangacaro* (*mUrongacaro*, sing.), who are experts at settling disputes, decide the merits of the plaintiff's case and use their influence to get the guilty party to admit to his guilt and pay whatever fine is due. The only sanction behind the elders is their senior status, but of course these men acting together can exert great pressure. An important factor in such disputes is that Turu are great legalists, preferring always that the guilt of the accused be beyond dispute. As a result, lying is a refined art. The accused typically maintains his innocence against the most over-whelming evidence. If the accused has injured the plaintiff and is convicted, he will be asked to agree to give soup made from a sheep to the plaintiff as admis-sion of guilt, and he will then pay his fine. Giving of the soup is very important in this process; it is meant both as a practical measure, to help heal the injury, and as a symbol of guilt, signifying that a fine will be paid to additionally balance the wrong. Soup is not given in *njUγUda*. For an attack on status the guilty one cannot rectify the wrong by restoring material well-being, even though gifts may be given the injured party to settle "out of court." No property has been damaged. It is the social order that has been upset.

In sum, while rights in property are clearly understood among Turu, the protection of these rights is achieved in a diffuse manner. Possession is truly nine-tenths of the law, encouraging aggression by men against each other's property. It also encourages self-help, which is so marked in Turu society. An example appeared in 1960, when a man and his three sons were arraigned on a charge of murder after the sons, at the direction of their father, had killed another man of the village who had aggressively intruded on their grazing land. Because rights in grazing land are not easily maintained, the first reaction of Turu to invasion is to attack the invaders.

Until recent times *njUγUda* was utilized by the colonial courts to protect the authority of chiefs. The courts could judge that a man had committed a viola-tion of authority in his village and command him to do *njUγUda* for the elders there. It has even been suggested that teachers be protected by this sanction in their relations with their pupils.

LEADERS

We may end the account of Turu norms with a word about leaders, even though they are not normative. Turu have a word for a "strong man" (*mUxaI*, sing.; *axaI*, pl.), who is one able by his skill to command and receive obedience. In warfare such men were the leaders of groups of warriors. There is evidence that during the early years of occupation of UnyatUrU by the Germans all villages, and perhaps even Level III lineages or higher, had men recognized as leaders and often described as *axaI*. Understandably the opposition to the Ger-mans when they first arrived came from these men, whose power was threatened. The Germans, recognizing the existence of such leaders, attempted to promote a stable take-over by making them the chiefs (*jumbes*) of their villages. Today one finds that certain men are looked to by others in the villages as leaders.

Perhaps the best way to describe these leaders is to say that to some degree they were and are charismatic. They did not usually commit serious violations of existing norms but did sometimes act as fonts of authority. When the Germans arrived in UnyahatI, there was the infamous Mwati, described as a *mUxaI*, who was able to terrorize a large part of the clan. He is said to have beaten and killed enemies and strangers and to have appropriated cattle and other wealth. His actions finally led to a revolt by the people of UnyahatI, who attacked and killed Mwati and all those close to him, burying them in a mass grave that exists today along the road north of Ikungi. The expression of charisma, we therefore see, was not confined within the village but could extend over a larger area. The most famous example of a leader is Mgeni, the Paramount Chief until the position was abolished about 1944. From 1926 to 1939 he was able to control the whole tribe by his charisma and is remembered today with great fondness. Significantly, his charisma was never successfully routinized, and the position was abolished because his son was unable to hold it successfully.

It seems possible that the rise of these village and supravillage leaders was due to the operation of the lineage system among the Turu, where the norms of the system can only be fulfilled by political action. The vague status of *arongacaro* suggests this interpretation. These persons themselves are to some extent fonts of authority. When disputes arise, there are norms governing them, but settlement is achieved not merely by reference to them, but also by the good offices of the *mUrongacaro* who is able to persuade or cajole disputants into observing the norms for the good of the society and themselves. But even though leaders are therefore emergent in this society, Turu reject institutionalized positions of authority, preferring the greatest amount of individual freedom.

5. THE MARKET SYSTEM

Cattle are our banks, our stores, our farms, our wives, our clothing, everything.
MWAJUMA

T HE central aim of Turu economic activity may be visualized as the acquisition of cattle, sheep, and goats, as is implied by the quotation from Mwajuma, one of the rare Turu women who by circumstances and enterprise has managed to approximate the role of a man.

Each homestead is a complex small "firm" in the economic sense of the unit that makes production decisions. It produces the staple food—principally millet—to feed its members, and it has as its primary aim the production of surplus food for sale to other homesteads that desire it in exchange for livestock. Other products made for sale include honey, various utensils, and tobacco; services, such as medical advice and temporary labor, are also provided. The most valuable of the services exchanged in the market is female productive labor, obtained through marriage, for which bridewealth is exchanged. In this case, however, rights are partly leased and partly sold, as will be explained. In the market, livestock are stores of value and media of exchange for all valued things. As well as storing value against emergencies, when production of grain or other necessities falls below needs, cattle are the means of increasing production of millet and livestock by investing them in land, wives, and tools, and they are ultimately desired for the prestige they give their owner. All these considerations are in addition to their value as real capital in the production of hides, milk, meat, and manure.

THE ORGANIZATION OF THE HOMESTEAD

Seen from the outside, the homestead is a unit. The participation of the homestead in the external market is through its head, who is usually a male. These days the Swahili term *jamaa* for "family" or "collectivity" is frequently used to describe the household, although traditionally Turu household heads merely called it "my people" (*ana akwe*), or "the people of my homestead" (*xaya*).

The organization of people in the homestead is analogous to the physical model of the homestead. However, the terms *xaya* ("homestead") and *nyUmba* ("house") have relational connotations that do not always conform to the physical model. When Turu speak of the "ownership" of any wealth (as they do by using the possessive pronoun, since there is no term equivalent to our word "ownership"), it is usually by reference to the house to which it belongs. While the reference may literally be to some woman's house, it means more specifically the woman who heads the house and her sons. Each house is viewed as an independent unit for the production of goods, provision of subsistence for its members, and the holding of all wealth produced by that house—livestock, land, grain, children, and so forth. Nothing is held in common among houses. Transfer of goods from one to another within the same homestead is accomplished by normal market processes unless the house head has some special arrangement or except in the case of transfer from a mother's house to that of a son's wife— the process of inheritance. This independence of houses is physically displayed by their separation, the storage of the house's grain within its confines, and the separation of the farm lands of each house from those of others by boundaries. Even the livestock held by a homestead head at the time of marriage and those acquired by borrowing are assigned to individual houses, which then control them. In a sense the homestead head owns all the property, but the women are the channels of descent. Property must therefore always be assigned in such a way as to insure clear inheritance. The tools in a homestead are much more specifically male property, while a woman's clothes, certain utensils, and her stool are specifically hers, brought with her at the beginning of the marriage from her mother's house. Land which the homestead head also technically owns, however, is assigned immediately upon marriage to his wife and from then on is under her control.

Ownership—by which I mean the right, in whole or in part, to hold or exchange some form of wealth, whether goods or services—is therefore not a simple matter, and its clarification is essential to this account. The head of the homestead speaks of himself as "owning" all the wealth of the establishment while admitting that the house heads "own" their wealth. The female head of a house owns her livestock, grain, and other goods in the sense that they are assigned to her, mainly because her labor produced or nourished them, and she can veto their use in the market if she disagrees with her husband's plans for their disposal. The only exception to this rule, beside the clothes and utensils she owns, or his tools, are chickens, eggs, milk, and cream, which are handled somewhat differently. A house head may independently sell the milk of her cows, and chickens and eggs are independently owned, even by children, and can be sold any time by their owners.

A woman's rights in such property are, therefore, best described as usufructary. If her husband divorces her, all her property reverts to him. In order to sell any of her property, the wife needs the husband's agreement. In this way a balance of power is established within the homestead that can manifest itself in constant tension.

The house head may cooperate with the homestead head's managerial efforts to coordinate the activities of the various houses and to sell and buy goods because she needs him to help in her productive process so as to increase the wealth of her house. In turn, the homestead head will respect the house head's wishes because she may refuse to cooperate with him and thereby make difficult the increase of wealth he desires for the homestead as a whole. In its most extreme forms non-cooperation by a house head takes the form of complete or partial withdrawal. She may return to her father or brothers, leaving her husband with a broken unit containing wealth but no further productive potential, since that rests mainly on her labors. (Typically, whenever a wife—especially a young wife—is upset with her husband, she tends to run home to her family, sometimes most inconveniently, as when she is in the middle of planting.) If there are two houses in the homestead, she may demand construction of a totally different *xaya* for herself and her children, in this way continuing to live in the village of her husband (or whoever is head of the homestead, since it does not have to be a husband) and continuing to control her property but refusing to have much to do with him and his other wife, thereby increasing his problems of coordination.

In the village of Utatuu there were five instances of separation of *xayas* in an area of about fifty homesteads. Some of these may not have been due to disputes in the homesteads but to the desire of the head to exploit land in two different places, since two of the cases were of homesteads in different villages, between which the husbands divided their time. Even this illustrates the productive independence of the house units. The identification of property with houses is revealed in cases of violent disputes between the head of the homestead and the house head, in which cases the man often rejects the woman by repudiating the property of her house. He may throw her porridge to the chickens or refer scathingly to the behavior of "your children." When a husband dies, a woman such as Mwajuma, who was quoted at the beginning of this chapter, may invoke her right to refuse to be inherited by his brother and carry on alone. There are some women of this sort in most villages.

Behind the power of the woman is the incomplete control of her by her husband. He can beat her if she is unreasonable, but if he goes too far, her family can demand compensation for damage to her insofar as it can be determined that the beating materially reduced her productive capability. The letting of blood is sufficient indication of such damage. The wife can appeal to her father or brothers to help her, and they can take her away from her husband if they are willing to return the bridewealth. On the other hand, the husband's ultimate weapon against an unreasonable wife is to appeal to her father or brothers to discipline her.

The tension of marriage is revealed by the frequency of divorce and the commonness of separation of husbands and wives, resulting in the return of the wives to their natal homes together with their smaller children. There are no exact figures on divorce, but it is a rare man who has not been divorced at lease once. There is a case of one ambitious man of UnyahatI who had three wives, all of whom he divorced for laziness and replaced with three more. Even von Sick comments on the frequency of divorce, which he said was used as a threat by the owners of the wife in order to increase the bridewealth. Tension is also revealed in the great formality of relations between husband and wife and in such rituals as *imaa*.

A further consideration in the power struggle is that it is sometimes to the husband's advantage that the wife's family be reluctant to allow a divorce for fear they will lose the bridewealth, while under other circumstances the husband may gain by encouraging a divorce. The extreme weapon that can be used by a woman forced to remain with a husband whom she does not like is to work so indifferently as to produce no wealth for him. In the end it comes down to the need for striking a balance of interests in the family.

Tension in the homestead may also be caused by the competition between women heading different houses (who call each other *mwirUwane*, "my jealous one"). A complex homestead is not necessarily polygynous but may contain women who are attached to it by some other process than marriage—for example, a widowed mother. The mother of a homestead head is senior to all his wives, but in fact the first wife is usually senior, since there are many fewer widows. The senior house is referred to as *nyUmba nI nkUU*, "great house," while the houses of junior women are *nyUmba nI nyUUii*, "small houses."

Technically the senior woman "owns" the juniors. She provides the livestock by which they are acquired, and in case of divorce or death of the junior, she is residual heir to all the property if the junior wife leaves no sons. Even if the junior wife dies and leaves a son, the senior has claim to all the grain in the dead woman's house but not to her livestock. Nevertheless, as long as her house is viable, a junior wife operates it independently, although she defers and is servile to the senior wife. The source of tension is in the competition between the houses for land, livestock, and the managerial aid of the husband as well as for his actual help in cultivation and other productive chores. The junior has a severe handicap in most cases, since she can expect to receive less help than a senior wife. The motive of a junior wife in entering such a marriage is the hope, sometimes possible of achievement, that she may prosper greatly despite her handicap. Her advantage often consists in the greater amorous feelings the husband has for her.

In complex homesteads the managerial problems faced by the head may be especially complicated, even though there are problems for him in an establishment of any size. The head desires success for his whole homestead, while his wife or wives desire it mostly for their own houses, even at the expense of the other houses. He sees himself as the founder of a lineage and a potentially respected elder and ancestor. If he has sons, they help protect his property and herd the livestock, and he thus gains prestige by being free of such labor. The wife's aim is simply to boost her own sons and thereby also to insure high status for herself, especially when she is old and widowed. An old woman who is poor and without sons is a pathetic figure. In one such case the old woman, nearly blind, lived in a ramshackle house, where she cared for the small daughter of her son, who had gone off to work in the mines. Her husband's brother and other relatives living nearby tried to ignore her. A woman summed the situation up by saying that she desired children so they could honor her father, help with the work, inherit her estate, and give her a goal to work for. She said that she also valued them for the honor she acquired by having them. If she had no sons, she said, her husband would be unhappy and she would suffer for that.

It is a wise man who can maintain peace in his homestead. One folktale, "Mpahi The Orphan Child," deals with the whole constellation of relations and conflicts in a homestead. The tale tells of a man with two wives, each having a son, although the second wife is richer than the first as a result of her superior industriousness. (The substitution of industriousness for advantage by junior wives is a common theme.) The first wife bewitches the second, with a view to killing her and obtaining all her property for her son, but after doing so she is faced with the problem of disposing of the dead woman's son, Mpahi, who would otherwise inherit his dead mother's property. An important element in the story is the devotion of the father to both his sons and their devotion to each other. By a ruse this woman succeeds in burying Mpahi in a hole in the backroom of her house, from which he is subsequently rescued by his devoted half-brother, who informs the father of his mother's perfidy. The father, greatly angered, cuts the woman to pieces and throws her to the hyenas, saying, "It is better to live with my two sons and without you than to put up with the loss of the rest of the family because of you!" In actual instances where one of a man's wives dies leaving a son, the father is likely to wed a woman to take over the estate and care for the orphan rather than put him in the care of the remaining wife.

If a homestead persists, some modus operandi will be reached and there will be some degree of synchronization of the activities of the houses. The husband will attempt to weld the units into a whole rather than allow them to proceed without any reference to each other. In the nature of the productive system, however, there is no attempt to submerge houses, and coordination is never complete.

MEDIA OF EXCHANGE

The exchange of valued goods and services is accomplished with a currency consisting principally of livestock. Reciprocity does not account for the flow of most goods. While mutual obligations among members of the same lineage are important in certain respects, they apply mainly to rights in persons, not in such goods as livestock, land, and grain. We can therefore speak of a sphere involving exchange of these goods and of another sphere dealing with the flow of rights in persons, which relates to the corporate aspects of lineages. This chapter is devoted to the former. Both spheres use the same media of exchange, however, and are part of the same general economic system.

The monetary system includes items other than livestock—such as hoes, cowrie shells, and arrows, which are the smaller denominations of the currency. Nowadays cowrie shells and hoes have disappeared, to be replaced with money introduced by the British—shillings and copper cents—while goats, sheep, and cattle remain. The goats and sheep are the "small notes" and are equated in value regardless of sex, both types of animals normally being referred to as *mbUri* ("goats"). Three goats are equal in value to one young steer (*mUjikU*), and five are equal to one heifer (*ndama*)—that is, a young prebearing cow. The terms *mbUri*, *mUjikU* or *njikU* (a steer), and *ndama* are to a certain extent to be considered monetary terms, for although an *ndama* is actually a heifer in most transactions where the term is used, it can be used to designate a full-grown bearing cow when used as currency, or it may stand for its equivalence in goats.

This currency has sufficient divisibility to make possible transactions involving all valued goods: grain, wives, land, hoes, and the like. It is also amenable to arithmetical manipulation. Two examples will suffice to illustrate its actual use. When bridewealth is being arranged, it is normal to speak only of cattle and to designate the purpose for which each animal is paid. For example, *ŋombe a mUsae*, "cow of the corral," is the one paid at the beginning of negotiations as a peace offering between hostile lineages. When the actual payment is made, the "cow" may, in fact, be represented by five goats. When inheritance is being calculated, a cow or steer may, if necessary, be mentally divided into its component goats in order to establish the proportionate rights of the heirs. If a steer is the subject and there are two brothers, the eldest will receive the equivalent of two goats and the youngest will receive one, but the steer is not necessarily exchanged.

A ranking of types of livestock from highest to lowest, ignoring their monetary use, is somewhat as follows:

1. *mboɣoma* and *nxama*, cows that have bred but are not old
2. *ndama*, heifer
3. *njikU* or *njaɣamba*, steer or bull, full grown
4. *mUjikU* or *mUjaɣamba*, steer or bull calf
5. old cows or bulls
6. female sheep
7. female goats
8. male sheep
9. male goats

Numbers 6 through 9 are differentiated on the basis of sex and the fact that sheep also have ritual value, being used for cleansing and sacrificial rites. This ranking shows not only the superior value of cattle in general, but that of cows in particular, especially those that have demonstrated ability to breed. It also shows the values of large males for prestige and sacrifice. However, these factors affect the monetary use of the animals only in the following ways. A breeding cow is used for exchange only in extreme circumstances, so that to designate the heifer as the currency is almost literally accurate. A person who has a breeding cow withholds it from trading precisely because he expects it to

produce calves, which he can then use as money. On this basis trades are sometimes made in anticipation of the birth of calves. A young male is differentiated
in value from a fully grown animal on the basis of size. Sometimes a heifer is
traded on an equal basis for a very large steer or bull. The very large animal is
prestigeful and necessary for sacrificial rites, so that the value of the young male
rests also on its potential for attaining large size as much as for breeding. Most
males are castrated because only a few are needed for breeding. In dealing with
goats and sheep, the sexual difference between males and females is considered
insignificant because the value of their offspring is so small.

Standard prices for most commodities and services can be quoted in this currency, although fluctuations in prices naturally occur. The currency has been in
existence since before contact with the West, as is shown by lists of prices
quoted by von Sick. According to him, 100 cowrie shells were worth one goat,
and even the *matambi* necklaces served as money. Of livestock, goats (and
sheep) were most frequently the media of exchange because they are the smallest
denomination of livestock. In other areas von Sick found the Colobus monkey-
skin headdress worth three goats; a hoe, a spear, and a bow with five arrows
were each worth one goat. A lion-skin cap sold for five goats. He also discovered a ball of cured tobacco to be worth from one to two goats or from one
to three hoes. So usual was the use of goats in exchanges that the White Father
account of the Turu, written about conditions before the First World War,
explains that Turu did not eat goats (certainly an incorrect claim and now
untrue), but used them entirely to facilitate exchanges. While von Sick did not
mention that cattle are also used as media of exchange, there can be no doubt
that they were so used in his time as well as at present.

Standardization of quantities by the use of measures as an aid to exchange is
common. The *klu*, or bark storage bin, is a standard measure, even though the
amount of grain it holds varies from as much as 30 to 60 *debes*, each of which
holds 40 pounds of millet. *Debes* as standard measures of grain have replaced
other measures that were more generally used in von Sick's time, such as the
wooden trough or *nsUa* and the *mUsUta*. The *mUsUta*, a cowhide bag, holds
about 200 pounds of grain. Von Sick found that three of the troughs of the
variety called *sori a ŋombe*, "cow trough," filled a *mUsUta*, equivalent in value
to a steer. Further, a third of a *mUsUta* was equal to a male calf, a sixth to a little
female goat, and an eighth to a little male goat (showing that apparently in those
days the sex of small livestock was more important). Arrows are used today
only in the bridewealth, but the term for "arrow"—*mUyI*—also has the general
meaning of a small fee for services.

Much has been written about what money is (Weber 1947; Herskovits 1948).
Perhaps at the heart of its definition is the notion that something is money if it
can act as a store of value and medium of exchange for all valued goods. The
formal characteristics claimed by some anthropologists for money—portability,
divisibility, durability, and homogeneity—are relative to this view. For example,

when it is asserted that money must be portable, the implication is that it must be possible to exchange it with ease for goods and services. Whether money is actually carried on the person of the buyer is irrelevant. Livestock are eminently portable in a functional economic sense; they can be driven from place to place with ease. That Turu have standardized ratios of value between livestock demonstrates sufficient homogeneity among them to serve as money, and their divisibility is clearly adequate to effect exchanges of the type necessary to the Turu economy. Durability is relative also; the life span of a Turu cow is probably about ten years, which is obviously sufficient for Turu purposes.

Looking at Turu currency in these functional terms, two characteristics are noticeable. One is its exchangeability, despite its massiveness. Grain has value, so much so that a man who has much grain but no livestock is considered to be potentially wealthy. During high-production years it takes almost 500 pounds of grain to equal the value of a steer, or approximately equal weight, but the grain is poor in portability. More important, however, the value of livestock as money rests on their ability to reproduce. While cows literally reproduce themselves, male cattle are reserved for sacrifices that in addition to their avowed purpose serve to obligate members of the community to the giver, who thus has a necessary source of credit on which he can draw to aid him in the production process. Grain, by contrast, will multiply only with the expenditure of much labor.

For any product to act as money, it must be in constant demand. Of all goods, livestock are probably the only ones for which there is always a demand. There seems to be one restriction on the use of livestock as money, imposed by the impossibility of holding more than a certain small number in the homestead corral. The average homestead seems to be crowded when it contains thirty head of cattle. This restriction is removed by the operation of the system of *Uriha*, whereby an owner can loan his cattle or small animals to other persons, who are rewarded for keeping them by receiving the use of the milk and manure they yield. The constant demand for the loan of livestock makes it possible for some people to own over 1000 head of livestock. The system of *Uriha* has other values for the lender: he distributes his animals about the country, thereby counteracting the effects of localized epidemics, droughts, and theft; he also hides his wealth and thus improves his position in the market insofar as the deals he makes are affected by other people's knowledge of his actual wealth; and he avoids the envy and hatred of the less well-to-do—a very important consideration to Turu.

The equation of livestock with money is further verified by the existence, at the time of this study, of a standard of convertibility between livestock and sterling. The rate was 100 shillings for a heifer, which makes a steer worth 60 shillings and a goat 20 shillings. The principal role of cattle in the currency is aptly expressed by one Turu who said, "Cattle decide everything."

PRODUCTIVITY

In order to discuss productivity, it is necessary to refer occasionally to the two villages that were studied most intensively—Utatuu-MUmbII (or Utatuu for short) in UkahiU and of SUnja in UnyahatI.[1]

For the successful accumulation of livestock the producer must in most cases possess three essentials: land, livestock, and laborers (mainly wives). Many men talk as if success is due to mere chance; though chance is a not unimportant element, the Turu know that the odds can be turned in favor of the hard worker who utilizes resources efficiently. The incentive to try to acquire riches is due largely to the success that is possible by skillful manipulation of resources. This is not to say that it is possible for anyone to control completely the variables of production; the system would not work if this were so. As long as an important element of chance exists, it is impossible for the wealthy livestock owners to use their wealth to dominate the system, while the poor always have the hope of achieving wealth by a stroke of luck or by hard work. In this society nature puts controls on the market that are equivalent to normative controls in the sense of making the game possible.

That there is incentive to excel and that resources can be manipulated to gain success is best illustrated in Table 5.1, which shows the wide range of variation in the amount of resources controlled by thirty homesteads in Utatuu and the grain (both current and reserves), reckoned in *debes,* that each producer held after the harvest of 1959. There is clearly a correlation between the amount of available manure (calculated from an index in which a small animal arbitrarily equals one, a calf two, and a cow five), the amount of land, and the number of females in the homestead. The figure for cattle, which includes loaned cattle, is of interest because it shows a correlation with the other factors, arguing that, in general, houses that produced well during the 1959 harvest had also produced well in the past. That the correlation is not higher between grain produced and the other factors illustrates the element of chance as well as the basis for incentive.

Before continuing, it is necessary to say something about how the data shown in Table 5.1 were gathered. Land holdings were mapped, and acreages were calculated from the map. The manure index was calculated as explained above, and the animals in each homestead were counted to obtain this index. The number of wives or woman in a homestead was determined by a survey of all the homesteads and by use of such data as genealogical charts. The number of cattle owned and grain produced was determined by conversations with the owners, making this the weakest point in the survey. However, it was possible to get a good degree of reliability by cross-checking informants' statements and by using as a rough measure the ranking by wealth of members of a village, facts known to all. At the end of the survey it was found that the ranking of persons by wealth based on the survey agreed exactly with ranking of them done by

1. Maps 2.3 and 2.4.

TABLE 5.1

Grain Production in Utatuu in 1959 Correlated with Resources Needed to Control Grain Production and the Actual Number of Cattle (but not Small Stock) Owned.

Farmstead	1. Acres	2. Women	3. Cattle Present	4. Manure Index	5. Wealth Index	6. Grain Pro- duction
1. Muhomi	4.1	4	34	187	315+	189
2. Sunas	4.7	3	35	177	160	95
3. Nkango	6.4	3	25	148	272	335
4. Kinyisi	5+	3	23	130	336	150
5. Ikoti	4.6	1	22	130	268	57
6. S. Masaka	6.8	5	30	127	188	195
7. Lisu	3.5	2	24	113	156	205
8. Mudemis	5.2	2	16	98	31	72
9. Petero	3.1	3	18	90	28	90
10. Sunja	2.6	1	16	87	57	75
11. Ibi	8.8	4	18	85	92	163
12. S. Mosi	2.6	1	16	82	109	53
13. Chima	2.7	1	20	79	179	96
14. Mtinangi	4.3	2	11	71	66	95
15. Mutinda	2+	3	10	70	28	55
16. Nkuwi	2.6	1	18	69	27	75
17. M. Mpondo	6.7	3	16	69	1	58
18. Mutatuu	2.3	1	9	61	75	36
19. Ghula K.	4.2	1	13	56	17	76
20. Ikita	4.0	1	13	54	2	125
21. Samahii	4.0	1	6	54	40	45
22. Msumari	6.1	3	11	51	45	90
23. Ibunka	2.7	1	9	50	22	37
24. Ntui	2.6	1	10	41	15+	35
25. Nkongolo	4.1	2	6	39	14	41
26. M. Sinda	1.8	1	6	35	8	40
27. Mujou	2.0	2	8	34	33	61
28. Bula	3.0	2	8	34	5	49
29. Ngua	3.3	1	4	17	0	40
30. M. Nkese	1+	0	0	0	0	4

trusted informants (showing that Turu do have a pretty good idea of each other's wealth, despite attempts to hide resources).

The freedom with which informants divulged these data demands some explanation. It has been the experience of anthropologists that East African pastoralists refuse to reveal this sort of information. Among the Pokot of Kenya I had great difficulty getting such data. In the case of the Turu it can only be conjectured that, in harmony with their extreme cordiality to strangers and their belief that outsiders can do them no harm, they are willing to confide in them.

The number of intentional distortions of data on cattle and grain ownership was small. Similarly, Turu were always quick to give me intimate details about their most private affairs.

Turning to an examination of the variables of production, beginning with land, the most important type of productive land is *iyanda*, the farmland that is actually under cultivation and that has been manured over the years. This land is represented on the map of the village of Utatuu (see Map 2.3) which contains the thirty homestead units listed in Table 5.1. Of fifty-five homesteads in this village, the sizes of holdings range from .4 to 8.8 acres, averaging 2.95 acres, with a median of 2.65 acres. More significantly, the size of individual house plots varies from .4 to 4.4 acres with an average and median of 2.1 acres. Discussions with owners about the adequacy of various sizes of plots indicates that 2 acres is the smallest that is considered sufficient to effectively utilize the labor of one wife.

Of all the factors necessary to obtain good production, land is relatively the least important. Although No. 1 in Table 5.1 has needed all his land to attain his total of over 300 *debes* and is actively engaged in securing more, and although the poor production of No. 25 is strongly affected by his small land holdings, the number of workers in the homestead and the amount of manure available are more important, since land is seldom used to its fullest extent because of lack of manure to fertilize all of it or lack of women to cultivate it. No. 2 got high production on a relatively small plot because of the amount of manure he had and because he had two wives. No. 5's success is due more to the number of women in his homestead than to anything else, although the large area available to him was, no doubt, an important factor. Because the size of the plot so frequently exceeds manure or labor available to exploit it, there is always danger that both resources will be scattered. It is therefore the custom to mark out for special attention a small section of the land—perhaps half an acre—to which attention is given first to insure its high productivity.

Land is still valuable and in demand, however, especially in a long-established and growing village such as Utatuu, where it has special value because it has been regularly manured for many years and produces better than virgin land. In a number of instances in Utatuu (including Nos. 11 and 1, to mention only two), the need for land is acute, making it a prime variable. Land in a village also may be of special value if it is contiguous to other homesteads on which the owner depends for various types of help. As population increases or men acquire more wives, the demand for land also increases, and land shortage becomes a problem in any old settled area.

The question arises of the method by which more land can be acquired. There are those who maintain that in African societies—especially in societies with corporate lineages—land cannot be thought of as a commodity. To do so, it is argued, violates the people's way of thinking about and allocating land. The tendency of the corporate group is to perpetuate itself, leading to control of land to insure this aim. Allowing individuals to buy and sell land leads to its dispersal or alienation from the lineage. In the Turu case, the high coincidence of lineage and land would seem to verify this thesis. In the village of Utatuu, as shown on Map 2.3, the heavy line running approximately southwest to northeast is the division between the Level II lineage of the People of MUhUri on the south (which consists also of the affiliated lineage of the Tatuu People) and the Level II lineage of the People on NtUnduu on the north, whose portion of this area is also sometimes called MUmbII. While it is unusual for two distinct Level II lineages to occupy contiguous sites, the situation nevertheless illustrates the normal pattern of lineage-land coincidence and the contiguity of holdings of men of the same lineage. As previously noted, it is believed that the founder of a village site and his patrilineal descendants own the land jointly, a situation that seems to demand a normative prohibition against alienation of lineage land to nonmembers. There is even support for such a belief, since usually people of the same lineage do not buy and sell *iγanda* from each other. They may loan or give it, and it is usual when someone leaves a village for his kin to occupy and use abandoned land, but they feel they should not buy and sell land among themselves.

This argument notwithstanding, the proper interpretation of the evidence is not that land is jointly owned or normatively excluded to alienation, but rather that various constraints usually lead to preservation of land in the lineage; when those factors are absent, the situation may not be the same. The notion that the land of a lineage belongs to the senior member is an ideal that combines with other factors to help to conserve the land. The quality of relations between people of the lineage and with people of other lineages is more important, however. If the owner of land does not part with his rights, it is because it is unprofitable for him to do so, whatever other reason there may be.

This point can be demonstrated by again looking at the situation within the area of the People of MUhUri in Map 2.3. The only land any member can be sure will be his without question is that which he has received from his father or that which he has pioneered. If anyone takes land of a kinsman with or without permission, the land is subject to reversion to its original owner on demand. We see this in the instance of *a*, whose inheritance was only a small portion of what he now holds. He has taken land belonging to his paternal parallel first cousins, who have left the village, and he may have to give it up, should they return. (However, they will have to establish their right to the land, and *a* feels that there is always the possibility that he could find some way to beat them out of it.) Their argument would be, "You got your land from your father, and we got ours from our father." Nevertheless, almost everyone in a village is using land technically belonging to someone else. Another example is furnished by *b*, who is engaged in a private feud with his paternal kinsmen who forced him to migrate to a nearby village. In his anger he has refused to let them use his land, which includes not only the bounded plot shown on the map, but also the indentation to the southwest adjoining his plot. His exclusive right is honored, although to enforce it his continued presence in a village nearby is probably necessary. In both these cases we see expressed the individual right to land.

Sale of farm land normally occurs only between members of different lineages above Level II, but it may take place within the lineage under certain circumstances. It is most likely to happen between men who are distantly related and is more likely if the land for sale was cleared and thus created by the seller rather than being inherited. Even in these cases, however, the exchange is not effected in a direct way. For example, in one case the land was transferred to pay off a debt.

The usual kind of sale, between members of different Level II lineages, may be illustrated by looking at the eastern portion of Utatuu, which is divided from the rest of the heavy line running approximately north and south containing most of the members of the lineage called Tatuu. Mythology explains their affiliation with the lineage of MUhUri as resulting from the marriage of their apical ancestor with the daughter of MUhUri, the founder of the lineage of MUhUri. It is said that MUhUri dictated that after the union his line and the Tatuu should not ever again intermarry. The Tatuu, however, can marry People of NtUnduu and other people of the clan of AkahiU, even though MUhUri belong to this clan. Despite this fusion, the foreign origin of the Tatuu continues to be remembered.

It is of interest to note that c in Map 2.3, although a legitimate member of the AkahiU like others in the lineage of MUhUri, is also of a different Level II lineage, which was fused to MUhUri although its "foreignness" is also remembered. He and his brother are the last of their line, even though the fusion took place two generations back. In the cases of both these fused lineages, the remembered "true" genealogies are the basis for reassertions of separateness whenever the competitive situation is such as to warrant it.

These fused people share cooperative labor and other activities characteristic of members of the same Level II lineage, but paradoxically, land exchanges between MUhUri and the accreted groups are accomplished by sale. This situation is exactly equivalent to the case of d of NtUnduu lineage, whose southern plot was purchased from a member of MUhUri lineage. The partial fusion of Tatuu and MUhUri and the contiguity of NtUnduu has thus created special situations in which sale of land is possible and makes economic sense. As a result of the shadowy relationship between Tatuu and MUhUri, two members of Tatuu are situated on the west of the village (in what is labeled the Tatuu pocket), where they are isolated from their line. At one time, and for many years, the plot of e was also occupied by a Tatuu, who had bought the land from f and thereby cut the MUhUri into two sections.

A further example of alienation of land is represented by the mere presence of the Tatuu in this village. These people are living on land that normatively belongs to them only by grace of the MUhUri, and insofar as their fusion to the MUhUri lineage is incomplete, they have no rights to it. They justify their possession by reference to the length of time they have lived on the land, and they could not,

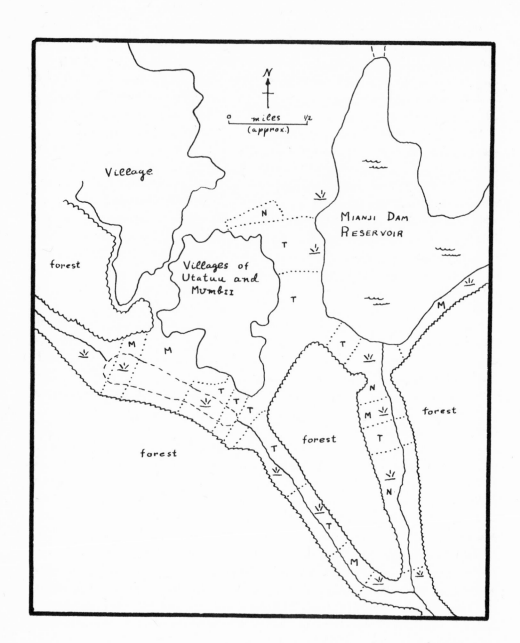

MAP 5.1

Ownership of Marsh Grazing Land by People of Utatuu And MUmbII.
Broken lines show limits of wet portion of marsh. Dotted lines show boundaries of grazing property. Initials indicate lineage to which owner of plot
belongs. N for NtUnduu; T for Tatuu; M for MUhUri.

in fact, be removed by any legal process. If length of residence did not count for a good deal against claims of original ownership, almost every Turu would be without real claim to his land.

A further aspect of individual land ownership is illustrated in Map 5.1, showing ownership of marsh grazing land by members of the lineages of MUhUri (M), NtUnduu (N), and Tatuu (T) in the area of Utatuu. While the owners tend to possess grazing near their homesteads, ownership is interspersed. In contrast to the general lack of exchanges of farm land, members of the same lineage exchange grazing land with each other. Grazing land is not exploited by lineage work groups but by private herding groups, formed contractually around the owner of the land. Hence contiguity of the land of members of the same lineage is not necessary. An owner of marsh land who decides to sell the land is, however, expected to offer it for sale first to a member of his own Level II lineage. Since it is not necessary to actually own grazing land, its loss is not as serious as is loss of farm land. There are cases of village members who own no grazing land and who use land belonging to others, with whom they herd.

In Wahi the amount of group cooperation in the use of land is not a function of norms but one of strategic considerations. The greater the scarcity of land, the greater the limitations on the individual's use of it. This proportion generally holds for farm land but varies with respect to marsh. At one village where grazing was very scarce, joint control of marsh by a group of brothers was extensively practiced, and the land was not broken up. At Utatuu, where more land is available, brothers did on occasion split plots, and ownership of the land was more mixed because of the greater tendency to market it. At Isuna, however, where there is a surplus of grazing, it is said that each individual has his own plot and does with it as he pleases.

It is a norm that any type of land sold by an owner may revert to him on demand, with the qualification that sometimes he must pay to the buyer an additional amount, usually twice the original selling price. While such transactions cannot therefore truly be spoken of as sales, the provision is not as restrictive as might seem. Since the rights of the holder of land obtained by purchase or squatting increase with time, it is necessary in order to implement this norm, for the rightful owner to act without too much delay. For example, MUhUri of Utatuu sold some of his land to a member of the Tatuu lineage. Some years later, after the Tatuu had lived on the land long enough to have dwelled on two different sites, the son of this MUhUri returned to the village and demanded return of his land. The Tatuu refused, and the case was taken to court. It was determined that the Tatuu had originally paid a cow plus some other goods in the amount of a cow for the land, and the court ruled in favor of the MUhUri—specifying, however, that he should pay the Tatuu four cows for the land, the additional two being in consideration of the amount of time elapsed since the original sale (and probably for capital improvement).

To summarize, the preservation of the coincidence of lineage and land is accomplished within a framework of private ownership of land. It is true that the mobility of land in the market is inhibited by various considerations, but as much can be said about land in any society. For a Turu who wishes to expand his farm land, there are a number of possibilities. He can borrow land in his village, in which case the plot he borrows does not have to be contiguous with his other holdings (as can be seen in Map 2.3, where two full brothers, g, have borrowed plots to the north of them). He can also buy land, as was done by d—that is, from someone of another village—if the opportunity arises. If these possibilities are closed, he may leave the village and open new land elsewhere or he can buy land in a new area, where the village is not yet stabilized. He also can obtain land from another person in his village in repayment for debts, and he can pioneer a plot in the forest near to or far from his village.

The wide range of variation in the size of land holdings shown by the figures in Table 5.1 demonstrate that those who remain in a village are apparently able to expand their holdings by varying degrees in accordance with their needs (although none of the forest acreage, which is small, is taken into account in that table). A study of the position of ancestral trees in a village testifies to a constant flux. While outright sale of land does not usually occur among members of the same village, there is indication that the loan of land is subject to reciprocity, of which cattle loans, sharing of beer, and the like are part. Finally, grazing land is freer of restrictions on sale than is farm land. Lest it be supposed that the individuality of land holding is a new development, it should be noted that Reche also indicated that real estate was individually owned and was the cause of much fighting.

It has been emphasized that the principal source of labor is women. The main way to increase the labor force is through polygyny. In Utatuu the incidence of polygyny is exactly 33 per cent. But Table 5.1 shows that the numbers of producers per homestead is not determined simply by multiple marriage.

Women become part of a homestead in various ways. Commonly, a woman continues to exploit her own resources until she is quite incapacitated, so that a widowed mother's house may be included in the total homestead of a youngest or only son, with whom it is customary for a mother to live after the death of her husband. In Utatuu a sample of fifty homesteads yielded five containing widowed mothers of the homestead heads. Other classes of women operating houses who are not the wives of the head are: married daughters who have returned home because they are separated or divorcd from their husbands; brothers' wives, whether inherited at the death of the brother or simply incorporated into the homestead when the brother deserts or is away for a long period; sisters separated or divorced from their husbands or simply returned home because none of their husbands' brothers chose to inherit them; father's sisters; widows of fathers' brothers; wives or other women in those circumstances where the widow takes over direction of her dead husband's estate even though she remarries. (This occurs when the widow has no sons and it is agreed that the line of the dead man should be maintained. In order to do this, another wife, one who may produce children, is obtained for the dead man.)

Most of these can be summarized as: either the inheritance of rights in a woman by the heir of a deceased male or return of a female member of the lineage to her home after dissolution of her marriage for one of various reasons. In Utatuu the largest aggregate of productive females was five, and in one of the several instances where there were four, they consisted of a wife, a mother, a brother's wife, and a father's sister. Perhaps in order to properly assess this situation, it should be added that my impression is that the best producers are usually a man's wives; because they have the opportunity of having children to whom their wealth can be passed, they have the greatest incentive to work. Women detached from their husbands—except older women who are widows—tend to be more indifferent.

A homestead containing multiple houses is not always a blessing. If it is created by marriage, an orderly development of homestead organization may take place because the wives are clear about their status in relation to each other, and the resources of the homestead are efficiently utilized. In other cases there may be disruption. Wives resent the presence of a mother, whose status always exceeds theirs. An inherited widow may be especially disruptive. If she was the senior wife of the dead brother, she must assume an ambiguous position in the new homestead. The trick is to multiply units of the homestead without disrupting the organization, and the desire to attempt this aim is witnessed by the high incidence of polygyny.

Various elements lead to a pattern of variability of production between wives or women in the same homestead. The senior wife (or the mother, if she is present) usually has the highest productivity. The reason for this fact is that she normally receives the largest share of assets, such as manure, and is favored by the head of the homestead. If a second marriage is contracted before there is sufficient land to fully exercise the labor of the second wife, the senior wife must agree to the match. In one case in Utatuu the second wife had no land to work at the homestead, and she was therefore required to wander around the village and even go to nearby villages, borrowing small plots for a year in expectation of the day when more land would be available at the husband's homestead. Some men marry second or even third wives to utilize different talents. If a first wife is a good farmer, she will not be divorced if she produces no children; a second may be obtained specifically to get them (although, of course, if a man cannot afford a second, he may divorce the single wife he has in order to get one who can produce both crops and children). Another wife may be married simply because she is a good cook. Whatever the case, behind all multiple marriages is the expectation that production will be increased.

The payment for the initial marriage is, in a sense, the obligation of the lineage, as is the provision of some land, which is accomplished through the inheritance rule requiring land to descend to a son from his father. In this way two of the essential forms of capital for production are guaranteed to most new homesteads, with the exception that the senior brothers are favored. After the first marriage a man is solely responsible for accomplishing further marriages and for obtaining other capital by utilizing whatever resources he has. Since wives are sometimes accidentally acquired, there are cases where a man finds himself with more wives than he has use for.

Livestock are especially important in order to provide manure. Obtaining them is the responsibility of the homestead head. If he has inherited enough, he has no problem. If he gets rich selling grain, he also solves his problem. But the usual solution is through borrowing and loaning *(Uriha)*, in which almost all men are engaged to some extent and for various reasons. Other than those already mentioned, *Uriha* has advantages that make it valuable for both rich and poor. The most prominent reasons for a large owner to loan cattle are to hide them from the envious eyes of neighbors, to obtain the services of persons with good reputations as husbandmen, and to make possible the possession of large numbers of animals. Avoiding decimation of the herd by local disease and war has already been mentioned. The poorer persons desire the loan of animals principally to get manure and milk, but also because by being diligent guardians of such livestock over a long time, they obtain certain rights in them. The holder of another man's livestock sees them as potentially usable by himself as marriage assets, to pay fines, and for other important expenditures. The owner will not refuse such use if he has received exceptional return by the arrangement, although he usually expects later repayment of the animals. Whether any man is able to acquire livestock this way depends in part on his willingness to exert himself to become a desirable prospect. Since almost all nonowners of animals are able to borrow some livestock, ownership is not the only consideration. Analysis shows that most livestock are loaned outside the local area. They tend to be sent to areas with which there are marriage ties, probably because it is possible to learn more about the adequacy of petitioners in those places. Within the local area most of the livestock are loaned to members of an owner's village. This process is not inevitable but probably reflects the feeling on the part of the wealthy that they should help needy kinsmen, and it is a way to elevate status and to counter the envy of the poor.

The evidence in Table 5.1 graphically shows the role of the *Uriha* institution for solving the problem of production when the homestead possesses few or no livestock. Only one person is without manure, but six people own no cattle (they may own some small stock, but these would produce little manure), and among those owning cattle, fifteen own four head or less. It is significant that the one person neither owning nor holding livestock is a widower living alone—an extremely rare condition for any man. Since without a wife no production of grain is possible in any significant amount, this old man has no agricultural use for livestock and makes his living by begging and by selling beeswax.

Incentive is an important factor in production. I have tried to show that in this economy managers have great incentive to seek wealth because of the good chance of success by skillful use of the main resources. As a result, most men and women have a consuming interest in the productive system and in its rewards. Some, however, do not exert themselves. When asked to comment on

these people, other Turu tend to shrug them off as lazy. This behavior is probably a symptom rather than a cause. There are many chance factors affecting
production—drought or disease may ruin the crops or disease may kill the livestock in large numbers, and sickness may lay low the productive force or part of
it. As a result, some people become demoralized.

Countering demoralization is one of the chief effects of the multitude of diviners. They are consulted whenever misfortune strikes, and they are expected
to determine its cause. The method of divination is simple, consisting of attributing blame to whatever the client thinks is the cause. The diviner usually discovers
this by the answers his client gives to his questions. The accused is usually a neighbor or an ancestor thought to be angry with the client. There is also a class of
diviners who are members of the various Watatuu-derived lineages scattered over
the tribe of which the Tatuu of Utatuu are but one. These are specialists in
production problems. While Turu vary in the descriptions of how these work,
at least some said that they give the client not only medicine to induce success
in production, but also some advice on how to use resources to get the best
results. In many instances diviners are greatly respected; they give their clients
hope and a course of action to follow when normal efforts fail.

Among the examples of poor production in Table 5.1, there are several people
whose incentive to produce is low. Nos. 26 and 29 are both old men; since
neither of them has sons living with him, they are doubly disinterested in
achievement. Their efforts will not aid the preservation of their names, since
their sons are gone, and they are too old to begin long-term production programs
aimed at acquiring wealth. In contrast, No. 10, who is almost the oldest man in
the village, has a son and a daughter living with him, and he works as hard as
ever while worrying as much as ever about success. No. 19, with all his advantages, seems cynical and uninspired for unknown reasons. No. 28 has little incentive to produce in the usual way because he is a fairly successful diviner and
lives on the income from his profession. To him production of crops is a poor
competitor to his divining, which brings in a reasonable profit each year in the
form of livestock and cash as well as prestige. No. 23 is probably paranoid; he
is the senior descendant of the genealogically senior lineage in this Level III
lineage, but only he and his brother remain to represent it, and the poor luck of
his family forced their fusion to the lineage of MUhUri two generations back,
as was previously mentioned. He now bewails the loss of his high status and
feels that everyone in the lineage of MUhUri hates him.

Contrasting with these are the first eleven people in Table 5.1, all of whom
are highly motivated. The first is so aggressive that he is in danger of turning
the whole village against him. His propensity to appropriate the land of others
and his indifference to the threats of the leaders of the village verge on the
irrational and could result in retaliation, as has happened in two other places
from which he has been ejected. One of these people is strongly motivated for a
very practical reason, namely that he has so many mouths to feed.

The data in Table 5.1 illustrate better than words the conclusion that land, labor, and manure are the three principal variables to success in production. The talent of the homestead manager must be devoted to bringing these factors together in efficient interplay in order to achieve profitable production.

THE MARKET

Dependence on marketing for livelihood has been described as a prime element in a money economy (Dalton 1961). By marketing is meant the exchange of goods and not simply the existence of market places, which Turu do not have. While this generalization is open to debate, it can be said of the Turu that they are dependent on the market system to a very great degree. The poor need it to obtain goods to stay alive, and the rich to sell goods to increase livestock wealth. The fact that much of the time the marketing process is slow and that many people are not engaged in high-level exchange does not alter the importance of exchange in this way of life.

The basic process in the Turu economy is the production and sale of grain. The existence of the market rests principally on the fact that a significant proportion of homesteads do not produce enough to feed themselves, while others produce far more than they need. This fact must be seen in combination with the circumstance that inferior producers can remedy the failure only to a small degree by borrowing grain from others; they must buy in the market. The mechanics of this system include two seemingly paradoxical elements. On the one hand, producers must feel that they have a significant degree of control over production or they will have little incentive to strive for increase in production, and our data show them to have this control. On the other hand, if the poor are not to get poorer and the rich richer until the whole system is destroyed by the polarization of wealth, there must be a significant amount of luck, both bad and good, to filter off wealth from the wealthy and give advantage to the poor. Put another way, the people to some degree must be able to control the system for their advantage but not enough to command it. From year to year there is a continuous flow of livestock and grain back and forth as the wealthy fail to produce and the poor produce surpluses, although the market favors the wealthy, who have superior resources to invest in production. Looking again at Table 5.1, No. 7 has had exceptional success in producing grain, although he owns no cattle. On the other hand, No. 19, for reasons already explained, has livestock but produces poorly. No. 21, whose success in accumulating cattle in the past is well known and who is still relatively well off, has suffered a severe drop in production by risking a move to a new site on the edge of the village in order to get more space; he has found the soil there so poor that he can do little with it.

Calculations based on various data from Utatuu show that the average amount of millet required for an adult person per day for all purposes—including the manufacture of beer, feeding guests, and the like—is between 1.5 and 2.5 pounds. Anything exceeding this amount can be considered to be surplus. Examination of sixty-seven houses showed that in the growing season of 1958-1959 almost

50 per cent (thirty-one out of sixty-seven) did not achieve minimum subsistence requirements, despite the fact that this was a good year for production. Table 5.2 showing the same thirty houses listed in Table I, indicates their grain surpluses or lack of them, based on grain produced combined with reserves in 1959. It is possible that my calculation of requirements for consumption are too high and that some of the marginal-subsistence producers listed here did, in fact, produce enough to satisfy their requirements, but I feel that this table gives a true picture because it is verified by other data, among which is the fact that all those producers listed as deficient admitted to having had to borrow grain to reach the harvest.

That this proportion of surplus to deficient producers is probably not unusual is shown by comparison with the village of SUnja, where in 1959 and 1960,

TABLE 5.2

Sample of Thirty Homesteads in the Village of Utatuu at the Harvest of 1959, Showing (1) Their Surplus or Deficiency of Grain in Relation to Subsistence Requirements (Including Reserves) and (2) Livestock Owned

Homestead No.	Grain in *debes*	Cattle
1.	+209	53
2.	+145	29
6.	+90	59
11.	+61	4
15.	+42	5
14.	+38	6
7.	+35	0
8.	+33	38
23.	+28	2
9.	+14	76
5.	+14	17
13.	+13	3
4.	+10	71
17.	+9	9
26.	+4	0
30.	−12	0
27.	−13	3
22.	−14	0
25.	−14	0
28.	−17	3
29.	−19	3
3.	−21	40
18.	−23	0
19.	−33	48
10.	−36	11
12.	−37	7
24.	−37	1
16.	−46	3
20.	−56	3
21.	−92	19

another reasonably good year for crops, fifteen out of a total of twenty-eight houses produced less than was needed to subsist. Some of the deficient producers were also those with the most livestock. Typical of both villages is the occurrence of a few very superior producers, usually people with many livestock, and a few very inferior producers, while the rest can be grouped in the range of somewhat superior to somewhat inferior.

Those producing too little food are not necessarily required to part with livestock to buy grain. If the underproduction is small enough, they can borrow a few *debes* from kinsmen or friends to tide them over to the harvest, at which time they repay the loan; 2 *debes*, which amounts to eighty pounds of grain, is sufficient to feed two adults for more than a month. Deficient producers can also begin to eat their crop at the earliest possible moment, sometimes a month before the usual harvest. Cutting back on consumption to stretch supplies is no doubt resorted to on occasion, but it is characteristic that Turu seldom consider reducing consumption at any time of the year, an attitude that probably indicates the relatively high supply of grain in the entire system. If a youth whose house is an inferior producer has his mother living with him, he may receive help from her. Probably in good productive years slight underproducers are able to make up shortages in some way without resorting to the disposal of livestock. In modern times a favored method of making up deficiencies is by brewing and selling beer, a practice which will be described in some detail in Chapter 9.

The slowness of the grain market in years of high productivity is probably the reason men visualize profit making in terms of a coup, to be accomplished by storing large amounts of grain (called *unkwama*) against a famine. Everywhere people accumulate surpluses when they can, while waiting for a disastrous year or a personal calamity to others in order to convert the stored surpluses into livestock by the sale of high-priced grain. Even during slow years, however, there is a regular circulation of livestock for grain. In 1959 fourteen surplus producers in Utatuu admitted to selling grain in amounts ranging from 1 to 70 *debes*, averaging perhaps 10 *debes;* but much of this was sold to Arab and Indian storekeepers, who then sold it back to other Turu at a mark-up. They have merely become middlemen in a broadening market. On the other side, inferior producers regularly sell some livestock each year, although many of the males are disposed of in the government livestock markets. Later something more will be said about the effects of the juxtaposition of the indigenous and Western market systems, which has led to some alteration in Turu marketing. For now it is enough to point out that when government livestock markets are available and Arabs and Indians act as middlemen for grain sales, exchange becomes somewhat more complicated. The producer of surplus grain acquires his livestock (as well as paying taxes and buying clothes and certain other introduced commodities) by selling grain for cash, which he then uses to buy female livestock from other Turu. The seller of male animals in the government market does the same, because he sells males and hopes to use the cash to buy heifers as well as pay his taxes. Some men talk as if accumulation of cattle were strictly a matter of good husbandry, but this view is an ideal one. Few men have livestock that came from their fathers, showing that livestock are a highly volatile form of wealth.

During years of high production the price of grain tends to stabilize. The stable rate during most of 1960 was 20 *debes* per heifer, or 4 *debes* per goat. Toward the latter part of the season, when supplies of grain were low, the price began to rise, until at the preharvest period there were instances of the sale of 2 *debes* for one goat and 15 *debes* for one heifer. Among the many stories of coups that were managed in bad years, an example is that of one well-to-do man who claimed to have established the basis for his present modest fortune by selling grain at the rate of 3 *debes* per heifer in 1938. Famine years are essential to such an economy; these, however, must be distinguished from the disastrous years when no one profits and even the cattle die. The last such disaster is said by the Turu to have occurred just after the British took control of Tanganyika in 1918. According to historical records and Turu accounts, the more usual famines occur generally every ten years. The last of these before this study was made occurred in 1952 but there was another in 1961-1962, after the study was completed. Where these strike, there is probably a violent circulation of wealth, although these "disasters" must certainly vary in intensity. Thus, the man mentioned above sold grain at the rate of 8 *debes* for a young steer in the year 1953, a price much lower than he was able to charge in 1938.

While market activity is relatively slow in years of good production, it must not be thought that the economy is ever static. A few statistics from Utatuu for the year 1959-1960 show certain normal fluctuations. With a total cattle population of 550 at the time of the survey, the year previous to compilation of the figure witnessed 110 cattle born and 80 slaughtered or dying of some disease. These figures represent a turnover of 20 per cent per year if this is a normal rate. Forty cattle were sold, mostly in the government markets, and thirty-one were involved in bridewealth transactions of which twelve were gained and nineteen were lost.

While the sale of grain is central in the market process, other goods also circulate, though in smaller amounts. Some men process tobacco into blocks, which they sell for as much as a heifer. Blacksmiths sell metal parts of tools for varying rates, of which four axe heads for a goat is an example. Since land is seldom sold, it is difficult to name prices, but a rate of one heifer for about five acres of marsh land is an example of a price once quoted to me. While sale of goods other than grain is not central to the economic process, it is essential; all homesteads must expend wealth to buy tools, land, services of various kinds—especially those of diviners—and the like. It is noteworthy that labor can be hired on a short-term basis. A person wishing to stretch his grain supplies can work for a wealthier person, for whom he can haul wood, draw water, and cultivate, in return for some grain. This practice has declined in modern times as workers prefer to manufacture and sell beer to fill out their stores.

The investment orientation of Turu is apparent in every type of loan of goods.

It is always possible to detect some sort of desired compensation, although it is not always livestock. When grain is loaned to a neighbor who is in need, the grain that is returned at harvest time is considered sufficient compensation because it can replace the old stored *unkwama*, whose durability may have reached the limit. Persons with much stored grain depend on such loans to turn over their stores.

Compensation for the loan of cattle in the *Uriha* system has already been discussed, but to show that the parties are conscious of the equilibrium of values, it is useful to observe what happens in some of these loans when rights are violated. If a man loans a heifer to another and then takes it back as soon as a calf is born, the loanee will without fail complain that the transaction is not fair. He reasons that he cared for the cow all during its pregnancy, and his reward, beside the manure he has obtained, should consist of the milk the cow will give while the calf is suckling. On the other hand, if a loanee keeps another man's animals for a long time and they prosper, he will expect the owner to let him use one or two of the animals for marriage or some other important expenditure, with the understanding that he will repay the animal at some future time, perhaps even after an indefinite period. In fact, he may never repay the loan, but the owner may not object if the loss is overbalanced by the value he receives. Of course owners deny that loanees have any such rights. In the early stages of an *Uriha* relationship the loanee can expect almost nothing other than the manure and milk produced by the animals he has been loaned, because at that point he is the one obtaining the greatest value from the relationship. Typical of all Turu exchanges, he appeals to the animals' owner for help and is at the disadvantage of being in a seller's market, so to speak. During this period the owner's right to possess his animals at any time without explanation can be most fully exercised.

The most glamorous investment process is speculation. A discussion of it is included here not only because it is part of the system, but also because it illustrates so well the business acumen that is not lacking among the Turu and that allows for profiteering by skillful men. To show this fact it is necessary to shift the scene somewhat and make reference to the juxtaposition of Western and Turu markets. During the culling or destocking campaign that was in progress in the 1950's, Turu used to complain bitterly that it only made the rich richer and the poor poorer. This complaint was not mere idle carping. In various ways destocking upset the balance of the indigenous system and accelerated the polarization of wealth. The process had been designed by the colonial government to reduce livestock across the board in order to improve pastures. The goal was to be accomplished by setting quotas requiring owners—or rather holders—to sell surplus livestock in the official government livestock markets at a rate of 1 in 10 in the first years. Subsequently the quota was raised to 1 in 6. Needless to say, the government was not aware of Turu uses of livestock as money, and it was this ignorance that finally resulted in the failure of the campaign, because disruption of the indigenous economy gave rise to severe unrest.

In the indigenous economy, as we have seen, a heifer or cow is worth more than a male animal, whereas the reverse is true in those markets where size of animals for beef is more important than sex or breeding potential. Given this difference and the pressure to sell, the stage was set for certain manipulations by farsighted Turu. Various possibilities presented themselves, of which the following was one: faced like everyone else with the requirement that he destock a certain number of animals, a man with acumen, who happened to have a heifer, would exchange it in the indigenous economy for a very large steer. The owner of the steer found the heifer more valuable to him, but the buyer had reason to value the steer more. Our speculator would then wait for a slack month on the government market, when prices were up, and he would sell the steer for 200 or 300 shillings. He would then hold on to the cash until others were forced to sell as the deadline neared for obtaining papers to show that they had met destocking requirements. With his cash in hand, he would find some unfortunate outside the market who was prepared to sell a heifer because he had nothing else to sell. It was a rule that any animal brought to the market had to be sold, and at this time prices, especially for cows, would be low. Our farsighted man would offer a higher price than the market. The seller would then use part of the money to bribe a clerk to record that he had destocked an animal. Thus he would come out of the transaction better off than if he had sold his cow in the official market, and both buyer and seller were satisfied. As a result, a regular system of bribery arose, whereby clerks charged 10 to 20 shillings to mark off one animal. In the end our speculator might come through the long process of manipulation with two heifers instead of one because he would get his heifers for about 100 shillings each and would also have credit for destocking one animal as well as some extra cash. He could then proceed to repeat the entire procedure.

A permanent variant is a form of arbitrage. The owner of a large steer sells it in the external market for 200 or 300 shillings and then takes his cash back into the indigenous system, where he exchanges it when the opportunity arises at the standard rate of 100 shillings per heifer. He then finds someone with a large steer who will exchange it for a heifer, takes the steer to market, and sells it for 200 or 300 shillings, so beginning the cycle again. The men who go in for this process must have capital to start with, but they also are of strong will, refusing to be seduced by the lure of imported consumer's good as they seek to turn a profit. They are patient, willing to wait for someone who wants to make an exchange and for good prices. To a certain degree all Turu share in these traits. They typically begin a transaction with a firm idea of what price they will offer or pay, and they refuse to budge. Sellers are more characteristically of this attitude, however, so that Turu markets are typically seller's markets.

One of the puzzling aspects of Turu attitudes—to say nothing of people in other herding societies in East Africa—is that goats are to some extent valued for their own sake; that is, sometimes goats will be preferred to cattle. The reason for this preference may lie in the fact that goats breed faster than cattle, making it possible to convert a cow to goats and to keep them until they have bred, after which they can be reconverted to cattle. This process has the effect of increasing the reproduction rate of cattle—a kind of increase in rate of interest.

While the ways a man can become rich are known to most Turu, they are difficult to follow. Generally speaking, Turu feel that a man must possess fifty head of cattle to be considered rich. One informant felt that a hundred was closer to the mark. A man with five head is hardly removed from one who has none, or so some informants think. In such terms there are few men in either of our villages or anywhere in UnyatuUrU who can be considered rich—only four in Utatuu, out of a sample of thirty homesteads. The largest holders are in Wilwana, some of whom are reputed to have over 1,000 head. The richest man in all the western subclan of AnyanhatI possessed no more than 400 head.

It should not be thought that each village is a closed exchange system. The data on Utatuu merely illustrate the conditions that make necessary a market system; they do not prove that exchange occurs only in the village or between nearby villages. Trade is conducted within and between villages and also between different areas of the tribe and with neighboring tribes. Trade within the villages is not very apparent, probably because trading with close relatives is prejudiced by familiarity. A better profit is to be obtained by dealing with strangers, but these may only be people in the next village, who are as ignorant of the economic status of their neighbors as they are of other aspects of their lives. In fact, the usual underestimation of the amount of marketing that goes on in East African tribes no doubt stems in part from its unobtrusiveness. Just as a Turu youth declares that he is in the marriage market by parading through a foreign village carrying a shield and spear (Plate 5.1), the person seeking to buy grain wanders around, perhaps driving his animals before him, looking for a seller. When a Turu decides to buy grain, he will go as far as necessary to find a good price, traveling from friend to friend in other villages, seeking information. In any village or group of villages people generally know which of their kin have surpluses. However, it is a good guess that grain is obtained from far off only when the price is low because of the difficulty or cost of transporting it on the backs of the few donkeys Turu own.

The amount of international trade (so to speak) engaged in by Turu should not be underestimated. Von Sick was impressed by the trade between Turu and Iramba, leading him to describe UnyatUrU as a "bread basket" of the Central Province. Von Sick tells of one famine in Iramba in the 1909-1910 season that led to widespread sale of grain to these unfortunates by Turu, who received a large steer or heifer calf for each "bag" of grain. Evidence from other early accounts gives a clear picture of the international trade situation at that time. In normal years Turu were deficient in certain desirable products, of which raw and finished iron, pottery, tobacco, amerikani cloth, ornaments (particularly beads) and, of course, livestock were the principal items. They, in turn, commanded various resources demanded by other surrounding tribes. Before the coming of European markets Turu exported salt obtained from Lakes Singida and Balangida, but otherwise their main export was grain. While von Sick was

PLATE 5.1
Young Man with Shield and Spear,
Signifying his Search for a Wife

of the opinion that Turu were better off than their neighbors, they too had bad years, during which they sold livestock and children to obtain grain. Stanley, in discussing one of his trips through UnyatUrU, mentions that even women were being sold.

The various early explorers make plain that trade was conducted with all the neighboring tribes, with the possible exception of the Barabaig, with whom Turu still have unfriendly relations. But in any case, the main direction of trade was to the east, south, and west. The Sandawe, Gogo, Nyamwezi, and Sukuma were the sources of the most desired good, iron, and it was mainly to them that live-stock and children went for grain and to whom grain was at other times traded. Reche gives us some indication of the prices in this trade. He says one goat was given for an iron cowbell or for a few arrow points and a fowl or some grain for a metal bracelet. In more recent times the foreign traders, who have moved into the district, have substituted for all these previous international connections.

The pursuit of wealth by the Turu should not be visualized in negative terms as the desire to avoid starvation. When production conditions are very poor, as they rarely are, some Turu may starve, but this outcome is quite unusual. By one means or another all the people get fed, the rate of intake of food being remarkably invariant throughout the year. Turu have a horror of the disgrace of poverty rather than of starvation. The poor man feels overdependent on others and unable to control his destiny. One such person summed it up: "The worst thing about poverty is that one is not happy. It is not possible to get money to pay taxes or buy clothes, and one may even be driven to sell livestock to do these things. When there are no livestock, there is no manure and poor crops. It is even hard to get married because parents don't want a poor son-in-law."

On the other hand, people defer to the rich man. His future is under control. He is called *mUnyampaa* ("sir") or *tata* ("father"). People come more readily to help him cultivate his crops. If he chooses, he can with greater ease increase the number of his wives and can afford to buy the *kIsaγwida* (an orange stone necklace worth one heifer) for his wife to wear and to proclaim his wealth. He is listened to carefully, and when he visits he is given the best stool or chair to sit on. He can afford to sponsor circumcision rites, give sacrifices to his ancestors, and loan cattle to obligate his poor neighbors, and he generally has the power to influence other people to follow him because they hope to benefit from his wealth.

To a non-Turu variations in wealth are not usually evident. Turu can read each other more accurately, detecting various signs of fortune. The most important of these, besides the number of livestock in the homestead, are:

1. The amount and condition of the standing crop, which correlates with the number of livestock in the homestead and the amount of manure available.
2. The number of people who come to help a man cultivate or perform other cooperative tasks, which they do both out of deference and because of the amount of food that will be given them in payment.
3. The size of his *nyUmba*, or houses, principally the width. It is necessary that the width increase as the number of storage bins increases and as the number of small animals, who are penned in the house, increases. Such a house takes more material and labor to build.
4. The number of wives in a homestead is generally a sign of wealth, not only because of the cost of obtaining them, but also because it is necessary to endow their houses with enough livestock to make them viable.
5. Food is more lavishly provided, and there is cream, milk, and meat to eat.
6. The wealthy man's dress is more varied and nowadays may include European clothes.

6. INDIVIDUAL RIGHTS
AND CORPORATE RIGHTS

When people exchange cattle, a calf is a calf.
TURU PROVERB

A TURU depends upon others, particularly on men of his village, for the successful accomplishment of his economic ambitions. In this chapter the nature of such cooperation will be assessed.

A revealing area in which to compare joint and individual rights is ownership of livestock. The norm of joint ownership of livestock parallels that of land. Men talk as if the elder brother is the real owner of all the animals held by him and his brothers. As with land, this "ownership" must be seen as ideal, derived from the elder brother's favored position in relation to the ancestors who are the ultimate "owners." They are supposed to give him the mystical power to render proper decisions about use of the animals. In practical terms, once the inheritance has been divided, the elder brother cannot exercise further direct control over animals he has given to his brothers. Significantly, this situation is not true of an immature brother—one who has not been circumcised and is thus not yet socially existent, who is not "known to the world." In such a case the elder brother is acting principally in the role of guardian rather than as one who knows what is right in a mystical sense. Similarly, in one instance where a man had two wives (the second giving birth to a son long before the first), the son of the second wife acted as guardian of the wealth of the son of the first, who was rightful *mUkUU*, until that son reached maturity.

The rules of inheritance specify in general terms how the father's wealth shall be parceled out among his sons. Although the eldest son is ideally the only inheritor of the wealth, he is actually obligated to share equally with the youngest brother, the *mUtInampafo*. Even this is an ideal, however, for the youngest brother seldom receives as much as the eldest unless the inheritance is very small.

The exact amount of the division is not specified but is worked out in conference with senior members of the lineage, unless the father has already determined it. The seniors weigh various factors, such as the number of animals previously used by the various sons for bridewealth or other payments. Ignoring such variables, if there are twenty-five cattle, the elder brother probably gets about fifteen and the younger ten. If there are more cattle, the differential is greater, for example sixty to thirty. Each of the senior brothers is then obligated to share with the middle brothers *(va mUxati)*, all those from the center up being the responsibility of the *mUkUU* and those from the center down of the *mUtInampafo*.

89

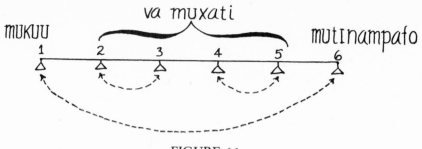

FIGURE 6.1

Division of Brothers for Inheritance

These middle brothers get far smaller shares than the favored brothers. For example, if there are four brothers and the division is of twenty-five cattle, as in the first example, the ratio might be ten-five-three-seven or twelve-three-one-nine. In one actual case involving four sons, the division was 40-5-5-25, and in another with three sons it was ninety-fifteen-sixty. It is a fundamental principle that all the cattle must descend to the offspring of the woman to whose house they are attached. This qualification can lead to the unusual circumstance that if a man dies leaving a herd that he mostly inherited from his own father, the cattle must be divided among the sons of his several wives as if they were full brothers—that is, as if they were the sons of the wife of their grandfather and belonged to her house. In one such case, however, the division worked itself out as follows:

FIRST WIFE	SECOND WIFE	THIRD WIFE
1 son	1 son	3 sons
70 head	10 head	4-3-0 head

Ideally the sons of the third wife should have gotten much more than the son of the second wife. That they did not was due to certain circumstances that do not concern us here but that show the rule of inheritance to be a guide, not a prescription.

Frequently the division of the inheritance presents no problem because there is little to inherit in the way of livestock. When a division must be made, however, the inheritors must publicly declare their satisfaction with the formula arrived at, so that if they later raise objections, their words of acquiescence will testify against them. As one might guess, few but the senior brothers are ever really satisfied, and animosities between middle and favored brothers concerning the division of inheritance are endemic in this society.

To cope with the problem of residual legatees in the case of the death or disappearance of a brother, the formula of inheritance includes the further factor, the pairing of brothers (see Figure 6.1), as previously discussed. The eldest and youngest are paired, after which the second goes with the third, the fourth with the fifth, and so on. An absolute middle brother—that is, the odd man, if there is one—is allied with his next senior brother, although in the division of inheritance he receives some livestock from both youngest and eldest brothers. If the youngest son should die, the eldest is his legatee and vice versa. Similarly, two and three are residual legatees of each other, and so forth. If both of a pair of middle brothers should die, the property passes to the other middle brothers, who divide it, but never to the senior pair unless all the middle brothers are dead. In such a case the eldest and youngest divide the property on the basis of which of the brothers each owned.

In this ideal system is illustrated the corporacy of the lineage. It may be speculated that the effect of favoring the senior brothers, particularly the eldest, is to insure the continuity of the lineage by concentrating the capital to control production. Though the seniors do not really control all the wealth, they do control most of it. These are the brothers who, upon the father's death, are obligated to give a steer apiece to sacrifice at the funeral. The middle brothers are forced to display more initiative to make their way. This situation is made apparent in the Turu folktale "The Widow and Her Three Sons," which tells of a widow who had been left many cattle by her husband and during a year of drought had to seek water very far from home. Favoring the eldest son, and after him the youngest, she sends them in turn to seek water for the cattle, but they are frightened off by a sound at the pool; the middle son, after he finally is allowed to seek water, discovers the sound to be made by a small bird. Not only is the middle son in this story not favored, but his mother aggressively dislikes him, calling him ugly. As a result of his success, his mother now praises him for caring so well for "your father's property" and gives him all the cattle, disinheriting the other sons. While the story is a kind of sop to middle sons, its moral seems to be that, although the senior brothers are favored, a middle brother of initiative, like a junior wife, can make his fortune, and senior brothers should be careful not to feel too secure in their positions.

The encouragement of opportunistic behavior is contained in the system of pairing, which brings brothers into balance alliances and mitigates anarchic tendencies. We saw earlier that the pairing of brothers is a structural principle having the effect of combating centripetal tendencies in the relations of Level III lineages which during feuds pair off in balanced opposition on the basis of genealogical charters associating or opposing them as descendants of the senior or middle sons of the founding ancestor. This structure is an example of how norms guide and contain individualistic behavior and how individualistic behavior, or strategy, is encouraged within the structure. The control of wealth as a necessary element in the continuity of the structure is achieved, even though individuals control their own wealth by the channeling—rather than dictation—of individual actions.

This process is made clearer by looking at the sharing of wealth among members of the lineage. It is the duty of agnates to help each other assemble bridewealth and pay fines, and there is the feeling that help should be given a "brother" (here used in the classificatory sense) if he needs help for a "good" reason, and that such help need not be repaid. The giving of aid, however, is always considered in the light of two factors. The first is whether the applicant is a real friend or not. Some kinsmen do not like each other and consider this dislike sufficient reason to ignore moral obligations, rationalizing the rejection as resulting from the applicant's not having honored his obligations in the past. The reverse of this situation is that people who are friends may share with each other, regardless of kinship ties.

The second consideration is degree of relationship. Men know exactly their degree of relation to all others, and when anyone needs aid, he will appeal first to the closest relations. As a result, most aid is rendered among fathers and sons and full brothers, with decreasing amounts among remoter kin. Five degrees of reciprocity are illustrated in Figure 6.2.

1. Father and son render aid to each other "without a reason"—that is, without specifying why the animals are needed. Even so, the person being petitioned may refuse a request for animals if he can marshall arguments strong enough to defend his refusal. In this relationship, repayment is not considered, since the persons are joint owners of the animals according to the norms of inheritance. The nature of the relationship can be illustrated by the case of a young man who tried to sell to his father a piece of land he had cleared; the father explained to him that this would be a silly business because the land would be passed to the youth when the father died. Even so, the son who displeases his father could badly prejudice himself in disposition of the inheritance, although the father could not truly disinherit him. Ownership is not absolutely corporate, therefore, but is based on the logic by the son that "I might as well give him the animal, because I'll get it back anyway," and the logic of the father, "I might as well

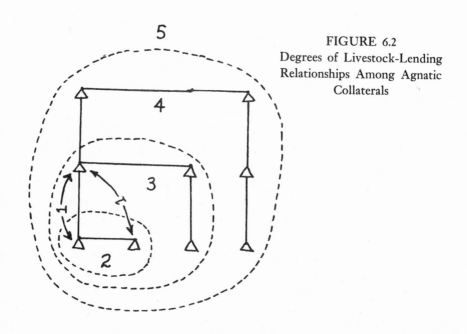

FIGURE 6.2
Degrees of Livestock-Lending Relationships Among Agnatic Collaterals

give him the animal, because he will get it anyway." Of course, this attitude presumes that the property under discussion is attached to the house of the son's mother; the son would not ask for property attached to other houses. It also presumes that the son is an only son. If he has brothers, the complication of division of property arises.

2. Among brothers of the same mother the divergence of interests, muted in the relation of father and son, now causes an alteration in the pattern of sharing, even though there is the ideal of common ownership. Full brothers render aid "without a reason," or so it is said, but it is understood that in instances other than those subsequently to be described, repayment is expected, although no time limit is set.

3. The third degree includes those to whom livestock are given only for a good reason—that is, if the applicant can make a good case for his request. If he is given the loan, he must repay it, but no time limit is set. This category includes father's brothers, and paternal first cousins and half-brother, as well as father-in-law.

4. The fourth degree includes the members of the same village other than those already dealt with. These also can obtain animals only if they can give a good reason to back up the request, and they must repay the animals within a set time period, usually a year.

5. The fifth degree is a residual category. It includes people outside the Level II lineage. They do not loan animals to each other unless they are special friends, particularly if they have the *waiyembe* relationship.

Relationships of sharing are conceived according to this schema by some men. This neat picture must be qualified, however, by recalling that people who are friends will loan livestock to each other regardless of relationship, although such loans must be repaid at some time. In certain cases the friendship is transformed into a father-son relationship through the adoption of a person, who then becomes the "son" of his benefactor. The loss of independent status as members of a senior lineage by the two brothers of Utatuu, which was previously mentioned, is explained as based on the fact that their grandfather was given cattle with which to accomplish his marriage by a man of the MUhUri lineage, who then became their official father. The founder of the Tatuu lineage of Utatuu was similarly adopted by MUhUri.

To the types of loans or gift giving so far discussed may be added the free gift of livestock to sister's son by mother's brother. While this resembles the relation between father and son, it differs in that, if mother's brother borrows livestock from sister's son, he must repay them. The symmetry in this relationship, which from one point of view is that of a father and son but from another is that of collateral kinsmen, again points to the contradiction in the Turu system.

It is thus clear that the essence of corporacy is not the joint use of livestock by two or more individuals, who look upon them as truly common property, which occurs to some degree only between persons of the relation of father and son.

The moral obligation to share with collaterals derives from the realization that all are descended from a common "father" or ancestor, but the actual corporate relation is less ideal. This fact is graphically illustrated by a certain incident related to me by one of a large group of brothers. He said that one of his brothers had gotten into trouble and at the chiefdom court was fined a cow, which he was unable to pay. The chief then sent a messenger to confiscate a cow from the defendant's brothers, on the grounds that the property of one was the property of all—a principle bitterly rejected by this informant, who, however, had himself previously informed me that "brothers are one."

In truth, the extent of the moral obligation to aid each other is even less than suggested. Men are reluctant to loan animals to others for any reason other than to pay bridewealth or fines; some insist that they have no obligation to give animals even to a full brother except for these purposes. On the other hand some men feel they should extend to paternal first parallel cousins the same liberal terms associated with loan to full brothers.

Certain other customs throw light on the reciprocal relations of men of the same lineage. It is considered superfluous to establish the *waiɣembe* relationship with a man of one's own village, presumably because such a relationship already exists between full brothers. One man called this situation, not a case of mutual aid, but *majlɣana*. The significance of this statement lies in the fact that *majlɣana* refers to an act of altruism, implying the giving of a good thing to make another person happy; its essence is that the gift is voluntary, not compulsory.

It is especially enlightening to examine ancestral sacrifice to understand the relations of father and son and of a man and his kinsmen. Sacrifices are made to ancestors when they are angry because of the failure of their descendants to share their wealth with them. It is said that these ancestors lack a hide to sleep on or a cow to give them milk. It is now the responsibility of the descendant to make the sacrifice but, significantly, the act is classed as an act of *majlɣana*— voluntary and altruistic. To perform the rite, the principal invites his collaterals within the village to attend, but he himself is the one who obtains the animals to sacrifice, who conducts the rite, and so forth. In short, it is his special relationship with the ancestor that is being reinforced; the attendance of members of the lineage is equivalent to the sharing relationship that exists among them in that they aid him in carrying out the rite. Put another way, though the rite is in fact an individual affair, the members of the lineage are brought in on the principle that they should cooperate with each other.

It is also clear, of course, that the rite is a public declaration of a desire, based on individual choice, to continue a corporate relationship that has been allowed to lapse, so that again we see the exercise of individual choice even in the most corporate property relationship. The ancestor is thought to be threatening his descendant for not honoring a moral obligation, which is indication that the desire to maintain a corporate tie is a function of its profit to the individual. There are no regular sacrifices to ancestors; they occur only when trouble arises. In contrast, the rain-making rite of a Level III lineage involves the whole group in action as a group because all are threatened together; in this case, however, only a sheep is sacrificed "because this is medicine, not a gift."

Sharing of rights in livestock, then, is a result of a set of mutually beneficial relationships created for the individual. The lineage does not completely contain beneficial relationships, however. The *Uriha* relationship may be established with strangers and is a type resembling that between third- or even second-degree relations. (See Figure 6.2). It is also occasionally the case that a mother's brother who has no sons may choose to pass his wealth on to his sister's sons. Normatively this wealth should pass to his paired brother or to his paired brother's sons, but respect for the individuality of rights is often strong enough to permit such an anomaly. Paralleling this exception are those cases in which men voluntarily attach themselves and their property to foreign lineages in the manner of the founder of the Tatuu lineage of Utatuu.

Yet the ties among members of the same lineage must not be so understressed as to give a false impression. For most men it is the ties established by birth, with their emotional overtones, that provide the most permanent basis for mutual aid. People living in villages other than those in which they have lineage ties feel uncomfortable and unsure; becoming accepted in such villages is a long process.

The division of land has also been previously discussed. A few details remain to be added in conjunction with the question of privacy of rights. Land rights are even more individualistic than those pertaining to livestock. Once a young married man has been given a piece of land out of his mother's plot, and once he presents this land to his wife, the plot comes under her control and will not be shared with others in any way. The male members of the lineage of the village "own the village," it is said, but this ownership is manifested rather indirectly. Unless his wife divorces him, a husband does not even have control over the land he has assigned to her.

The division of land follows a pattern similar to that followed in the division of livestock in that the eldest and youngest sons get the largest share. Because it is not possible to borrow land the way livestock are borrowed to complete the formation of a productive unit, the father and mother must try to provide sufficient land to make a married son's homestead viable. If we examine Map 6.1 we see how this goal was accomplished in one large family, where seven sons had to be provided for. The first son was given a large plot and the next eldest got a somewhat smaller but sufficient one, but as the other sons successively married, their shares got smaller and smaller, so that the fourth, fifth, and sixth could not manage with theirs and had to move to other areas. The last son had no problem, since the mother retained a large plot for herself until she died, after which he inherited that, as was his right.

WIVES

From the fact that all men of the same generation in a Level II lineage call each other's wives "my woman" it might be deduced that all have equal rights

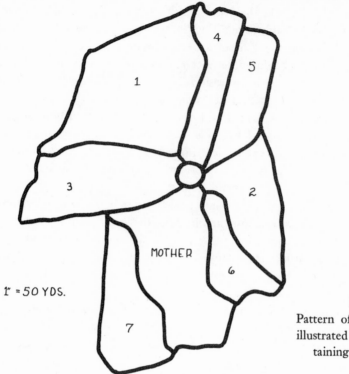

1″ = 50 YDS.

MAP 6.1
Pattern of Land Inheritance
illustrated in a family containing seven brothers

to them, including sexual access. But from what has been shown, one must doubt this deduction, and the evidence supports this doubt.

Joint use of the productive labor of wives must be immediately ruled out. Each man jealously conserves his wife's labor, sharing it with no one. The wife herself would not agree to such sharing, and in most instances she does not even help her co-wives. As to sexual access, it must first be noted that a woman asserts the right to a lover—called *mbUya* or "friend"—and may even obtain a divorce from her husband on the grounds that he denies her this privilege. This procedure implies, of course, that men object to philandering, although at the same time they themselves carry on with the wives of others. A husband can do little except object to or perhaps attack a full brother who sleeps with his wife, but he may fine others. This fine, which is normally three goats, applies to men in and outside the village who have relations with his wife. While there is no understood rule, the evidence indicates that a woman usually chooses as a lover a man of equivalent generation to her husband in another Level II lineage of the same Level III lineage, (that is, a man from a different village). This selection appears to result from a process of elimination; beside classificatory husbands, the only other men available to her, practically speaking, are classificatory sons and fathers-in-law, with whom relations are strictly forbidden, just as they are with persons who are not of the same Level III lineage, who may be fined a heifer for being caught with her and who are prevented from perpetuating the relationship, whereas the legitimate lover cannot be prevented except by exercise of the authority of the husband over his wife. This authority, if used, is universally considered a sign of selfishness and is difficult to enforce in any case. Lovers of the legitimate type many institute a kind of quasi marriage by the process of being formally discovered in the act of intercourse.

There is some question about the size of the fine for adultery. Some say it is always twice the amounts stated above because both the husband and the wife receive an equal amount. Thus, for the "permitted" relation the fine is actually six goats, and for the forbidden relationship, ten. Von Sick claimed it to be seven goats, paid to the husband.

Here the balancing of forces is again demonstrated. There is no question that classificatory brothers do believe that in some sense they have sexual rights to each other's wives (aramu), and the smallness of the fine as well as the right to continue an established relationship supports this belief. That a fine can be levied and that husbands tend to be angry about anyone else's use of their wives argues for the conclusion that wives are seen in ideal terms as private property and that husbands only allow these relationships because they cannot prevent them.

The free access to each other's wives by full brothers grows inevitably out of the nature of their relationship. Men die or disappear for long periods of time, and their wives cannot be left alone (in fact, most women fear being alone). It is the right and duty of the paired brother to take such a wife into his homestead and to treat her in all respects as his own. But, of course, when her legitimate husband is present, he will object if she has relations with his brothers. Even though a woman may be absorbed into the homestead of her husband's brother, the individuality of her husband's estate continues to be recognized. Not only are all children born to his wife ascribed to him—even when he is away or dead—but in a case where a widow is left with no sons, she may contract a marriage in the dead husband's name and try to arrange production of a son through his new wife, so that the estate will be kept together. In many cases strong minded widows refuse to be absorbed into the homesteads of their husband's brothers and carry on the estate alone. The particularity of the relation of a man and his legitimate wife is such that if he dies, even if she is absorbed into her dead husband's brother's homestead, she does so by choice, and her new "husband" must pay her owners an additional cow to legalize the union.

WORK GROUPS

Cooperative labor is essential to production as well as to ritual. It is utilized for land clearing, harvesting, housebuilding, ancestral rites, funerals, and other tasks requiring a large investment of time in a short period. When such aid is desired, it is possible to ask any friend for it, but it is only men of the same village who normally have obligation to honor such requests, and even they may refuse if there is a good reason to do so. Again, however, the familiar pattern of balance exists between what is morally required and what is practical. It is represented here by the fact that he who invites others to help must pay them with beer and a chicken. The men work on the joint task during the morning and at noon stop to drink and eat for the rest of the day. If the host cannot provide the beer and meat, he will get no help, although he may put his workers off with the promise of feeding them a goat at a later date. (The case of the sons who would not help their mother with her cultivation, forcing her to con- vene a work party at some expense to get the job done, will be recalled.)

Investment of beer and meat to obtain aid is not insignificant. Some of the poorer producers cannot afford it and must do the work alone. Some purposely refuse to ask for aid, even when they can marshall the payment, because they hope that the resources of their homesteads will be sufficient to do the job and to save the additional cost. When there is house building to be done (Plate 6.1), the women of a village work as a group to draw water on the day before the framework is to be plastered with mud. The following day they cook porridge to feed the workers at the morning meal. While each may contribute grain from her own stores, it is the responsibility of the woman for whom the house is being built to do so.

It is noteworthy that when a man needs less help than is given by a whole work group, he may hire one or two men and pay them with some grain. One

PLATE 6.1
Work Group Building a House. Note the grain bins already installed and
the ridge pole.

rich man explained that he never honored requests for aid by members of his lineage, but when he himself needed help, he paid them like hired help. Another explained a new method he had worked out for getting better compensation for his investment of beer. To defeat the lazy members of a work party, he marked out his plot in squares and assigned one to each man. The worker got no beer until he finished his section. (This man is one with rather progressive agricultural ideas, which he picked up in school.)

It seems apparent that the value placed on mature male cattle, used in most rituals to feed participants, is precisely that they purchase the participation of members of the community in the rites and establish obligations for the future, of which communal labor is one. In a sense it is true, therefore, that Turu do not slaughter most cattle for food, in the way we do, but their main value is nevertheless as food.

FOOD

The pattern of sharing food is also pecuniary. Raw grain is not shared except in small amounts, and any given out by a woman to anyone must be repaid. Milk in excess of requirements is sold. There is sharing of certain kinds of food in certain circumstances, however. It is considered unlucky not to offer cooked food to visitors when they are present at the time the food is served. Beer is classed with food, and the same rule applies to it. The etiquette of beer drinking is elaborate and sheds light on the whole pattern of food sharing. Beer is a highly desired food, and enormous quantities of it are drunk by individuals at any sitting. A perennial problem whenever beer is made is to keep the event secret so as to avoid too much sharing. The work is done by the wife in the darkness of her inner room. When the beer is ready, she and her husband may attempt to drink it alone, but it is almost impossible to refuse a share to full brothers, who are usually invited to help drink it anyway. If others in the village hear of the beer, they may also invite themselves. In this event the method of control is to put the invited guests into the darkened back room, where the stored beer is located, while others must stay in the outer room. They are given small shares but are excluded from the main party. There is no need to share beer with any person outside the village, even though good manners would lead to their receiving a token drink. When affinal relatives visit, they must be served. In this case others in the village who have beer, particularly full brothers, must honor a request of a host for a loan of beer to serve his guests if he has no beer of his own.

There are, then, three classes of relations with respect to sharing of beer: full brothers and affines, who must share fully (if they find out about the feast), and probably also members of the herding group of the host; members of the same village, who receive consideration but are not necessarily invited to participate fully in the drinking; "strangers" who need be given no consideration unless the host is so inclined.

The etiquette of beer sharing is illustrated by a party I gave for some close friends in a village in which I was living. I bought the beer and sent special invitations to certain men in the village while ignoring others. This procedure was naive. On the day of the event, it became apparent that all the men and women of the village had come and that they felt it proper for them to be there. When the close friends were invited into my tent, all the other men elbowed their way in with proprietary certainty; only a few strangers from another village and the women planted themselves outside. There is a proper method of coping with such an exigency. My adviser in the matter held back some of the beer without my knowledge. He had quietly passed the word to the close friends that they should remain at the end of the event. This they did, and when all the others had gone, they drank the remainder of the beer. One "stranger" who did not leave was given none of the beer and felt no offense, since he understood that he was intruding. This device does not always work. It sometimes happens that when a host asks his close friends to remain at the end, they invite *their* close friends, and no one leaves. It was apparent from the way my affair developed that I was considered to be a quasi member of the lineage of the village and that I had, by inviting one of them, invited all. Normally, when there is a large group, however, the guests are given quantities proportional to the degree of relation to the host.

HERDING GROUPS

The method of constituting herding groups goes farthest toward ignoring ascribed lineage relations for the sake of utility. Ideally a group of brothers or close agnates would constitute a herding cooperative. In such a group—which would hold undivided grazing land inherited from the father because the land can be more efficiently utilized that way—the brothers would take turns herding the animals. However, because of the differences in men's responsibility, variations in size of sibling groups, size of grazing land, and other factors, this ideal does not work in practice. Brothers do tend to herd together; in fact, they may even keep a common herd on rare occasions when the herd has prospered in the past, on the grounds that it would be unlucky to break it up. More often, however, outsiders are brought into the group. Ordinarily only men of the same village herd with each other, but occasionally men of other villages are invited. Such strangers have no grazing land of their own and join the group to exchange service for grazing. From time to time the composition of the groups changes as new men join and others, even full brothers, voluntarily leave or are thrown out for neglect of obligations. The groups must occasionally be reduced as available grazing declines in the dry season. If one of a group of brothers acquires grazing land by purchase, he is most free to dissociate himself from his siblings.

The nature of the relationship between brothers is generally illustrated by one case of a dispute over grazing land. A group of five brothers held grazing land in common, but one of them had moved his homestead to a new village near the old one but on the opposite side of the pasture. For the sake of efficiency, he felt that it would be better if the land were divided so that he could have his share to use in conjunction with a herding group in the new village. His brothers, who as a group had to make the decision about the division, refused his request. While this dispute shows the joint action that a group of brothers is capable of, it also illustrates the idea that each member of the group has personal shares in corporate property and can convert them to a private holding under certain circumstances. By denying the request, his brothers were not asserting common ownership but only stating that this division would not bring a common advantage.

During the time a group of men herd jointly, they occasionally share beer to mark their relationship. It happens sometimes that a herding group breaks up because a member is not invited to share beer with others of the group; this, one suspects, is an aspect of the politics of herding groups and a way of easing an undesirable person out of the group.

Because the composition of herding groups is so free of ascription, the number of herding groups in a village becomes a measure of the degree of factionalism. In one village there were no herding groups larger than two members, and informants considered that the size of the groups accurately pictured the amount of antagonism between members of the village. It is quite possible to find men who are rejected from all herding groups in their village and are forced to scrounge the forest and other free lands for fodder or actually to pay a few shillings a day to obtain access to grass in the land of an agnate.

Nevertheless, the notion of the unity of the lineage is seen in the fact that though in some places the main portion of a marsh is exclusive for the use of the owner, he will not prevent his lineage mates from letting their cattle nibble at the edge. It is felt that this is their due, because they will help defend the pasture against intruders from other areas. If ever such a person should blithely intrude his animals into the main portion of the pasture without permission, however, a fight would surely develop.

GIFT GIVING IN GENERAL

Perhaps the essence of the relationship among cooperating people is that the parties trust each other or feel that they can depend on each other. The ascription of obligations by birth in a lineage is the main frame for such trust; but it is important to realize that it is only the most important source. It can be extended to people outside the lineage, as is done in the *waiγembe* relationship, which may now be more fully described. It consists of picking a man, usually not of one's lineage, who seems likely to be trustworthy. He is approached and asked, for example, for a hoe or perhaps for 10 shillings—in any case, a small gift. It is in the nature of this particular relationship that if he refuses, the petitioner will give to the petitioned the object for which he asked. The purpose of his petition is not to get the object requested, but to attempt to establish the relationship by creating an obligation. The receiver of the gift will return the same object or something of equivalent value to the giver, but not before a year has elapsed. Next a more valuable object—perhaps a goat—is given, and the same exchange ensues. The parties go through this exchange for a long time, up to the point where cattle are exchanged. The effect is to establish a tie that is even more intense than either party may have with his own brothers. Afterward the *wai-yembe*, who may become destitute, can be taken into the home of his friend and given a plot to cultivate until his fortunes improve. He is in a position to ask and receive of his partner almost anything for any length of time. It is quite ordinary for a man living in a strange place to give small gifts to people around him, in hopes of establishing to a small degree a *waiyembe* type of relationship that will insure him friends in time of need. There can be no doubt that, whatever the emotional content of this relationship, it has a clear pecuniary content. It is this that is referred to by the proverb that opens this chapter, which means that when a person gives a cow to another, a cow must be returned—that is, for value given, value must be received, or "value is value."

The relation between corporate and individual rights may thus be summarized. Livestock ideally belong to the eldest brother, yet rights in them are given to each individual brother, who jealously defends his claims. Grazing land is jointly exploited, but individual brothers assert private rights to their shares. Members of the same village honor the call for help in work groups but expect payment. Wives are looked upon as accessible to any classificatory husband, yet husbands are angered when wives actually engage in such relationships. Grazing land is exclusive to the person who owns it, and he allows his fellow villagers to freely graze only on the edges. In short, there is a balance between individual rights and the moral obligation to the group.

Furthermore, there are no hard and fast rules about ownership, and this flexibility in some ways makes more difficult the protection of individual rights. Thus a Turu, as a last resort, often makes use of the most individualistic of rights —the right to attack another who invades his property—because he fears that he is unlikely to rectify the wrong with dispatch in any other way. One mission-educated Turu said that Cain and Abel are symbols of the Turu, killing each other for wealth although they are brothers.

Insofar as it is possible to state the nature of the situation with precision, we can say that possession of property is clearly thought to reside in the individual, although ideology gives only vague support to this belief. The system is ideally corporate, but this fact must be seen as a charter for cooperation between individuals, essential for success in the pursuit of private ends, not as a merging of rights.

All this may sound very pecuniary, but the fact is that true altruism is as hard to assert in Turu society as in any other. Any person who chooses to give to others without thought of return must take into account not only his own inclinations, but also the feelings of those to whom the gifts are given. When he gives the gift, if he denies to himself that he seeks any hold on the person to whom it is given, the receiver may nevertheless feel that such a right is being asserted and may resent the gift. I found that there was no advantage in giving gifts freely in this society; the receivers soon felt such an overwhelming obligation to me that they cut off all contact in despair of ever repaying.

7. PEOPLE AS WEALTH

A cow can split a boulder.
Turu Proverb

PEOPLE can be thought of in one respect as social beings and in another as property on the same order as cattle, grain, and the like.[1] Turu recognize this dual view in the distinction made with respect to "conflicts between people" and "conflicts between cattle." The former concern disputes about violation of social position, such as an unjustified attack on a senior by a junior. The latter concern disputes about property, for which the word "cattle" is simply a symbol referring, not only to cattle as such, but also to other goods and people insofar as they are property. For example, if the beating of a woman gives rise to a dispute between her husband and her owners, it is a "conflict between cattle." The issue is damage to her as property.

ASSIGNMENT OF RIGHTS IN PEOPLE

Corporeal rights, as we may call them, are assigned, not to the whole lineage, but to individuals. Looking back to the system of inheritance, we saw that while the father in a sense owns all his sons, in fact rights in them are the monopoly of the house that produced them. If rights in any person in a particular house are by some means vacated, compensation must go to that house. Furthermore, brothers are paired, and in cases involving them the compensation becomes the property of the paired brother of the alienated member. Before a male is circumcised (between about 12-15), he is not yet a person in the social sense. In former times such young men could occasionally be sold. After circumcision, however, rights in men are not involuntarily alienable. They are given up only when forcibly taken by acts of assault and homicide or by capture in warfare. Short of murder, rights in a man reside with himself, compensation for injury to his person being received by himself. In fact, sale of corporeal rights in any initiated person is considered morally wrong.

Implicit in ideas of ownership of other persons or self is a dualistic concept that it will be helpful to explain. A person is thought to consist of two parts. The

1. This distinction is also made by Radcliffe-Brown in *Structure and Function in Primitive Society* (1952, 32 ff). I have not used Radcliffe-Brown's terminology (rights in *rem* and rights in *personam*) to avoid leading the reader to conclude that my conception of rights in *rem* is as restricted as his.

first is the corporeal body, which is a shroud for the second, the spirit, or what Tempels in *Bantu Philosophy* (1959, 30) calls "vital force." This latter part is called the *mwimiimi* or *moyo* (heart), which is the essence of a person as a social being. It continues to dwell in the realm of the ancestors after the death of the body. *Mwimiimi* stands for the disembodied spirit; *moyo* is the spirit when in the living body. The term *kiungU*—derived from the root *-ungU* "ancestor"—refers to this ancestral spirit when it acts on living people. A person's body may be diminished or killed, but the spirit cannot be killed. Because the body is finite and a kind of wealth, it has value, loss or diminishment of which requires compensation. This concept is coupled with the belief that the body will not diminish or die except by the action of some human force. In theory people are corporeally immortal. It is for this reason that people with unusual growths on the body refuse to have them removed and are proud of them. For purposes of calculating compensation, there are accepted measures of diminishment of the body, of which death is one. Spitting blood is a common measure to determine whether a beating has exceeded allowable bounds resulting in actual decline in the value of the body. Loss of parts of the body, breakage of bones, or even mental derangement are other measures.

Men may have rights in themselves and others, but women may not. If a woman is injured, compensation is paid to the man or men who own rights in her. Because of the mixed status of a woman, compensation for violation of her corporeal wholeness goes to the man who owns her in the house from which she came at marriage. Violation of her productive talents, as in the case of adultery, brings compensation to her husband.

As was previously indicated, ownership of a woman's body is assigned to a brother, according to the ideal that each brother should have one sister for himself. The manifest reason for such assignments is to provide bridewealth for the brother; he expects to accomplish his marriage by using the livestock received from her marriage. Since the ratio of male to female siblings is bound to vary in most families, principles relating to assignment favor the senior brothers. If there is only one sister, the feeling is that she should be assigned to the seniors, except that if in a family of four brothers she is born in a position between the two middle brothers, they have claim to her despite the lack of a sister for the seniors. A sister born on either side of the senior brothers is theirs, a rule that gives seniors a special edge.

Even when rights in a sister are split between two brothers—as would be the case if an insufficiency of sisters required paired brothers to share—the senior of the two brothers has principal rights. The owner becomes the prime mother's brother to his sister's sons and has rights and obligations with respect to them that are not shared with his brothers. His ownership of his sister is partially extended to her children, resulting in a conflict of claims to rights in children between mother's brother and the children's father, as well as a conflict between him and the male children themselves, who identify with their father and his lineage.

As is now apparent, this conflict rests on the condition, previously discussed and here recapitulated, that for any person there are always two persons who claim rights in him or her. At the same time that any man or women is owned by his or her sibling (or in the case of a man, by himself), he or she is claimed by mother's father, mother's brother, or mother's brother offspring, whichever holds the estate. Hence, when any demand for compensation is made, two people make claims. This situation gives rise to situations thought to be peculiar even by Turu. For example, if a man is injured, his mother's brother will extend sympathy to him and solicitously attend to the recovery of his health, mainly by giving him sheep soup. He will also demand compensation from the injured person on the grounds that, since he is a member of a foreign lineage, he can be accused, with all his agnates, of having injured his own body in violation of mother's brother's rights. The distinction between the patrilateral spirit and the partially matrilateral body of Turu is no more apparent anywhere. This conflict between members of affinal lineages over rights in persons is one of the most striking facts about Turu society.

MWANDU

Earlier it was explained that *mwandU* means a discussion about compensation for death or injury. These cases can conveniently be divided into two types—those having to do with assault or homicide against men and those having to do with women. Since Turu have no distinction between the types of *mwandU*, it is clear that to them the exchanges of values are of the same order, even though the former are involuntary, and even behind the marriage process there seems to be a feeling that it is wrong to voluntarily alienate rights in people, so that marriage is viewed as a lease, not a sale.

When compensation for death or injury is demanded, the elders representing the disputing sides discuss the circumstances and decide the legitimacy of the claim. Sometimes it is difficult to decide the cause. Overt aggression poses no problem. Where the defendant is the actual physical agent of the injury, he is considered guilty whether he consciously wanted to injure the plaintiff or not. Facts speak for themselves. Von Sick, acting as magistrate, tells that this attitude offended his notions of justice, even though he wished to respect Turu customs, and once led him to reduce a fine from fifteen to five head of cattle for a man who had "accidentally" killed another.

If a person is injured by other means than overt contact of persons, this act can be interpreted as the result of different kinds of spiritual forces. One may be witchcraft, or sorcery. Another is a person with an "angry heart"—that is, one who has reason to wish harm to the subject but is not consciously aware of doing so. In fact, it is felt in some cases that the harmful force is not actually that of the suspect but that of an ancestor (as *kiungU*), who takes vengeful action for him. Finally, an ancestor may be thought to cause harm for his own sake. In cases where the ancestor is the cause, no penalty can be assessed. Instead, the injured party may find it in his interest to make a sacrifice to placate his rampaging forebear. In this type of case it is important to note that the injured party is being injured by someone who owns him—a lineal ancestor. When injury is due to vengeance by an ancestor in the name of someone the subject has harmed, the remedy is to right the wrong to that harmed party, rather than to sacrifice to the guardian ancestor. In the case of a witch, his or her actions are outside the pale of human intercourse, and the witch is ideally exiled or killed.

Thus, *mwandU* for injury to the body is leveled only against a person who has been the willful or "accidental" agent of overt aggression against a plaintiff, the other agents being considered to have the right to injure the person, with the exception of the witch, who is outside society.

The matter of how much compensation is paid for homicide against men and who receives it is somewhat unclear, because fines and payments for this offense have almost disappeared since the Tanzania courts judge such offenses. In the case of assaults, however, since they are still to an appreciable extent judged outside government courts, there is no such difficulty.

The cessation of *mwandU* for homicide was a reflex of the abolition of inter-lineage feuds by the Germans and the British. The colonial authorities pre-empted the prerogative of judging such cases and removed the feud claims, which sanctioned *mwandU*, with the result that people were often forced into the courts. Turu have subsequently learned to distinguish between murder and accidental homicide. One who is convicted of murder is hanged or imprisoned; his relatives then claim that the compensation has been sufficient. One who is acquitted argues that he owes nothing to the owner of his victim because the death was an accident—even though, as we have seen, accidental homicide is not recognized by Turu. Today there are numerous instances of long-standing bitterness between persons over the matter of compensation that was not paid because of acquittal or punishment by European standards. However, compensation for the death of a wife, which is classed as homicide, is still regularly paid, and since the process is analogous to the other form of death payment, it helps us to deduce how the matter was handled.

Knowledge of what happened in former times in the case of homicide is available today from old men or from others who have been told how disputes were conducted and settled. We also have the account of von Sick, whose experience as a magistrate adjudicating such disputes corroborates other data. It is worthwhile to quote from von Sick's account, in which he generalizes from his experience (Von Sick 1916, 32):

> By far the most disputes originated at the watering places and pastures. Following is such a dispute as they occurred over and over with little variance in the old days. "A" heards his cattle and in the course of this, on purpose or not, comes to be in the pastures of "B" of the neighboring sib, perhaps even in a part which is carefully fenced with thorn bushes and saved for the calves until the end of the dry season. They do not waste time with words but take up the weapons which are always at hand when

herding. "B" kills "A." Having been called by the children and wives, the friends of the two gather in a crowd. An extensive brawl then develops whereby, of course, there occur some injuries. The old men try in vain to stop it and they are usually not successful until the fighters are tired and stop anyway. The Munyaturu does not permit the opportunity for a brawl to pass. . . . But here instead of the spear they use the well beloved dueling stick, their *vademecum*, which is quite a dangerous weapon. After the fight ends, a delegation of "A's" relatives come to "B" to demand the compensation which, however, is at first always refused for nobody will without question part with fifteen head of cattle. The people of "A" now do not wait long; if they cannot manage to get the cattle of "B" by stealth they simply take away those of a man of "B's" sib, who is not personally involved, and remove them from the pasture. If it is the case mentioned above, they take more than 15, let us say 30. This has the advantage that the people of "B's" sib are now afflicted and put pressure on "B" to pay while having the old men apply to the old men of "A's" sib to get back their cattle. A delegation from "B" arrive to get their cattle and are scornfully laughed down when they request all of them so they merely demand 15 and thus acknowledge that compensation is due. The people of "A" agree but keep as punishment a few more head than is proper. That, of course, arouses the anger of the "B" sib and gives them reason to take back these few head at the first opportunity of stealing them. One does not need great imagination to see that this brought about an infinite chain of robbery, homicide and theft. As a matter of fact, in Turu there was permanent civil war of all sibs against each other which was not ended until the German rule began.

While in close agreement with informants, this account is unclear or in disagreement about some important facts. It is true that fights did most frequently occur in the pastures and about pastures, as they do now, and that they were between neighboring "sibs." The evidence suggests that von Sick's "sib" is a Level III lineage because no organized fighting between kin occurred within a Level III lineage and because lineages above Level III tend to be separated by grosser geographic features, while Level III lineages are commonly separated by marshes. It is true that dueling sticks, rather than spears, were used because the intent was not to kill but to "teach them a lesson," as one old man put it. Turu distinguish between two types of combat—*wlxhul*, using sticks, and *Uroɣoo*, using spears. These stick fights could be quite damaging, however, and the high feeling accompanying them did result in house burning, still a favorite form of aggression. However, it seems that a death would stop the fight. These groups had important relations, not the least of which were economic, that would have been upset by perpetual warfare. Most disputes were settled without a fight, and the *ifaha* dance, held subsequent to settlement, was a way of making the settlement official (see Plate 7.1). It has already been noted that some Turu classify those encounters as *njUɣUda*, indicating that they were institutionalized.

Von Sick's account, therefore, seems to have missed the regularity of the procedure for settling disputes of this type. The old men mediating the battles did

PLATE 7.1
Young Men at Fair Dressed in Old Style *ifaha* Costumes

not take part in the fighting. They had definite ideas about how much compensation should be paid; when it was paid, a feast of peace was held to stabilize
relations. The stick fights were so formal that the White Fathers in their account of them expressed puzzlement that the warriors should take them so
seriously that sometimes participants were seriously injured or even killed. In
other words, the White Fathers viewed them strictly as ceremonies, just the
reverse of von Sick's view. An illustration of the role of the elders in these fights
is obtained from a case involving a fight between two different Level II lineages
in more recent times. The elders of the villages discussed the case and decided
impartially who the guilty persons were and what the fine should be. In the name
of peace they were able to transcend their sectional interests.

By present accounts, the feast ending the feud required cattle in excess of the
fifteen mentioned by von Sick for a feast for the group. While Turu tend to
think of compensation for homicide as consisting of fifteen cattle, in fact the
payment is variable with the degree of relationship of the disputants, to name the
most important variable. Even von Sick was aware of this variation, although he
did not understand the meaning of what he saw. He says that he was surprised
that "brothers"—by which he undoubtedly meant men within the same Level III
lineage—paid less compensation than did others when they were in conflict about
homicide. In short, it is apparent that while von Sick's account is generally accurate, it covers only disputes between immediate Level III lineages, which were
probably the most frequent type, and it has nothing to say about the amount of
compensation paid between closer or more distant groups.

As far as can be ascertained today, the amount of compensation paid was determined as follows. In the first place, norms of mutual aid were brought into play both for defense of the lineage during the actual fighting and to pay compensation, but the number of persons cooperating to pay did not always vary with the level of alliances formed by feuds. While it is not entirely clear that paired Level III lineages did not cooperate in payment, most evidence places such mutual aid entirely within Level III. Lineages at higher levels, as has already been explained, did ally with each other, but if the dispute had to do with homicide, the exchange of compensation was only between the Level III lineages acting for the principals. This is additional reason to suppose that the blood-wealth is quoted at fifteen head because disputes most frequently occurred between units that would expect such an amount.

There was also mutual aid for paying compensation in disputes between Level II lineages, but Level I lineages did not line up on the model of higher lineages; their disputes were settled by informal negotiations.

The variation in rates with the degrees of relationship seem to have been as follows:

Homicide between subtribes: 60 head
Homicide between Level III lineages of the same subtribe: 15 head
Homicide between Level II lineages: 7 head
Homicide within the Level I lineage: 3 head

It therefore seems that the amount of compensation is a function of several factors, of which two are most important. It is, first, a function of the size of the units in dispute, increasing with increase in size. Of course, this would be an expression to some degree of the factor of supply. In one case in precontact days, a whole village gave up its land to another Level II lineage to settle a homicide claim for fifteen head of cattle, showing that at this level fifteen head is a very large claim. Additionally, the more distantly related the conflicting groups, the larger the number of people brought into opposition and the greater the likelihood that nonpayment will result in serious trouble. Secondly—and this is a dominant idea in the minds of the Turu—the closer the cooperative relations of the group of the plaintiff with the group of the defendant, the less is demanded of them for fear of creating lasting bitterness. This function is, of course, in part merely the obverse of the first.

MwandU of this type did not disappear entirely with the coming of the Germans, and there are examples of cases remembered by people of the village of Utatuu. Particularly remembered are cases of conflicts of the Tatuu people with other lineages within the Level III lineage of Wijue. In every one of these cases the compensation paid was seventeen head. This amount may seem strange, considering that the Tatuu are fused with the Level II lineage of *MUhUri* in the larger lineage of Wijue, but it becomes understandable when we remember that this fusion is incomplete. The amount of the compensation is one indicator of this anomaly, because for purposes of paying compensation the members of Wijue clearly consider the Tatuu to be a kind of foreign Level III lineage.

One of the gaps in von Sick's account of disputes is any clear indication of who pays whom. The answer is an important illustration of the individualism inherent in the system. When homicide is committed, the procedure is for the person who commits the act to be personally accused, and compensation is demanded of him. We saw this in von Sick's account, where the members of "A's" family demanded compensation of "B," who refused to pay. It was only subsequently that they stole cattle from others of "B's" lineage, as if there were no difference between them and "B." I say "as if" because by their actions the plaintiffs showed that they do recognize a difference, or they would not have approached "B" first. The defendant then had the right to turn to his lineage mates and demand help in paying the fine. It is such cooperative payment (along with the typologically identical claim for help in paying bridewealth, which Turu most frequently point to as the only indisputable claims to mutual aid) that exists among members of the same lineage. This fact is verified not only by the tendency for the plaintiffs to take cattle from anyone in the offender's lineage, but by the willingness, even insistence, by members of a lineage that they help pay such fines, even when the offender can himself afford to cover the entire amount.

Nevertheless, when claim is made against an offender, it is expected that he will bear the brunt of payment and that appeals for aid will in fact decrease in intensity with distance of relationship, so that the offender's full brothers will have the greatest obligation to help, other members of Level II will have a lesser obligation, and so forth. In a dispute between Level III lineages, the claim for mutual aid can radiate out within the whole of this lineage, but people outside the Level II of the offender will contribute the least. When only injuries are being compensated, claims may never go outside the lowest level of lineage, which is commensurate with the small cost compared to compensation for homicide. The conclusion must be that if a person kills, it is not seen by any of the parties as if his whole lineage had performed the act. The responsibility of the lineage in helping pay the fine is moral, not automatic, and is based on enlightened self-interest, not on slavish acquiescence. It is, for example, for this reason that when homicide occurs between full brothers, the lowest level of lineage, compensation must be paid, whereas if the lineage were corporate, there would be no point in such actions because the persons would be joint owners of the animals.

Turning now to a consideration of the receiving of compensation, in contrast to the paying, it is not received jointly by members of the lineage of the offended party, but by the owner of the dead person. If the deceased is a married man, the compensation is paid into his estate—that is, to his wife to hold for his sons. If he has more than one wife, the compensation is probably divided according to seniority, although there is no direct evidence of such division. If the man is not married, his paired brother will receive the compensation; if he has no brothers, it goes to his father; and so forth. All the compensation goes to the owner of the deceased, and none is shared with members of his lineage. It used to be customary to give five or six of the fifteen head for homicide to the elders of the deceased's lineage, to remunerate them for their services in settling the dispute, but this gift is not the same as payment to the lineage.

In cases where there is only injury, the general pattern remains the same as that of *mwandU* for death, but the compensation is considerably smaller and the settlement procedure is less complicated. Von Sick, who studied Wilwana rather than Wahi, found that most injuries were compensated with a heifer or its equivalent—five goats or a very large steer, the *nxama*. This payment covered fractures of various types, chipping of the head, loss of teeth from the maxilla, and loss of eye or ear. Very serious injury to the chest or abdomen might cost from one to three heifers.

In Wahi today the rates are similar, although most of the injuries von Sick lists as costing a heifer can be compensated with only a steer or three goats. Because of the frequency of injuries demanding this amount, the people tend to think of *mwandU* for any injury as in the amount of a steer, even though the cost really varies. For example, in the case of one young man who was speared in the shoulder by a jealous husband, the cost was two heifers.

Although the situation in precontact days is not clear, it seems that payment of compensation for injury to a person outside the Level III lineage was rare; though occasionally it took place. There are examples of such payments, but there is no clear idea of variation in costs.

As to the matter of mother's brother and his place in such disputes, whenever a person is injured or killed, mother's brother may make a claim for compensation against those who have violated his rights in the victim. In doing so, he reasons from the premise that the injured person is under the protection and care of the patrilineage to which he is attached, as if he were loaned to it by mother's brother. He also makes the paradoxical assumption that the person who is his property is at the same time a member of the patrilineage into which he is born and is therefore accused as well as victim. Mother's brother makes his accusation against the men of the Level II lineage of his sister's child, all of whom he holds responsible for the welfare of his sister's child. He makes known his complaint by visiting his sister's child and giving the victim soup (in this case not as an admission of guilt but to establish the claim). The paradox is complete, as was previously noted, when he makes claim for compensation from the person who is the victim of the injury. The only exception is that if the victim is a woman, mother's brother makes claim for compensation when she dies during marriage against the patrilineage into which she is married, not against the patrilineage into which she is born.

The inherent contradiction does not escape the Turu, who feel, despite recognition of the right of mother's brother to make a claim, that the claim is somehow not really legitimate. Various devious methods are used to try to avoid payment. Subsequent to giving soup—which he may never do if he feels he does not want to exercise responsibility and has little hope of obtaining compensation —mother's brother is supposed to provide beer for his sister's son and his agnates prior to requesting a steer or three goats as compensation for the injury to his property. These men politely request that he bring the beer before discussing the compensation, but they phrase the request indirectly, saying that he should bring some "milk" for his sister's son. If mother's brother wishes to press his claim, he brings the beer. But he may be further put off by a request for something else—perhaps some honey. If he is sufficiently irritated by these evasions, he may attempt to retaliate by bringing the thing, such as milk, that is actually requested. Probably the extent to which these tactics are used is a function of the extent to which mother's brother has actually taken an interest in his sister's son in the past, has "shown that he is really his son." Even if he has demonstrated his real interest in his "son," he cannot expect to obtain much compensation. Probably for this reason it is quite usual after mother's brother has given soup to his sister's son for him to make no claim but merely to mark the event in memory, to be recalled at the sister's son's funeral.

The manner in which claims for compensation are worked out at funerals shows in capsule form the extent of ownership by mother's brother of sister's son. When a man dies, his mother's brother may and should come to the funeral bringing certain of his agnates, who are also classificatory mother's brothers of the deceased. The crucial issue in the debate occurring at the point in the month-long funeral rites called *mUpanda* ("path," from the path worn in the corral manure by the spokesmen for both sides to argue the case), is whether mother's brother ever showed by his actions that the deceased was considered to be his "son." This he proves mainly by recalling instances when he gave soup. In one recorded case the mother's brother insisted on compensation for an occasion when the deceased had been badly beaten and was given soup by him. The spokesman for the agnates of the deceased replied that the claim was ridiculous because at the time he was beaten, the deceased was living with his mother's brother who had, in fact, been the assailant. Despite this rebuttal, which was considered strong indeed by the spokesman for the deceased's agnates, payment of one steer was made for this legitimate claim. The principle underlying the settlement undoubtedly was that protection of the deceased was the responsibility of his agnates and that he would not have been living with mother's brother and exposed to danger if he had been properly cherished by his agnates.

While mother's brother and his helpers make extensive claims for compensation, recalling every instance of abuse to the deceased, it is unusual for them to get more than one steer; on occasion, however, it is said, they may get as many as three cattle. The one steer is given almost automatically and is usually the *ŋombe a Usale* ("cow of seriations"). When the deceased is prepared for burial, his stomach is seriated to allow for the escape of gases, so that the corpse will not move in the grave. This act, performed by his agnates, is equivalent to assault on the dead man's body; the knife with which it is done is therefore placed on the corral fence and is taken away by mother's brother after the funeral, just as he also claims possession of the instrument that causes injury to his sister's son in any instance of assault.

The lack of effectiveness of mother's brother's claim correlates with the vagueness of his rights over the bodies of his sister's children. In a sense he is considered to be the owner of his sister's children because he owns his sister. The fact that he makes claim for injury even from the injured sister's son, and that sister's children's agnates honor their obligation to help pay the compensation, indicates that sister's children are actually and more truly members of their agnatic lineages. This correlates with the fact that during marriage a special payment is made for children that acts to alienate them from their mother's lineage, although obviously the alienation is not complete.

There is no way to resolve the Turu situation into a consistent system. Two principles operate simultaneously: patrilineal descent and matrilineal descent; although the former is predominant, the latter persists in a vague form.

MARRIAGE

Marriage *(nxwe)* must be differentiated from the exchange of corporeal rights. The rights in services a person may perform are distinct from corporeal rights and can be purchased or leased. As with corporeal rights, only men can hold them, selling their own services and the services of women in whom they hold corporeal rights. When a wife dies in the service of her husband or is injured while serving him or by him, the event is treated as a violation of the corporeal rights of her father or brothers in her, as if these rights had been unjustifiably taken. Marriage has attached to it elaborate strategies by which owners of a woman pretend reluctance to allow her to live with a stranger, act as if it is in some way a temporary state of affairs, and when she dies, blame the death on her husband and his agnates, arguing that they abused their privileges in their use of her. In short, the relationship established by marriage is normatively a mutual loan of the service of cattle for a woman. In fact, it is a more complete alienation of rights than is admitted.

Women are usually compared with cattle. It is not that they are literally thought of as cattle, but rather that the roles of cattle and women are comparable. Cows provide manure, which is essential to the growth of crops, and milk to feed the children and calves. Comparably, women by their labors produce the crops and also the children, which they also feed from their breasts. When cattle are discussed, female animals dominate considerations. Although all children at circumcision and clitoridectomy are given liver of the sheep to induce fertility, it is girls in most of Wahi who are given beef liver in the special fertility ceremony of *ixanda*. The productive abilities of women are described in the same terms as those of cows; for example, women are called *baisa* if they have had one child. Some feel that just as in the case of cows, the first child of a woman is in some way deficient. The first-born male calf is not allowed to breed, and the first-born human child does not constitute adequate productive return to warrant immediate payment of the special charge for birth of children. This payment is made only after the second child is born, according to some. The comparability goes even further. If one of the bridewealth cattle dies prematurely, the husband of the bride must replace it, and if a man's wife dies prematurely or produces no children, her owners must provide a replacement—either a sister or a daughter of wife's brother—although the husband must pay some additional bridewealth.

The similarity between *Uriha* (livestock loaning) and marriage is striking. Normatively, marriage differs from *Uriha* only slightly. The marriage is a mutual loan of productive property, rather than a one-way loan, as in *Uriha*, in which the owner of the woman technically receives bridewealth to use, not to own, his profit being the same as that obtained by the holder of *Uriha* cattle. The holder of the woman receives her productive labors. One apparent difference between *Uriha* and marriage is that although in *Uriha* the holder does not own the off-spring of the cows any more than the cows themselves, in marriage the calves produced by bridewealth cows are the property of the owner of the wife, while the children obtained from her are to some degree also the property of her husband, as is indicated by the special payment made for them and their identification with father's lineage. That mother's brother still claims rights in them does not alter the fact that the major rights in them are possessed by their father. The similarity to *Uriha* is emphasized by the norm, almost universally violated, that bridewealth cattle should be kept in the herd of the owner of the woman and not sold. When a marriage is dissolved by divorce or the death of the wife, the husband loses his wife's labor but not her children, while the owner of the wife must return the bridewealth, but not the calves. There is, then, an equation of the general productive ability of cattle with the productive ability, in all respects, of the woman. That additional payment must be made for children is probably merely an expression of their superior value in comparison to calves.

Because of the norm that alienation of corporeal rights from their owners is not possible, marriage is a complicated process. The norm stresses wives station as social persons and members of their agnatic lineages, while marriage stresses their status as chattels. The inevitable conflict of these statuses makes the arrangement of marriage a lengthy process. When it is arranged, it is highly tenuous, particu-larly in the early years. Although the tie between a wife and her husband's line-age increases in intensity with length of marriage, becoming greatly strengthened by the birth of children, her tie with her own lineage never lapses, and relations with her husband's people are marked by a difference of interests.

A woman marries at a very early age, being eligible after the clitoridectomy rite at about the age of ten. Her equivalence to an *ndama*, or heifer, at this stage is unmistakable; heifers are the main female cattle to be traded. Hence, to marry a prepubertal women is to contract for her potential. An additional purpose of early marriage is probably to enable the girl to be better conditioned to her life with her husband's lineage, although the frequency of divorce would argue that she is merely conditioned to accept removal from her home rather than any particular person or lineage.

Settling the amount of bridewealth is time-consuming and is followed by a long term of brideservice—almost the only time a man trades his service, during which the suitor frequently visits the home of his bride-to-be to help her mother, father, or brothers to build a house, harvest the crops, cultivate, and so forth. This practice may go on for a year or more.

When the time comes to actually remove the bride, the bridewealth cattle, consisting of the portion promised for delivery at the onset of the marriage, are brought to the bride's mother's house, after which the groom attempts to leave with his bride. He is accosted by the bride's agnates, who demand "arrows" of him before allowing him to proceed. Arrows may actually be given, but nowadays it has also become usual to substitute East African 10-cent pieces. The bride also refuses to proceed unless she is bribed with arrows at frequent intervals during the journey. She is expected to put up a great show of resistance and even to try to break away and return to her home if she can outwit her husband and his friends who help him escort her home. While her resistance may have all the appearance of real refusal to proceed, and while in some cases she may in fact wish not to, this resistance and the hostility of her agnates to her husband and his friends is a formality. If, along the way, the husband should run out of arrows with which to bribe her, she may return to him all he has given her so that he may continue. After the girl has been successfully conveyed to her husband's mother's house, her family will come to visit and will be told by members of the husband's village at whose houses they inquire that nothing is known of the girl's whereabouts.

At her husband's home the girl is met with hostility. The elder women, especially, attempt to shame her and put her in her place. A simple rite is held to "cool" her—an expression of the conflict of interests, not only between the two lineages involved in the marriage, but also between women. The bride is accused of being a poor cook, and some of the flour she brings as a dowry is playfully stolen by the older women to discomfort her. Finally, consonant with her new status as producer, she is put to work immediately, a practice so striking as to cause one Nyamwezi immigrant to condemn Turu for what he considered the crudity of the status of wife in their society.

The wife, in turn, immediately demands a house of her own, so that she may be independent of the other women. She expresses her lack of true integration into her husband's lineage by returning home immediately. She may spend only one day with her husband and then go home to stay for a day. She returns and stays for two days and returns home for two, carrying on in this reciprocal way until the stay extends to ten days with her husband and ten days at home. After this she settles down but makes frequent visits to her natal home at irregular intervals, decreasing with the length of her marriage, so that in old age she may never go to her original village.

The propensity of wives to visit their natal homes frequently is so great that one man seriously argued that a reason for polygyny is to insure the presence of at least one wife around the place to do the cooking and other necessary daily tasks. When the young wife reaches the onset of menses, she again returns home for a period of six months or a year, to be confined and fattened in her mother's house. In order to manage her rapid re-emergence, the husband may have to pay her mother. Later on, the wife again returns to her home to participate in the *imaa* rites. When the time for the birth of her first child arrives, she again is likely to return home to give birth at her mother's house. Whenever her family sacrifices to the ancestors, she is invited home. And finally, whenever her husband abuses her beyond what she consideres tolerable limits, she runs home to her family, who may refuse to allow her to rejoin her husband until he pays for his indiscretion. As a result, men spend much time retrieving their wives, especially in the early years of marriage.

The bridewealth itself is not fixed. Theoretically it consists of a separate cow for every significant value lost to the wife's mother, as well as cows for certain other considerations. The market process involved in arriving at a price is, to a certain extent, disguised. Each cow exchanged is named according to the purpose it serves in the bridewealth; for example, normally there appears an *ŋombe a ndUγU* ("cow of relatedness"), whose purpose is to overcome the possible harmful effects of a union between a bride and groom who are too closely related. Turu believe that if closely related people marry, their children will be born defective or no children will be born at all. There is a special rite of *itIma* ("cutting") performed for young married people to whom no children have been born, the purpose of which is to ritually sever a possible unnoticed close relationship and thereby to make way for children. Behind this thought, however, is also the belief that the lack of children is caused by the bitterness of the girl's mother for not having received sufficient bridewealth. After this rite is performed, a special additional payment is made to right this wrong. The *ŋombe a urII* ("cow of the bed") may be charged for removing the girl from her mother's bed and the *ŋombe a ixanda* ("cow of the liver") for having performed the fertility rite and incurring the cost of getting the liver for the bride. In addition to these, special cows may be demanded for provision of clothing for the mother of the girl, removal of the girl from the service of her mother, or for breaking the rules of propriety in the courtship and bridewealth negotiations. During the negotiations between the representative of the groom, who is usually his father, and the father of the bride it is the task of the bride's father to think of as many special reasons for demanding a cow as he can, and it is the task of the groom's father to counter these demands or to agree to them. While it would not be accurate to say that the special reasons are a mere masquerade for a bargaining process in which the important consideration is to determine what the total market value of the bride is, it is true that marshalling these special reasons is, to a considerable extent, a pretense. If the father of the bride can think of no more than a few reasons but feels his daughter to be worth more than the number arrived at, he may simply demand certain "cows of marriage." The net result is that the contract for bridewealth shows variation from one marriage to the next, but the final determinants of the price are only partly, if at all, these special reasons.

Certain facts about payment of bridewealth make it difficult to say just how much a wife costs. For one thing, the bridewealth cows are not really a direct cost, since they must be returned. The cost is the values produced by the cows —milk and calves. These, in turn must be subtracted from the values produced by his wife. For another thing, whatever the amount promised in a contract, it is not all paid at once, the remainder being paid little by little over many years. Certain animals are paid only when conditions arise that demand them. Nothing is paid for children until they are born, and if the value of a wife exceeds estimates, her owners are in a position to exert pressure to increase bridewealth payments by recalling her. Moreover, separately from these service costs, the husband may be forced to pay for unpredictable assaults on her person. In the initial bargaining the representatives of the suitor arrive at a tentative figure, the highest of which I am aware being twelve head of cattle, of which eight were paid at the onset of the marriage, said to have been promised for an exceptionally attractive women. The lowest was one head for an old and unsightly woman. If we calculate in terms of livestock units, as Turu do, a unit being one sheep or goat, a heifer five and a steer three, the usual contract based on a survey of actual marriages, averages twenty-five units. Of these, the actual first payment averages eighteen units, or the equivalent of three cows and three goats. One informant claimed that the first payment is almost invariably two heifers and one steer, or thirteen units. The range of variation in total contracts calculated from these cases is from twenty to thirty-six, excepting the case of the beautiful woman, whose contract is equal to sixty units.

Von Sick, again probably referring to the Wilwana subtribe, found the bridewealth to consist of "not less" than two heifers, a steer, and some goats and sheep, which are paid later. The price varied with such qualities of the bride as beauty, diligence, intelligence, and good humor. Reche listed the price as two to six head of cattle and two to six goats, and he notes that Baumann put it at four to six goats only. We may conclude, Baumann notwithstanding, that the bridewealth is approximately the same among Turu today as it was in these early days of contact. This equivalence may seem to argue that bridewealth is not affected by market considerations, because it would have been expected to alter in conjunction with the growth of economic contact between Turu and Europeans; I think this is not a necessary conclusion, however, as will be explained in Chapter 9.

It is usual to make the first payment at the time a bride is first removed to her husband's house. At this point, as well as others, factors that are not directly related to marketability are interposed. For example, the marriage may be delayed if the first cows paid are not the ones considered proper by the bride's mother. If she feels very close to her daughter and does not receive a "cow of the bed" immediately, she may balk. However, her reluctance may also be seen as merely the initial note in the kind of relationship that is to be established—one in which the mother continually presses her son-in-law for advantage.

As in other forms of *mwandU*, the payments for alienation of corporeal rights in a woman include compensation for injuries incurred in the course of her marriage. It is an important consideration that whereas the bridewealth cattle are simply loans to the owners of the wife, *mwandU* payments for a wife are not returnable. They are compensation for any injury to the woman that is considered to have shortened her life or lessened her productivity. Furthermore, just as in the case of *mwandU* claims by mother's brother for injury to sister's sons, the payment need not be made at the time the claim is made. Soup is given to the injured woman to legally mark the event, and all such instances are then totaled at the time of her death. Such claims include compensation for all the various types of injuries already described as well as some particular to marriage. The husband is held responsible for his wife's death, whatever the reason of her death, on the grounds that he worked her into the grave.

The amount of payment made for a woman during the length of the marriage is thus a result of a dynamic process in which the claims against the husband for wife's services and injury to her must be balanced against the value of the woman to her husband. If the wife's owners can enforce their demands by taking her home, the husband can resist by terminating the marriage (*kIreka*, "leavetaking" or "divorce") and demanding return of the bridewealth cattle, less any *mwandU*. The process is best observed when the marriage terminates. The bargaining positions of the two parties are as follows: the husband has the right to demand the return of the bridewealth cattle, less one for the birth of children. The wife's owners have the right to retain sufficient animals to cover *mwandU* claims. If *mwandU* exceeds the number of contract cattle, the wife's owners are at a disadvantage. On the other hand, if the husband owes *mwandU* that approximates the number of bridewealth cattle he has paid, he is likely to lose all his bridewealth and is the one in an unfavorable position. When a marriage has been long and fruitful, the total number of cattle contracted for will at least equal claims, so that there will be no return. If the known *mwandU* claims are considered insufficient to equal her value by wife's owners at the time of her death, others may be created. For example, a husband can be fined for the slightest impropriety during his wife's funeral, but if the marriage has been short, the husband is to receive back some of his cattle. In one case of a relatively short marriage, during which the husband had paid five head, no return was obtained at the time of the divorce because he had beaten his wife so badly that he injured her womb. In fact there was no divorce, but for all practical purposes the marriage was terminated. The man made no attempt to go to the home of his former wife to get his livestock, for fear her kin would kill him. In another case a man received back none of his bridewealth at the death of his wife, who was his third in succession to die. Her father argued that he had a record of dying wives and was known not to consult diviners after these events, raising the suspicion that he had killed the women. (Intimate acquaintance with this man led me to think the reason he did not consult diviners was that he was a skeptic; his action may therefore be considered a strategic error.) After the birth of sons the bargaining position of the parties is affected because the husband and wife now wish to maintain the marriage to insure an estate for their descendants.

Turu see the following as the most important points for settling claims at the termination of a marriage: (1) whether the wife had children; (2) whether she suffered any injuries during the marriage; (3) whether she died at her husband's or at her mother's home. They like to believe that if a woman has had no children, has suffered no special injuries, and died at her husband's home, no compensation has to be paid, except perhaps for "breaking her horns"—that is, living with her for such a long time that her breasts began to droop. It is true that some marriages may last quite a long time before any claims for compensation arise. During this time the owners of the wife are receiving value from the bridewealth livestock. As noted, however, the longer a marriage lasts, the greater the claims that will pile up, partly because any injury to a woman while in the service of her husband will be charged to him. For example, if she should die in childbirth at her mother's home, this incident will be charged against the husband on the grounds that if he had treated her properly, she would not have run off to her mother. The greatest amount of compensation will be claimed in those situations where the wife dies (in contrast to being divorced), where the marriage has lasted long, and where children have been born. The following two cases illustrate this situation.

A young man had paid four cattle (three cows and one steer) for a girl whose parents now demanded a divorce. The youth wanted all the bridewealth cattle returned, since there had as yet been no children. However, the father of the girl refused, claiming that his son-in-law had defamed his daughter by telling people that she had a small vagina. He demanded *mwandU* payment of a steer, and both sides agreed. The case was prolonged, however, because the father-in-law returned one of the cows in the form of a hide, saying that the animal had died, and since he was entitled to a replacement, he had only to return the hide. The youth disputed whether the hide was that of one of his cows. The case was further prolonged because all gifts that had passed from son-in-law to mother-in-law had to be returned, and it was difficult to determine what these were.

In another case of a young wife who had died, for whom twenty-eight units (one steer and five heifers) had been contracted, the compensation claimed was thirteen units, for a net return to the husband of fifteen units, even though several children had been born.

These two cases, in both of which some return was made, are to be contrasted with the following, in which a young wife died, the event occurring at her father's home while she was in childbirth. Up to that point the husband had paid two heifers for her, and since he would have been charged three heifers because of the circumstances of her death, he simply let the matter go. In another case six cows were paid in compensation, exceeding the bridewealth, because very serious charges were brought against the dead woman's husband, including the claims that he called her a witch, that she died at her father's house while having a baby, and that she had had various serious illnesses, for all of which charges were made.

To settle affairs at the end of a marriage, the process is for the owners of the woman to demand first the payment of all *mwandU* debts, after which the remainder of the bridewealth may be returned. In other words, the owners of the woman, who hold the bridewealth cattle, are in the better bargaining position because of this crucial fact. However, it should be added that the settlement is not always conducted in an atmosphere of tension. Frequently when an old woman dies, it is her sons who must make the settlement if their father is dead, and they may express their gratitude to her by a generous settlement. One woman referred to the compensation payments as an "increase in the bridewealth," which in a sense is true, because when made during the continuation of the marriage, they increase the original number of bridewealth animals. However, this is only a manner of speaking, and it is clear that these compensatory livestock represent a different order of things. Perhaps the situation is best viewed in capsule form as an equivalent to that between feuding lineages after one has captured animals belonging to the other against whom the first has a claim.

The total cost of marriage to a husband includes brideservice, which, in addition to the initial service already described, may include occasional service during the life of the marriage when visiting with in-laws, as well as the occasional steer sacrificed at the grave of a deceased mother or father-in-law as a mark of respect. The son-in-law may also occasionally make gifts to his mother-in-law. However, it is only when divorce occurs that values beside the cattle are returned, and this includes only returnable things, thus excluding brideservice.

As in other instances of *mwandU*, a husband is eligible to call on members of his lineage to help him pay, and it is significant that the obligation to help pay bridewealth is weaker than the obligation to help pay compensation. While the men of the same village speak of each other's wives as common property because "we paid for them," in actual fact such payment is usually, at best, indirect.

Viewed from the perspective of the market, the *mwandU* charges are a form of payment for depreciation of capital, while the bridewealth is collateral held in escrow to cover the contingency of depreciation, as well as being an exchange of different forms of capital in an attempt at a rational capital mix. The question is why there is not an absolute sale of rights in the woman in the first place, the norm against corporeal alienation notwithstanding. We can speculate that since the value of a woman rests in large part on her ability to produce grain, and since grain is so fundamental to the acquisition of cattle, and since the success for production of various women is greatly variable, the marginal utility of a woman's services is too difficult to calculate, the door is left open to variation of payments as the capital resources vary in value. Nevertheless, husbands resent their partial control, attempt to increase rights, and are driven to desperation in some instances by the positions in which they find themselves.

It is necessary to point out that the market value of a woman in services is not always exclusively determined by reference to her potential as a producer of crops, milk, and children. Young men, particularly, tend to be romantics, choosing brides for their romantic talents. The danger that such choices will seriously prejudice more rational arrangements is overcome by the veto power held by the father, who both arranges the bridewealth and can refuse to allow the marriage to proceed. After a few years of marriage the youth learns that romance and marriage are incompatible, that his wife must be beaten if she does not pay attention to her duties, and that to accomplish her submission, she must be treated impersonally. If husband and wife can strike a compatible personal relationship, they may carry on the marriage with a combination of careful attention to duty as well as to love, but circumstances work to make affection out of place. In fact, the man who publicly shows affection for his wife may be ridiculed and suspected of being a poor manager.

The proverb that initiates this chapter has reference to the usefulness of cattle for accomplishing very difficult things, of which one is the compensation for injury and death to people. The discussion demonstrates that people are wealth of the same class as grain and other valued materials, because they can be valued and paid for like any other goods, but it also shows that rights in the corpus of adults is not ethically exchangeable.

There is a difference, however, between payment for rights in corpus and those in marriage. The market system does not work on the assumption of sale and purchase of corporeal rights. These are so valuable that the system of mutual aid in the lineage guards the individual against disaster claims resulting from injury or death to others caused by him; it also guards him from assault. The only intentional exchange is for services, the market for women's services constituting a labor market.

8. THE WOMEN

The hen does not crow.
TURU PROVERB

THE modesty of Turu women is literally proverbial. Like the hens with whom the proverb compares them, they flock together and decorously remove themselves from the center of attention when men are near. It is rare to see an inebriated woman in public, although men are continually drunk. However, while they do not "crow," and although in the pecking order they occupy an inferior position to men, they resist control; all women are regarded by men and themselves as witches; with this attribution they intend to convey a general tendency rather than a specific charge. "Witchcraft is the weapon of women given them by the Creator; it is their spear," an old man said. The word *muroyi*, most commonly used to refer to a witch, specifically means a female; a male witch is *mUtemea*. If men aspire to control their destinies, so do women. By virtue of their subordinate position, however, they are not allowed to express themselves fully. The conflict of interests between men and women is revealed in various forms of noncooperation and even hostility by women. This situation is the reason for the attitude of men toward women and for the particular female rituals designed to control the conflict.

WITCHCRAFT

Contrary to the men's usually unqualified ascription of natural potential for witchcraft to women, as if only they were ever accused of it, almost anyone can be designated a witch under proper circumstances. The main circumstance is that the witch and victim be in intimate relation involving some kind of right the possession of which is disputed. Whenever misfortune befalls anyone—when a cow dies, when property is stolen or destroyed, or when injury or disease is inflicted on someone over whom the victim has rights—suspicion usually falls on a witch or on an angered ancestor *(kiungU)*, acting for himself or for someone over whom he is guardian.

While conflicts can occur between almost any persons, certain types tend to clash or to harmonize. Very old people and children are seldom accused of witchcraft because the former are beyond involvement in the mundane pursuits of the younger people and the latter are too young to have become involved. Euthanasia is sometimes practiced on very old people, on the theory that since

123

they are beyond being bewitched, they will never die unless they are killed. By comparison, the older members of the society—those in the prime of power—are natural suspects, since they are intimately involved in the affairs of life.

People believe that no one can or should bewitch anyone outside his own village. The possibility of someone's attempting to transcend this limitation can be imagined, but the attempt is felt to be futile or so dangerous that the power of the witch will turn back on him and drive him mad. Nevertheless the assertion requires some qualification. A woman's lover, it is believed, may bewitch people or things of her village, even though he lives elsewhere, because of his special relationship to the woman, which brings him into intimate contact with affairs in her village.

If the powers of the bewitching rocks in the Ihanja region, such as KImaI (Plate 8.1), MUgUngusu or Mpembu are utilized, it is possible for the whole of one village to bewitch the whole of another. The rocks called *tita* at Puma once were used to bewitch other tribes. Where people live in a new village composed of a mixture of lineages, residents are thought to be able to bewitch each other. Because of the affiliation of the lineages of MUhUri and Tatuu, bewitching can also occur.

The most striking exception is a new development, a type of witchcraft called *Utambo*. An *mtambo* is a stranger to the village of the person he bewitches, but he has relations with his victim outside the context of the village. For this reason the victim knows for certain who the *mtambo* is who bewitches him and can name him. In the traditional pattern, the accused is not named unless resentment against him in the village is so general that to do so could not cause general disturbance in the equilibrium of relations. The witch is named by the diviner or by a group who seek the diviner's advice rather than by any individual, who, by naming names, might find himself in deep trouble if he could not make the accusation stick. To accuse a person of witchcraft in any instance except where the evidence is overwhelming is a grave insult that may arouse and cause conflict between factions in a village and may even lead to demands for compensation. There is no such danger in naming the *mtambo*.

Granting these exceptions, the claim by Turu that witchcraft is confined within a village is substantially correct. They conceive of only one way around this restriction—to prevail on a friend in the village of the potential victim to either bewitch the victim or in some other way to do him harm; but it is felt that there are few people who would go so far. People who live in different villages, therefore, do not fear bewitchment from each other.

The Turu have few specific ideas about the classes of people who tend to bewitch each other except for the general feeling that women, particularly wives and mothers, are prime suspects. This may be because there are few specific patterns—that all persons, with the exceptions noted above, are potentially witches. Certainly in the actual cases not only women are accused of witchcraft. Some even assert that men are usually the ones to be accused.

Certain tendencies are discernible, however. Brothers frequently accuse each

PLATE 8.1
The Interior of the
Bewitching Rock, KImaI

other, as one may readily understand considering their competitiveness. Fathers
seem to have a tendency to bewitch their sons, rather than the reverse; it may
be speculated that this situation derives from the property relationship between
them: the son owns a certain portion of his mother's estate and desires to use it
for his own purpose, while the father desires to keep it under his control. Because
it is easier for the son to gain control than for the father to keep control, the
tendency is for the father to develop animosity toward the son, as is reflected in
the form taken by the ancestral sacrificial rite. The rite is based on the assumption that descendants tend to ignore the desires of the ancestors, who must cause
harm to them in order to acquire any livestock for use in the ancestral world.
The ancestor's spirit, *kiungU*, is the agent for this harm. The ancestral rite is
meant to assuage the anger of an unhappy ancestor and to remove the cause of
harm. As one informant put it, "The ancestor is envious of the herd he left behind and wants part of it back to provide a mat for his bed or milk to drink."

Other than these, conflicts of men and women as husbands and wives are basic
to the pattern of witchcraft accusations. Women are thought unable to bewitch
members of their own agnatic lineages, although in fact adult women living with

their fathers or brothers sometimes are accused, probably because they are part of the social life of the village. Otherwise they are thought to aim their bewitching activities specifically at their husbands' villages, most usually at the husband himself, at co-wives, or at mothers-in-law. If a woman's children die, she is immediately suspected. The term Uγokie (ritually pure) indicates little more than that the first son of the woman to whom it is applied lived to pass through the circumcision rites and that she, therefore, did nothing to cause his death. Ritually pure women are required to officiate at rites like imaa, funerals, and other events involving the relations of affinal groups.

The ultimate position of success for a woman is to have sons and be head of a rich house, or even a homestead, after her husband dies, so that it is unnecessary for her to be inherited by a brother of her dead husband. In this status she has the greatest amount of freedom available to a woman. A woman will always prefer to remain an independent widow, even if she does not have much wealth. If a woman's husband dies before she has sons, she has no choice but to be inherited or divorced. Before she obtains her freedom, she is under the dominance of her husband and his divergent goals. He desires to achieve wealth for his whole homestead and to perpetuate his name through his sons. She has no opportunity to perpetuate her name and is interested only in her own sons and her own freedom. He desires to maintain strong ties with his male agnates; she does not care about them. She always questions his attempts to use the property of her house for any other purpose than to increase the wealth of her particular house and will utilize what power she has to thwart him. It can easily be seen that the counter-pull of the woman is indirectly the source of the conflict of father and son or brothers.

It is common belief that women do not attempt to bewitch persons outside the villages of their husbands, and some believe that they confine their activities within the homestead. This belief correlates with the idea that witchcraft is most commonly performed by putting medicine in the food of the victim, which for a woman would normally be possible only within her own homestead and against people to whom she serves food. This group includes co-wives; not only do they compete for the favor of the husband, but it is often the case that the death of one wife, especially if she is childless, works to the benefit of the other, who thereby gains possession of the deceased's estate. They are, therefore, prime suspects. It may be reasoned that the belief that women kill their own children derives from the fact that the husband's status is in large part dependent on having children; to kill them is therefore to attack the status of the husband. Women are thought also to kill livestock, again affecting the status of a husband. The belief that wives attack their mothers-in-law stems from the fact that mothers-in-law are the true controllers of the property of the husbands and are therefore in opposition to wives' aspirations.

When females are seen as the source of conflict between men, it becomes clear how women can be thought of as the witches. Generalized from the patterns detailed above, women are in competition with men and can attack men through their own children and in other critical areas. The pressure they exert on their husbands by the autonomous impulses leads to conflict between husbands and their brothers and fathers. The belief follows logically that men "learn" witchcraft from the women. Men are thought not to have natural knowledge of witchcraft, nor do they have any means equivalent to the female secret organizations by which to acquire such knowledge, but must actually be directed by women or be introduced to it by diviners. Whether, as Turu believe, diviners give clients medicine for sorcery is irrelevant, although apparently they do. It is a short jump to this belief from the fact the diviners commonly dispense *mplγl*, or charms, to counteract sorcery and witchcraft. The term for a male witch, *mutemea*, is based on the root "to cut" and is derived from the method used by men to render infertile the cows of their enemies; which they do by cutting the vagina of the cow in some fashion. In this activity a man is said to be directed and trained by his sweetheart, who uses him to get at the men she hates. Similarly, when men go to the bewitching rocks to bewitch other people in their villages or people in other villages, they do so because they have no knowledge of these techniques and need the help of the owner of the rock.

Women are thought to work together to help each other bewitch. The pattern of relations of men and women and the cooperation among them is most clearly manifested in the beliefs and activities surrounding the system of *mbojo*.

Mbojo ("lion man") is a man believed to be transformed into a lion or acting as a lion under the direction of someone who hires him for the purpose of committing a murder. It is thought that since all deaths are caused by someone, and since wild animals do not kill people, when persons are killed by an animal, this occurs because the animal is metaphysically or directly controlled for the purpose. To be killed by a wild animal is a particularly unclean way to die, and the victim is buried in a shunned position. Thus, when a lion kills, evidence is brought forth to prove that the lion was not in control of himself but was controlled by a man or was a metamorphosed man or was a man dressed as a lion, using knives to imitate claws.

Not all persons accused of complicity in lion-man killings are women, but it is assumed that if a man is involved it is because he was brought into the affair by women. In various cases of *mbojo* killings that were investigated, it was found that if the affair was allowed to grow to a climax, there was a polarization of males and females of a group of villages into antagonistic groups. This situation was based on the underlying assumptions that women in general were the cause of the affair, that the actual controller of the lion man was a woman or women of the village of the victim, and that women of a nearby village cooperated with the procurer by hiding the lion man until it was possible to use him. Accusations were aired, and the suspected agents—if there was more than one— were isolated on the assumption that if they were allowed to get together, they would concoct an alibi. This separation of defendants is a well-tested inquisitorial technique, as Sargant's *Battle for the Mind* (1957, 183) shows. It allows the interrogators, in order to induce a confession, to apply psychic as well as physical pressure on the suspect.

PLATE 8.2

Armed Men Attending Meeting to Investigate Three Women Accused of
Procuring a Lion Man

In one such case (Plate 8.2), where three women of the village of the victim were suspected and separated, they not only admitted their guilt after varying degrees and kinds of torture, but even gave detailed confessions that agreed in minute detail as to how the lion man was obtained, where he had come from, and how he was used. They even agreed on the total price paid for hiring the lion man, each specifying how much of the total she contributed. It seems clear that the confessions were in large part suggested to the defendants by their interrogators, who were themselves nevertheless convinced that the confessions were original and true. It was not necessary for them to suggest the whole story, because all Turu know of the supposed method of procuring and using a lion man.

It is generally agreed that lion men are procured from a certain place in the subtribe of Unyiŋanyi, that they are men turned into lions, that they can be docilely led to a village neighboring the victim's and held until needed, that they are kept in the dark backroom, and even that they must kill someone once they are hired, so that if the proper victim cannot be reached, someone else must be killed. The belief is so strong that, on the basis of Turu help, a number of suspected procurers of lion men were actually hanged by the colonial authorities in

1948, mostly on the strength of their own confessions and the evidence of their alleged accomplices.

An important element in lion-man proceedings is the assumption that all the women of the village of the procurer and of a nearby village knew who was planning the crime and may even have given permission for her to proceed. As part of men's investigation of a killing, the women of these villages are brought to the interrogation place in separate groups, led by the old women who are considered the leaders of each group. In each case the leader speaks for all the women of her village. In the interrogation of women from villages other than that of the victim, it is assumed that they would not bewitch the victim because they are of different villages; but they can be accused of cooperating in the venture.

Like the men, these women believe in the existence of *mbojo*, and before the interrogation, the leading women in each village question the other women to see if one of them was involved. If one of their group is suspected, they rationalize the fact that they had no previous knowledge by asserting that the accused worked alone, and they use this reasoning to justify giving up the accused to the men for punishment. If the group is without fault, its leader will respond to the leading question from the men, "Are you implicated this time?" (or words to that effect), by answering, "No." By the way the men ask the question it is assumed that women do commit these acts, and by the way they respond the women agree, only specifying that in this instance they did not.

Thus the act of "interrogation" is a sort of rite of integration designed to force the interests of men and women into line. By treating them as a group, the men are asserting their belief that women generally are in opposition to them, and by acting together as a group, the women are admitting this to be true. In the case of the three accused women mentioned above, the interrogation by the district commissioner ended with his declaration that the lion-man beliefs are untrue and that the government refused further to prosecute people for these activities. The reaction of the men was one of dismay. One, speaking for the others, could only assert that "Now women will run wild and kill all the men."

It is interesting that von Sick found Turu men to believe that women are only valuable when kept in fear. Men commonly assert that, no matter how much women deny that they are opposed to men, the fact that they act as a group and sometimes hold secret rites and meetings as a group is proof to the contrary. Furthermore, the organization of women's activities represented by the existence of leaders speaking for all of them argues that among women there is a sub-society with secret elements.

The net result of a lion-man affair, besides the possible elimination of trouble-makers of both sexes, is the tightening of integration of the relations of men and women. However, if too many killings occur, as has happened, the situation merely generates hysteria. During the rites women publicly declare their responsibility to cooperate with the men, but by doing so they also tighten integration in their own subsociety. In the light of this, it is no surprise to find that a lion man need not have killed anyone who was actually hated by the procurer; that he must kill someone regardless of motive takes care of that problem. In one village the story is told of a female martyr who once gave her life to a frustrated lion man who could not reach his victim, thus releasing the village of the terror. It is not surprising, either, to discover that there is no evidence to support a belief in actual lion men. It is clear that almost all, if not all (as I believe), such killings are by real man-eating lions.

Though the system of lion-man beliefs can, therefore, act to keep women in line, there is no evidence that it existed in precontact days. It is possible that it developed its present form since the arrival of Europeans and was in compensation for the loss of ability to execute or exile witches by means formerly used. Europeans have believed in lion men and have executed persons for these activities, but they have not taken action against witches. However, belief that wild animals are controlled by people antedates contact, raising the possibility that something like the lion-man activities is older than the records show.

THE RITUAL SYSTEM

The system of rites of passage for men and women has two dimensions. The first (ngoi, meaning both circumcision and clitoridectomy) differentiates and fixes boys and girls in adult roles. The second, which applies only to women, is to achieve unity among them as adults. The basic fact about the adult positions of men and women is that when men have become adults, they are arranged in descent-based groups that are associated with spatial units—the villages—while women are dispersed from their natal groups and mixed among the men, leading them to join into a general cooperative union throughout the country. Men are forever among their own kind, while women are thrown into juxtaposition with strangers, consisting both of the men who are their affines and women who are the other wives of their affines. Therefore, the rites of passage for males are brief, almost perfunctory, but those for women are complicated.

By the time a male reaches marriageable age—traditionally at about fifteen years but now sometimes younger—he is already thoroughly integrated into his lineage and needs only to be impressed with the shift of status from child to adult. The circumcision of boys, which accomplishes this, may be combined with the clitoridectomy of girls or the different sexes may undergo the rite at different times, depending on circumstances.

Beginning in the period preceding the harvest, but after the final cultivation, the male initiates gather from neighboring villages or even from farther off at the home of a man who has decided to hold the event for his son or daughter or both. On the assigned day each boy is anointed on the head while sitting with his mother on her bed; he is then sent to the circumcision site—a place cleared of stover in the field next to the host's homestead. There, surrounded by the men and removed from the women—who are not allowed to watch—each boy,

PLATE 8.3

Turu Boys Being Circumcised. Picture *a* was taken in 1960; Picture *b* was
taken about 1910 by von Sick.

having in effect been torn away from his mother, unceremoniously has his fore-skin cut off (Plate 8.3) while his father and other adult men jeer at him. "I won't ever herd your sheep for you again!" the boy may cry out, and the father replies, "Who cares! You were never any good at it anyway!" Some of the boys cry and curse. Others proudly remain as stoical as they can. For the rest of the day the bloody, naked, and miserable initiates are kept in a temporary stover hut in the field, where they are alternately victimized by the men, who force them to stand and sing while doing the *UsUηgU* dance, or are left to languish while classificatory husbands and wives, as if to mock the boys, gleefully engage in the *Ujumya ngoi* (Plate 8.4), a dance overtly mimicking the act of coitus. The mothers who attempt to join the boys to comfort them are driven off by the fathers or are sent away by the boys themselves, who consider that they are men enough to endure the ordeal alone.

PLATE 8.4

Man and Woman Doing the Circumcision Dance *ujumya ngoi*. The dance mimics sexual intercourse between husband and wife.

The climax of the day occurs when the women, doing the *kIllmbIda* ("march-ing dance"), parade to the village water hole in the marsh and return to the homestead with water to cook *nxomba*, a thick porridge made for sick people, which is purposely dirtied and defiled by the women, who throw soiled skirts and other impurities into it. Dancing another *kIllmbIda* while holding aloft the stirring spoons covered with the repulsive mixture, the women present the food to the boys. The boys must eat it, accompanied by the further jeers of the men. Having done so, the miserable fellows are successfully expelled from the homestead. The following morning they are fed the liver of a sheep, which has here-tofor been forbidden food for them and which is meant to induce fertility. They are then turned loose to go to their individual homesteads, there to construct a temporary windbreak and shade near the entrance, to be used during the daylight hours for the next six months or so. (They are allowed to sleep in the house at night because of the danger from wild animals.) During this time they are refused entrance to their homes until after dark and are forced to seek rest in the temporary hut. From this shelter they wander about like strange beings, their bodies covered with soot, mud, and odd designs (Plate 8.5), forbidden to wash, seemingly driven to hunt wild animals, and fed by anyone of whom they request food. They molest women, whom they force to give them white beads and whom they threaten with their oddly shaped *igolyo* ("paddles").

At the end of the six months, when the rains begin, the boys wash, their temporary shelter is destroyed by the men as if a great war had been fought and the initiates had been conquered, and the boys are received back into their homes by their fathers, whom they accuse of having deserted them and from whom they therefore demand a cow for reconciliation. This is the cow by whose name father and son subsequently address each other. After paying the price of a bracelet made of the white beads he has collected, each boys reportedly succeeds in having coitus with an adult woman (one who is clitoridectomized), and the transition to adulthood is complete.

While the male initiation is thus principally a rite of attachment to the father's lineage and separation from the women, it also contains a vague bow to filiation with mother's lineage. After circumcision is over, it is the duty of the boy to go to the home of mother's brother and to ceremonially herd his cattle, like a bridegroom, for one day, for which duty he receives a gift, usually only a goat. The symbolism seems to suggest subordination to mother's brother.

While the rites of passage for females are similar to those of the males in the first stages, the total complex is more intricate and can be represented as follows:

Phase I
1. *ngoi* (Clitoridectomy), at about age ten;
2. *Unyambee* (menstruation seclusion), occurring at onset of first menstruation;

Phase II
3. *ikiIka* ("cleaning"), occurring immediately following menstruation rites;
4. *imaa ra nyUmba* (house *imaa*), occurring as soon as possible after cleansing and before a child is born;
5. *imaa ra ŋimba* (lion *imaa*), occurring whenever the occasion arises after the first child is born.

The manifest function of these rites is, as the description implies, to induct women into the role of motherhood. The term *imaa* as used by the Turu has the same denotation as it does in Kiswahili, where it means courage, uprightness, or stolidity. It refers more specifically to the uprightness of a woman as house head and mother. However, particularly Phase II of these rites also has purposes secret

PLATE 8.5

Turu Youths Wearing the Decorations of the Long Circumcision Seclusion and Carrying the *igolyo* Paddle. Picture *a* was taken in 1960; Picture *b* was taken by von Sick around 1910.

from the men that have to do with the relations of women and men as well as the relations of women with women. That the rites are not merely to carry a woman to the status of mother is indicated by the fact that a significant number of women are inducted into every stage, including the last, even though they never have children. Such women must delay taking the final step, however, until their infertility is proved by time.

Phase II is the truly secret portion, whose secrecy must be differentiated from the ritual separation of sexes during the first phase, with which it might become confused. Girls going through clitoridectomy and menstruation rites are separated from the men. These two successive stages are equivalent to men's circumcision, during which the women are unclean and relations between them and most people are therefore taboo. During the menstruation rite a woman is physically removed from the men, to be hidden away in her mother's or her mother's brother's wife's house for six months or a year; during this time she is instructed in women's ways. She occupies herself painting the walls of the sitting room with pictures (Plate 8.6) of Turu life and of women's objects—the sun and moon, pots, cloths, and gourds. The stated purpose of this seclusion is to fatten the initiate to make her more beautiful.

The most violent form of the sanctioning rite *(njUγUda)* occurs when men violate the seclusion of *Unyambee*, yet it is common for the initiate's lover, who must be an uncircumcised boy, to visit her, and it is not uncommon for a girl to emerge from *Unyambee* already pregnant. There can be no sanction against an uncircumcised boy who impregnates a girl under these circumstances, but the

PLATE 8.6
Wall Painting by *Munyambee* Showing Automobile and Its Occupants

situation may lead to a dispute between the girl's parents and her husband, because the husband views such a pregnancy as unequivocal proof that the child is
not his and that his wife has been sleeping with another man. His anger is often
great enough to lead to a divorce.

It is of significance that only during Phase I are the initiates truly considered
to be in a ritually unbalanced state, paralleling the condition of boys during
circumcision. Girls or boys who die during this time are buried in a shunned
position, near the outer part of the corral yard or even behind the house. During
this time girls stay in their mothers' houses and go about their usual domestic
chores. They carry beaded dolls, in imitation of the children their mothers carry
on their backs but also as a symbol of the role of motherhood to which the rite
introduces them (Plate 8.7)

Up to the beginning of Phase II, a woman has in effect been identified with
adult females in their role as producers as well as with her agnatic lineage. In the
Phase II rites, however, she in effect transcends the lineage system and is joined
to the female organization. Throughout Phase II the theme drummed into the
initiates at each step of the way is that they must not overtly resist the men

PLATE 8.7
Young Girl Carrying Her Doll as
Part of the Rite of *ngoi* (circum-
cision and clitoridectomy)

because to do so would shame their families and would cause the men to be angered, bringing disruption of the peace. The courage of women, referred to in the names of the last two rites, means accepting firmly and with propriety any command of the husband. Yet a wife cannot conform to all the husband's demands without being dehumanized. The lesson she learns is to conform to the husband's demands and to depend on the organization of women to keep the power of men in check. Whether any woman could phrase it just this way is questionable. Women correctly insist that *imaa* rites are not antimale; they merely control male dominance for the sake of peace. To the men, however, the secrecy of women's activities shows their hostility and resistance to men.

In discussing these rites it is necessary to recognize at the outset that much about them remains secret, closed to outsiders like myself. The content and meaning of the rituals is kept secret from both the men and the uninitiated females. The word *ikilka*, the name for the first rite of Phase II, means ritual cleansing. The ceremony is held in a homestead from which the men have been excluded and to which are taken all the young women of the neighborhood who are freshly out of menstruation seclusion or who would ordinarily emerge shortly. It is conducted by the initiated women led by the leaders, or *axaikUU*. The first secret is simply that this is not a ritual cleansing at all, the name being meant to mislead the men. The soot worn on the faces of older women is, therefore, deceptive. The second secret lies in the noise-making device made by placing a stool over the mouth of a pot; when rubbed, the stool gives off a sound that is apparently meant to imitate the voice of the red ground squirrel *(sIIra)*. The squirrel's color is symbolic of the menstruation with which the initiates have just become acquainted. Each of the three stages of Phase II has its secrets, or *mUrimU*, symbolizing the ideational aspects of the rites but also giving the women some sense of exclusiveness. One of the elements of the rites is the nakedness of the initiates, which alone demands privacy from the men because women are very shy.

The rite of *ikilka* may be said to introduce a girl to marriage, even though in precontact days she would normally already be formally married and would have lived for some time with her husband. Turu believe that the onset of menses, which they see as initiating the ability to bear children, is caused by a girl's husband. Under the colonial government it was illegal for a man to have coitus with a prepubertal girl, but this law, designed to combat traditional Turu marriage practices, was frequently broken. During *ikilka* the initiates are informed that they must never shame their parents by acting in unseemingly ways. To illustrate this requirement, the girls are tested by being prodded in various ways to induce them both to cry and to remain stalwart. The songs of the rite stress loss of her parents to the initiate, who is being "orphaned." The darkened room in which the initiate spent so many months in seclusion is likened to a womb from which she emerges in symbolic rebirth into marriage and subordination to her husband. The initiate is taken to the rite by her mother or her mother's brother's wife. The fact that it does not matter where she attends the rite shows that initiation is into the sorority of women. Initiates usually like to be with their mothers for the rite, since it is a day of celebration, but the association is not a necessary requirement.

This first rite of Phase II is a minor one, carried off with dispatch in a few hours during an afternoon. The most important rite in the view of the women is the next stage, the house *imaa*. Here the *mUrimU*, or secrets, are many and are most jealously guarded from the men. The men know much about the secrets, but they have seldom if ever seen them. The secrets consist mainly of various objects, such as stools, which are encrusted with beads in meaningful patterns. Each is put together for a particular occurrence of the rite and then disassembled until it is needed again.

House *imaa* lasts for two days, while the men of the homestead in which it is held are excluded. On the first day the ceremony is concerned with the relations of husband and wife, the role of husband being taken by his sister. The main secret object is a gourd of blue and white beads, representing the husband. Another is a representation of the husband's penis. The second day has to do with relations of the initiate and her family, and the main secret object is an egg-shaped gourd banded with differently colored beads representing the colors of the bridewealth cattle. House *imaa* is most commonly described as having the purpose of "teaching" the initiate, who is married but as yet has no children, to obey her husband and parents, to be stalwart in the face of adversity in order to maintain good relations with her husband and not shame her parents. It is also sometimes negatively described as teaching the young wife not to be promiscuous, not to have more than one sweetheart at a time, and to avoid visiting the sweetheart's home. It is, of course, implicit that the wife tends strongly to do the opposite, and an important aspect of the ritual is, therefore, the testing of the initiate. She is prodded, shamed, and otherwise forced to meekly accept pressures that she might ordinarily resist. The husband of the initiate is portrayed as a lion who cannot be resisted, and one of the traits often criticized in the initiate during the rite is her resistance to him.

The dynamics of the social situation with which *imaa* is concerned are best revealed by a Turu tale about a young woman who refused to play her role in marriage. After completion of the initial bridewealth payment, when the bride was supposed to go to one of the houses in her father's homestead to spend her first night with her new husband, she agreed but then managed to avoid the encounter. After repeating this maneuver several times, her father became quite angry and decided to teach her a lesson. He locked the girl out of all the houses, confining her in the corral yard, where she was killed and eaten by a lion, who refrained from eating her bones. Afterward the girl was recreated from the bones into a more acceptable person. The aggression toward a recalcitrant daughter shown by the tale is a measure of the frustration of both the father and the daughter.

While an initiate may perform house *imaa* in the area of her parent's home, frequently she goes to the Level III lineage area of her mother's brother. On the first day the initiate is brought to the site by her mother and by other female relatives. Women normally try to wear fancy clothes when attending this rite (Plate 8.8); these clothes are gifts from their sweethearts, giving implicit support

PLATE 8.8
Women Dressed
for House Imaa

to the custom of having a lover. The initiate is led by her husband's sister, who is dressed in a costume symbolizing her ceremonial status as a male and the initiate's husband. She wears the *ngaa* (war helmet) and carries a war shield and spear (not a stick shield and stick, although a stick may be used to imitate the spear). The spear is only used against foreigners or enemies other than kinsmen. As previously noted, the secret objects exposed to the view of the initiate on the first day have to do with her role as wife and include the *sato mUrimU*, which has four sections said to be symbolic of the four great adversities in the life of a married woman: loneliness; the need to be courageous before difficulties; child bearing; and the labor of cultivation and housekeeping. But the principal secret objects represent the husband, including the penis, which is modeled generally on that of her actual husband and which, in the later stages of the rite, is inserted into her vagina. This seems to be little more than the climax of many acts of the same order, designed to provoke the initiate in order to see whether she will stand firm. These objects and acts are meant to be strange things which will terrorize her but to which fear must not be shown.

Von Sick tells that he was able to get inside during the rite of the first day and observed the "*mwimo*" (for *mUrimU*) rite. From his description it appears that this event happened in Wilwana rather than Wahi, but the rites in the two areas do not vary greatly. The initiates were seated on the ground and were decorated with beads and caps. A covered tray was produced and from it was extracted the secret object, which was put into the initiate's lap. It was a caricature of the initiate's husband covered with beads. Von Sick notes that the doll exaggerated the worst features of the husband. A phallus was also handed around. Songs of the rite recorded by von Sick have as their theme the strangeness of the husband, and they ridicule the wife and her manner of performing the act of intercourse. My own experience is that this ridicule may have been directed only at particular initiates, since it is the practice in the *imaa* to concentrate on the particular faults of each woman.

The husband surrogate leaves after the first day of house *imaa*; the second day, concerned with the relations of the initiate and her own family, is conducted by the women of her home village and her mother's brother's wives. On the first day these women merely oversee the ceremony, to prevent the "husbands" from overstepping the bounds of propriety. On the second day they introduce the initiate to the *mwana*, or "child," *mUrimU*, the egg-shaped gourd. This gourd is decorated by the husband's sister and the female relatives of the initiate. The aim of this portion of the rite is to encourage the initiate to obey her own family and to cooperate with her husband to avoid shaming them.

The house *imaa* is arranged and conducted by the elder women of the area in which it is held and occurs in the homestead of one of the women, who volunteers to be host and who herself has at daughter or niece to be initiated. It is important to note the extent of female cooperation in arranging the rite. The co-wives of the initiate in her own husband's village cooperate with husband's sister to make a list of the shortcomings of the initiate with which she will be shamed at the rite. They also measure and model the penis of the husband. The songs of house *imaa* are for the most part enigmatic. One tells of the bringing of the penis to the place of the ceremony, and another refers to warfare and the death of children by bewitchment, referring to the suspicion that mothers are the witches who kill their children.

House *imaa* can be an excruciating experience for an initiate. Sometimes it evokes so much fear and guilt that participants become entranced. The initiators try hard to provoke a reaction from the initiate, and every complaint against her as a wife and resident in her husband's village or her home is aired. During the height of the affair small groups of women are spaced around the inside edge of the corral, each conducting the initiation of her own subject or subjects; the tempo is fast, and the women become glazed with emotion.

The last stage of Phase II, the *imaa ra ŋimba* or lion *imaa*, is held after the initiate has had one child or after it is clear that she will never have children. The principal secret object here is the "lion," a mortar covered with skin and rubbed in such a way as to produce the voice of the lion. Some say there are also two small, pure white, bead-covered gourds to represent the twins whose birth is the overt reason for holding the rite. Lion *imaa* is most secret but is apparently less significant to women than house *imaa*. The manifest reason for holding it is to purify the homestead of a woman or cow that has had twins. Bearing twins is viewed as a very courageous act, equal to the bravery of a man who kills a lion. Yet, like such a man, the woman is ritually unclean. She and her husband are purified at the time of the birth, and a special *mwandU* payment, said to be three cows, is made to her mother's brother for the event. After this rite a cooking pot, pierced on the bottom, is placed on the roof of the house of the mother of the twins and over her bed, to protect the family from *ufeto* (lightning), which is the spear of the Creator (Mungu), an avenger of evil.

However, lion *imaa* is more than a purification of the woman's household. It is also the medium for initiating women who have had children into full female adult status, and the central drama of lion *imaa* is the alleged capture of a lion in the forest in order to bring it to the house of the woman who had the twins, to be kept there during the rite. The night before the ceremony the initiated women go to the forest, capture the "lion," and bring it back hidden among their massed bodies, where its roar is produced by the mortar. The "lion" is placed in the backroom of the principal woman.

The following day the initiates are brought to that homestead; there they are required initially to take hold of one of the *mlxoa* (straps) tied to the "lion" extending out of the house to the corral fence. The woman being purified is dressed in a disreputable costume with a brief skirt, soot is spread all over her body, and the holey pot is put on her head. The "lion" is left in the care of some senior woman at the homestead, from which all men are excluded, and the rest go off into the marsh to a *mUhUi* tree, which is ritually cool and which is supposed always to be the site of such an *imaa*. At the tree the initiates are in some manner instructed, and all beat the tree with their skirts "to get children"; after this the principal woman demands to be purified by means of a slaughtered sheep. At the end the pot is broken signifying completion of the purification. When they return, the "lion" is taken back to the forest and afterward beer is drunk. The next day the women disperse to their homes.

It seems significant that occasionally and for a reason never made clear, lion *imaa* (and some say house *imaa*) used to be followed by another rite called *ifaha*, which means "twins." In this the young men of the village, who were the main participants in stick battles, attacked the *imaa* proceedings after first warning the elder women and getting their permission. They dumped the women's food and spilled their beer, acts normally causing the invocation of the *njuɣuda* sanction. Subsequently the men and women met in the open as if negotiating *mwandU*, and a time was arranged for the *ifaha* dance in the pastures, just as a feud battle was arranged. In this dance the men lined up facing the women, and the particular feature of the dance was the use of sticks by the men, who tapped the women on the shoulders. In short, the event dramatized a fight between two affiliated but opposed groups, like the lineages. In the end the women gave in to the men as if in defeat.

Lion *imaa* is held some years after the birth of twins and is sometimes, though not usually, delayed even to the time of their circumcision. The significance of this delay, like so much of lion *imaa*, is unknown. As the men say, the secret of lion *imaa* is so great that the women never tell the men about it.

We can only speculate about the meaning of lion *imaa*. One element is clear— the separation of men and women. On the one hand the rite seems to display the power of women, while on the other it shows attempts to control this power for the sake of peace. The rite seems to parallel the lion-man activities; the bringing of the lion resembles the belief that women cooperate to control lions. The husband is considered to be the cause of the principal woman's having twins and thus endangering her, which is why he pays a fine. Having twins is equivalent to killing or capturing a lion and is an accomplishment open to women. They are thus shown to have power to threaten men.

Also important is the significant alteration of status of a woman after she has had a child. Before this time none of the wealth of her house is firmly under her control. If she is divorced, it reverts to her husband and his other wives. When a child is born, particularly a male, her estate is more firmly attached to her. Women who have had children are more secure and more to be reckoned with by the men. Turu say, "It is hard to be divorced after children are born."

Lion *imaa* thus seems to signify the achievement of control of men by women as a group, both in their villages and in general. They have, in effect, conquered the men, who are the lions; but they use their power for good by allowing themselves to be conquered by the men, as in *ifaha*, in order to keep peace because peace is valuable to them.

Some comparative evidence from the small Isanzu tribe to the north,[1] with whom the Turu are related, adds to our understanding of Turu lion *imaa*. The Isanzu have a rite called *mUrimU*, which is equivalent to lion *imaa* and which is performed when the twins are six months old. The initiates are women who have had one child, and in the course of the rite they are abused with thorn bushes, which scratch their backs as do the claws of the lion. The wielders of these switches are the mothers of the initiate's husbands, suggesting that the rite is a means of establishing the female power structure in the village. Hence those women whose interests have most closely become identified with the interests of the men of the village assert their power to control the younger women, whose interests are now becoming like theirs because of the birth of children.

WOMEN'S VILLAGE ORGANIZATIONS

One male informant said, "*imaa* makes all women one." A woman put it similarly: "*imaa* is to develop cooperation among wives, who fill the blanks created by sisters who go out of the village." We have seen this process illustrated by the cooperation of women across village lines during lion-man proceedings. During the days of feuds, when stick battles went on, women stood to the side,

1. Private communication from Marguerite Jellicoe.

not participating but cooperating to shield men of both sides who were injured in the fight. Women are to some degree organized within Level III lineages. The *mUhUi* tree around which the lion *imaa* rites congregate seems to be particular to a whole Level III area. In the villages stronger ingroup feelings develop, and as one man put it, "Women must more actively cooperate than men because they come from many different places and need a special bond that men, who live among those with whom they were born, acquire through their relatedness." This statement aptly summarizes the situation. In effect there is a general sorority of Turu women, but in the villages each group has a different chapter.

In the village organization the leaders are usually the older women, those who have lived there a long time and whose sons are grown. Like *imaa*, the basic aim of the organization is to keep a check on the behavior of younger women, to prevent improprieties that would anger the men and would upset the peace. As during the lion-man proceedings, one of these leaders speaks for the women as a group and defends them from the men or gives up recalcitrants to the men for punishment. But also like *imaa*, the coordination of their activities is envied and feared by the men, who feel inferior in the face of such unanimity of purpose, just as they feel inferior to the government, with which the women's organization is compared.

The status of women in a village varies with commitment to the village. The highest status is that of the independent director of a household who has grown sons. Her stake in the village is almost equivalent to a man's. By comparison, the young bride has little stake in her husband's village. The elder women desire to keep these young women in line, and when a new bride comes, they show this wish by putting her in her place immediately. When there is peace, all women benefit; the young are made to understand this fact. The stake in the system for the young women is the protection and guidance they receive and the companionship of other women.

Women work together in many ways. One man expressed awe at the way they acted when one of his cows died. They all knew immediately and came to claim portions of the meat. They did not come at random, however. One group came to perform one act, such as skinning the beast, another group to cut it up, others to cook it. To this man such action was proof that they work together by means of some secret government; but when more cows died on subsequent days, he asserted that they also work jointly against men they hate and that they were bewitching his cows. To defeat them he then began to burn carcasses of further cows that died.

The "little *njUγUda*," or *ŋangU*, has already been described. Here the check on each other's behavior by women takes the form of joint contribution of grain to make beer for a meeting to expiate the harm to relations in general caused by one mother's injury to her child. Similarly, when there is drought, the women gather and secretly take action to bring rain. When her husband dies, the purification of the widow is done secretly by the women, who go away from the corral where the men are gathered. When the secrets of *imaa* or the privacy of *Unyambee* are violated by a man, the women work as one to attack the guilty man. They are constantly watching each others' behavior and reporting and correcting improprieties, such as overt consorting with a lover. In such cases, after the elder women agree, one of them reports the behavior to the woman's husband, so that he will punish her. Whenever a woman travels, she is expected to take another woman with her to chaperone her and prevent behavior that would anger her husband. During *imaa* and other rites women who get publicly drunk or otherwise disgrace themselves are chastened by the elder women in charge.

A striking example of the way women operate has appeared in recent years when the social-development department introduced a literacy campaign. The attitude of the men was negative. The women cooperated en masse; obviously it was decided through their groups that literacy held an advantage for them, and they encouraged each other to take part. There are other examples of innovations that succeeded widely when women approved of them, most notably the disappearance, almost overnight, of skin skirts, which were replaced by amerikani cloth. The move was initiated among the women of Ikungi, who jointly disposed of skin skirts in one movement. Subsequently this practice spread like wildfire among Turu women everywhere.

The most notable example of women's activities that are in opposition to the men is the system of dalliance relationships. Men object to their own women's being the mistresses of others, while the women uniformly wish to have sweethearts. The women therefore protect each other from the men, coordinating and controlling their love making in order to avoid antagonizing the men.

Despite the generally hostile attitude of men toward women, men are actually unsure how to think of women. On the positive side, men seem to understand and excuse women for the way they are, like the man who felt that witchcraft is women's means of protection from men. Women are generally viewed as the best of the two sexes because they are, like the moon to which they are compared, creators and cool, while the men are like the sun, hot-natured. Women's personal names are often associated with birds, like the little brightly colored *balima*, or with flowers, things Turu think of as beautiful.

The ambivalence in men's attitude fits the ambivalent roles of women in this society. When men speak of women as witches, they are thinking of them in the status of wife, not as sister or even mother. Sisters are supposed to be unable to harm their brothers, which means that they normally have no reason to. The passion between lovers expresses in another way the view of women as cool and beautiful when they are not wives, but lovers are usually of different villages. Their interests in each other are almost purely emotional and do not involve property, at least not in the conventional sense. If the flame of emotion dies, lovers separate with little difficulty. If a Turu should ever phrase the conflict philosophically, he would have to try to resolve the paradox of how women can be basically so good and yet so evil—a paradox not unfamiliar to other cultures.

9. PAST AND PRESENT

The past is brother to the present.
TURU PROVERB

C HANGE is occurring, or has the potential to occur, in Turu society in two different directions, of which one is now apparently outmoded and the other is inevitable. The former is change in the direction of greater or lesser patrilineal emphasis, dependent on general increase or decrease in livestock wealth, and the latter is westernization.

THE PATRILINEAL SHIFT

While westernization concerns us most because of its inevitability, it is necessary to say something of the patrilineal shift because it appears to explain certain features of Turu life that are otherwise enigmatic. I refer particularly to the sometimes disabling conflict between men and women and between affinal lineages.

In the livestock areas of Africa evidence shows (Schneider 1964) a clear tendency for societies to shift structure in accompaniment with increase in bridewealth payments. The number of societies in which there are matrilineally defined corporate groupings and in which livestock are used in bridewealth is statistically quite insignificant. On the other hand, as livestock occur in the bridewealth, the levirate appears, the bride goes to live at the residence of her husband, patrilineages become very important, and brideservice disappears. Ultimately marriage becomes almost undissolvable. The latter state is most pronounced when the bridewealth reaches about twenty head of cattle or their livestock equivalent. The Turu, while well along this road, are obviously far from its terminus.

In the Central Region of Tanzania, among what Murdock (1959, 358) calls the Rift Cluster of the Tanganyika Bantu, which includes the Turu, we see this process in capsule form. The Iramba (who seem most closely related to the Turu) still have matrilineal descent with some form of matrilocal residence; the Rangi are matrilineal with patrilocal residence; the Mbugwe have matriclans and patrilineages and are patrilocal in residence. While information about cousin kinship terminology is lacking for Iramba and Rangi, the Mbugwe use Crow terminology, which is usually associated with corporate matrilineages. The Gogo are patrilineal with patrilocal residence and Iroquois terminology, while the Turu

possess patrilineal descent, patrilocal residence, and essentially Omaha terminology. Significantly, the Turu and Gogo seem to have the highest number of
livestock, and the Gogo pay by far the highest bridewealth (about fifteen head
of cattle) and have the most stable marriage system (Rigby 1966, 11–12).

That some significant long term-shifts are or were occurring in these societies
is apparent. Central to the change was the tendency to accumulate livestock. It
may even be that the growth of segmentary societies based on livestock is one
of two major directions toward change in traditional Africa, the other—occurring among relatively poor people without livestock—being a move in the
direction of states. The high incidence of segmentary societies or age-set systems,
which are also stateless, among people with significant numbers of livestock is
suggestive of this trend.

WESTERNIZATION

Interesting as the patrilineal shift is, the matter now appears to be academic
because of the factor of westernization, which for the last fifty years has had a
far greater potential for determining the future of the Turu. In the foregoing
account of the Turu only parenthetical attempts were made to draw a sharp line
between the society as it was and as it now is. This chapter, which specifically
compares past and present, states the premise that none of the changes that have
occurred reflect significant alterations in Turu society and culture. The past, up
to now, is indeed brother to the present.

The claim of inevitable resistance by indigenous societies to influence from
the West is a romantic notion that used to be common in some kinds of anthropological writing. On the contrary, I have the impression that many, if not most,
Turu would be quite willing to become westernized if the change could be
accomplished with appropriate and dependable future rewards.

The simple fact is that the traditional society has an integrated method of
production and appropriate goals combined with a social structure that is suited
to these and for which no competitor has been found by either the Turu or the
Europeans in the last fifty years. In the eyes of some Turu, they are literally
condemned to continue with this system because they can find no way to accom-
odate European innovations with the same assurance of control and success. Von
Sick, when summarizing his account of the Turu, noted that in his opinion the
country was of little potential use for Europeans, for it seemed unsuited to any
kind of production other than that already pursued by the inhabitants. His
description of Turu modes of production and associated activities does not differ
in any important way from those continuing today. A review of other accounts
of the Turu by such early writers as von Luschan (1898), Reche (1914), and
Baumann (1894) confirms this view. This is not to say that in the future such
change cannot occur; but up to 1960 it had not yet occurred.

In general, what happened in the fifty years up to 1960 was readjustment of
various facets of life to maintain the integrity of the system. Mainly there was a

partial substitution of one form of government for another by the colonial powers, to which Turu reacted by utilizing portions of the new structure but not others, and trade developed with external markets in response to the need for cash to pay taxes and to buy clothing and certain other goods. Whenever changes posed a threat to the integrity of the indigenous system, however, they were successfully resisted, and the colonial authorities were reluctant to insist on change at the cost of peace. Only in the 1960's, with the postwar impetus to economic "development" and the rise of nationalism, did the threat to the traditional system become severe. This new decade, which has already seen the independence of Tanzania and a strong desire by the new leaders to revise the structure of indigenous societies to fit national ends, may possibly be a period of real alteration in Turu life, marking a true departure from the old ways.

By 1960 some of the patterns of future change had already been set. There were a few Turu who had gone far toward accommodating themselves to the new order, severing their dependence on the indigenous system because they earned salaries or wages sufficient to make participation in a new social environment possible. These were the men who had gone on to advanced schooling or who had government jobs. They usually removed themselves from the tribal system not only in actions, but also in body; defections of this kind tended to occur steadily as opportunities arose. This course was not open to all, however. The mass of people remained illiterate, or barely literate, while continuing their economic and emotional dependence on the traditional system. Following the general framework of this book, we will turn now to an assessment of change in terms of the constraints (material life and ideology, norms) on the one hand and strategies on the other.

MATERIAL LIFE AND IDEOLOGY

Speaking in the present tense of conditions in 1960, the manner of dress of Turu is misleading as an index to social change. Indigenously women used goatskins for skirts and capes and sheepskins for baby carriers, while males generally wore only a skin cape. The desire for cloth and Western dress has led to the almost complete eradication of precontact dress styles and adornments among men and to extensive alteration in styles among women. It is not clear why cloth was so immediately admired. When it first began to appear in the market, traded up to the Turu from the Gogo, it is said to have been so greatly in demand that men would search the whole country and pay as much as three goats to acquire a piece to wear for special occasions, such as the harvest dance *(ilanda)* or the *ifaha*. By the time the Germans were driven out of UnyatUrU about 1916, most men seem to have replaced skins with clothes, although young men still wore traditional dress, whereas women continued to wear skins up to about 1945, after which they replaced them with pieces of black amerikani cloth called *kaniki*.

Today the form of clothing worn by men and women is of two general types. Those men and women who have actively committed themselves to the abandonment of the indigenous system have assumed Western dress in its entirety, wearing shorts or trousers, suits, shirts, shoes, and the rest (see Plate 9.1). Needless to say, the number of such people is still small. It includes the government officials and clerks and political persons and a few schoolboys at the advanced levels. Some plantation workers and specialized laborers, such as cooks, may also be classed with this group. There are fewer women who have been able to accomplish this extreme shift, but they also do wear clothing not basically different from Western women's dress. To a large extent, then, this extreme shift is a measure of social change among a few.

For the vast majority of men and women the change in dress style is less extreme. The men no longer go naked, but usually cover even the top of the body. Their standard dress (as shown in Plate 3.1) is a *shuka*, a piece of white rectangular cloth worn wrapped around the waist, a shirt or pullover buttoning down the front, and sandals made of rubber ties. Nowadays the wealthier men also wear the Arab gown called *kanzu* on special occasions. In addition, a heavy wool coat or heavy blanket is worn over the rest of the costume during cold weather. The coat may be an old army-style one but is frequently a European female style, imported into the country by traders. It is startling to discover that already in 1910 von Sick was complaining on esthetic grounds about the importation of such coats. To his mind it was demeaning for a herder to be clothed in a Prince Albert.

The women who continue the traditional life have two styles of clothing, of

PLATE 9.1
Catholic Wedding Among a Group of Young Western-Oriented Turu

which the most common is the one featuring the amerikani *kaniki*. One sheet of this black cloth is worn wrapped around the body from the knees to above the breasts (as shown in Plate 8.4), and the other is used as a cape or a baby carrier when the sheepskin carrier, which is used only on special occasions, is not used. On more formal occasions women wear the *kanga*, a garment exactly like the *kaniki* but printed with bright colors and patterns on cloth of a better quality. For the rite of house *imaa* a red fez is worn in addition to the *kanga*, and rolled *shukas* are draped over the shoulders and held in place by a leather belt.

Clothing reform has reached the children last. Little boys still go naked much of the time except when in school. Girls continue to be covered from a very early age. Body scarification, which used to be done on the upper part of the trunk, is now disappearing among men because they prefer to keep the body covered.

As to the care of clothing, these new materials tend to be treated like skins— which is to say that washing of them is done seldom or not at all. A variable in change is proximity to centers of acculturative influence. The tendency to wash clothes, as well as to adopt new styles, varies with and is greatest near to the trading and administrative centers, such as the town of Singida or Ikungi, the headquarters of UnyahatI.

Jewelry has been greatly affected. Most of the indigenous ornaments have disappeared or are used only on ritual occasions. The highly valued *kisaγwida*, which consists primarily of a type of large orange stone valued at one heifer, is now quite rare. It has been replaced by other forms of adornment purchased in the shops of foreign traders, such as necklaces of various types and bracelets of bead or metal. The demand for foreign jewelry also came very early, long before the Germans arrived, and beads were traded up from the Gogo, who received them in payment from caravans traveling across their country.

Hair styles have also changed (as shown in Plate 8.5). While adult men and women who adhere to the traditional system still shave their heads and the elder men grow small beards, the young girls and boys do not allow their hair to grow long. The men imitate European styles, and the women braid their hair into the fashionable *usuke* style borrowed from the more sophisticated tribes.

The beaded *ifaṃpa* belt and *dIlanda* anklets are still common, as is true of other elements of female dress and adornment having ritual significance. These both have symbolic reference to birth and fertility and therefore to the integrity of the indigenous system, as does the style of dress in *imaa*, which has remained most conservative. Similarly, boys going through circumcision are the most conservative in male dress and jewelry.

Standards of body decoration, while not essentially altered from precontact times in the sense that decoration is still related to prestige and ritual, have therefore altered almost entirely to a new standard, modeled generally on European values. The men's styles more closely approach European patterns than do women's, and both are exceptionally conservative when adornment is tied closely to ritual.

The essential fact about these clothing styles is that they are supportable by small expenditures of imported money, as befits their use in an economy still traditional in orientation. The smallness of expenditures is suggested by the exasperated but exaggerated comment of an Indian trader, who said that the Turu will not spend more than 5 shillings for anything. The *kaniki* and *shuka* can be bought for about that, but shirts generally cost 5 or 6 shillings, the *kanga* costs about 12 shillings and the Arab gown about 20 shillings.

Turu technology is strikingly conservative. The only imported tool in general use is the hoe. However, this has been so for fifty years at least. Before the Germans appeared, iron hoes imported from tribes to the west were eagerly received and replaced the wooden-headed hoes that were still widely used when the Germans first arrived but that had already disappeared by 1918.

In those days some Turu acted as entrepreneurs, buying thirty hoes for a heifer and selling them for one goat apiece, which would give a profit of 500 per cent on the basis of five goats as equivalent to one heifer. Put in other terms, people were willing to pay the present day equivalent of 20 shillings for a hoe.

The art of smelting was unknown and the art of blacksmithing was poorly developed among the Turu. It is not that Turu did not have knowledge of blacksmithing but that they simply would not, and even today do not, bother with it. The conclusion is inescapable that blacksmithing was not considered a dependable method of livelihood, compared to livestock raising and grain production, so that few people went into blacksmithing. Even today most of the few blacksmiths are foreigners, such as Nyamwezi, despite the fact that, except for the hoe, Turu still prefer to use traditional-style tools made by itinerant indigenous blacksmiths. The *panga*, a machete that has been widely introduced and accepted all over East Africa, is not admired and is hardly used at all.

In other respects the technology has not altered appreciably. Grain is still ground on indigenously produced grindstones laboriously shaped by the women, food is cooked in clay pots produced by a few female potters (whose pots continue to be as crude as those that were critically remarked on by Reche in the early days of contact), solids are carried in troughs carved out of trees, liquids are carried and stored in gourds and clay pots, and grain is kept in the bark bins. Even the ancient gourd water pipe is still universally used. Imported aluminum *sufurias* are in general use because water can be heated faster in them, and *debes* are used to carry grain and to transport liquids, these being the only important innovations in utensils.

The amount of technological innovation is to a certain extent also a variant of closeness to centers of foreign influence. This fact is apparent in types of housing. Everywhere the form of houses and homesteads has remained the same as in the past, except that near the centers of influence the tendency is to build with sun-dried mud brick (Plate 2.2) and to plaster the outside of the house with mud to enhance its appearance. In the more usual traditional style only the interior is plastered and the walls are supported by upright poles rather than by brick.

Other changes run a wide gamut. Wooden spoons and troughs are made by specialists and sold in the marketplaces (which now exist alongside the livestock marketplaces); before, they were probably a product of each household or group of villages. Women who live in the towns continue to participate in *imaa*, but they now sew the patterned beads on pieces of cloth or put them on bottles. The use of cattle urine for washing seems to have disappeared before new ideas of cleanliness or at least in deference to the opinions of Europeans.

Swahili forms of greeting are now widely used, although they have not displaced the traditional KIrImi forms. The Turu word for Creator, *Matunda*, is now generally qualified by the Swahili form, *Mungu*, so that people refer to *Mungu-Matunda*, although in von Sick's time they spoke simply of *Matunda*. In fact, the Turu godhead is actually a trinity that also includes *Maγema*, the Thinker, and *Mahanya*, the Speaker, both of whom continue to be recognized.

Literacy in Swahili has so increased that a newspaper published for the Turu, called *Sayu-itu*—which in KIrImi means "Our News"—in 1958 sold 1,900 copies a month, enough to pay for itself. This paper is now discontinued under a government policy discouraging local papers.

Branding of cattle by inscribing designs on the hide with a hot iron has almost disappeared because it damages the hides, which are sold in the external market. The drinking of cattle blood and its extraction from living animals have also disappeared with penetration of Islamic and Christian ideas, although Reche, whose information is frequently incorrect, claimed that blood was only drunk during famines even in former times. While boys still construct toy corrals in the fields to play at house management, some now make toy automobiles of reeds. In surveying the paintings on the wall of the *mwango* by one girl who had been in menstrual isolation, it was discovered that among all the traditional patterns was an attempt to represent a car with people in it (shown in Plate 8.6) and in another place a painting of a framed picture, imitating the pictures Westerners have on their walls.

Extraction of the lower front incisors of children seems to have declined. Syphilis, according to one European doctor, is now widespread, where formerly it was rare or lacking. The shields used for stick and spear fights are not now used except for ceremonies, although spears and sticks are still defensive and offensive weapons. In some places the government has succeeded in introducing gardens into the marshes, where many vegetables and fruits not formerly grown are now grown willingly.

The younger generation is superficially more sophisticated than the older because of the increase of contacts with new ideas, largely in the schools. One elder man with whom I worked was so unfamiliar with European ways that he had never ridden in a car and tried to spit through the closed window because he was without knowledge of glass.

In contrast to these selected changes in life, attempts to induce other changes have quite often met with failure. The social-development program in the district has over the last few years succeeded remarkably with its literacy campaign, particularly among women. Windows, however—which some Turu have been induced to put in their houses—have been covered, for fear that they are possible routes of ingress by thieves, vandals, and enemies. The growing of elephant grass for fodder has been rejected, along with communal vegetable plots and communal stores, both of which operate on principles of corporacy that are foreign to Turu ideas. Past attempts to require planting of cassava and sweet potatoes as protection against famine failed. People have been encouraged to construct outhouses and have even been forced to do so in some places, but these are not understood and little used. Maternity hospitals go unused, there is still no attempt to calculate age or time in the European manner, and there is little acceptance of European styles of food or liquor, although certain foods—such as tea, sugar cane, sardines, and sugar—are purchased as occasional treats by the more affluent.

In searching for the reasons for rejection of desirable innovations, the cost must be calculated, not only in terms of money, but also in time and energy. Turu not only refuse to sell more than a small amount of their resources to earn cash to buy goods in the external market, they also refuse to devote time and energy to such activities as blacksmithing that would make inroads on more productive indigenous economic activities. Some cash crops are now grown, probably because they are competitive in the indigenous market. In Wahi maize is such a cash crop grown by a few, as is finger millet. The small amount of such crops is a measure of their inadequacy to challenge the traditional system. In 1926 the provincial commissioner reported that the main items of import were hoes, cloth, brass wire, and beads (*Report of the Provincial Commissioners* 1926). This situation has not appreciably changed.

The situation is summed up by reference to responses to the appearance of Islam and Christianity. At the time von Sick described the Turu, the Catholics had established the mission of St. Leo's at Makingu in UkahiU, which in 1952 was augmented by a hospital run by the Medical Missionaries of Mary. The American Augustana Lutherans appeared after the first World War. The Moslems have been an intrusive force since early times. At first none of these groups had much success. The Christians made the first gains, while conversion to Islam began to occur only in comparatively recent years, except among the chiefs. Nevertheless, Islam has overtaken Christianity and now well outdistances it in most places.

There is a fundamental difference in these religions with respect to their adaptability to Turu life. Islam, although the least prestigeful, can be taken over with a minimum of dislocation of traditional practices. The convert takes a Moslem name, adheres to some degree to fasting rules during Ramadan, eats only properly slaughtered meat, and conducts burial rites with some attention to Islamic law. Christianity, although more prestigeful, requires a severe readjustment. Monogamy is essential, and the missions in UnyatUrU have variously declared against such rites as *imaa*, the sexually suggestive dances of circumcision, *mwandU* at the death of the wife, ancestral sacrifices, *njUγUda*, and burial in the homestead.

It is possible for a person to become a nominal Moslem while changing almost not at all, while for a person to become a Christian requires a radical break. Because Christianity is more closely associated with the whole complex of European cultural and social goals that progressive Turu admire, many people attempt to convert to Christianity while compromising with the old system. This compromise does not work very well, and such people are likely to find themselves involved in uncomfortable conflicts. To compromise with the strict Christian regime, the vacillating Turu tends to use his Christian name but takes part in ancestral rites to the extent of drinking beer or even goes further in limited participation. He may keep an inherited wife but will not live with her. One group of Christian sons whose Moslem father died participated in the funeral but not in the Moslem rites. A son-in-law whose mother-in-law was a Christian did not kill a steer at her grave, but he made up for the omission at the death of his father-in-law by sacrificing it to him instead.

Some, though not all, of these compromises are serious challenges to the convert's role as a Christian. The non-Christian may express sympathy and understanding when Christians do not participate in traditional rites, but hostilities do tend to develop, and Christians tend to be rejected. For a Christian woman who has not done *imaa*, rejection by the other women is a serious matter and is probably inevitable. On the whole, the conflict of Turu and Christian practices is not a serious challenge to the persistence of Turu life because there are so few active Christians.

In the village of Utatuu, which is medially remote, the religious affiliations of 134 adult men and women were as follows: 59 Moslems, 37 *afIkani* (the term in general use by Turu to indicate an undeviating adherent to indigenous beliefs), and 38 Christians. At SUnja village, which is next to the important trading and government center of Ikungi, the force of urban influence is such that there were no *afIkani*. The relatively large number of Christians in Utatuu is a result of proximity to the Catholic mission headquarters. In both these villages the Christians tend to be mixed even in the same family with adherents to Islam, although there is a strong tendency for the whole family to convert if the head is a Christian. The set of figures from Utatuu should be interpreted to mean that there are 96 traditionalists, since the Moslems are only nominal and of the Christians there are only a few who are truly committed. When they become rigid advocates, the Christians tend to cut themselves off from the village or are cut off. It follows, of course, that young people who attain any appreciable degree of advancement in the educational system become Christians, but those who have risen in the civil service need not become Christians and the chiefs were Moslems of more than nominal variety.

NORMATIVE SYSTEMS

As one would suspect, the amount of change in the norms is also superficial, although the apparently radical change in government structure appears on the face of it to dispute such a claim.

Both the German and the British colonial administrations made very few attempts to alter any indigenous social forms except the government. Both intertribal and interlineage fighting were banned and disappeared almost immediately. The prohibition on foreign wars seems to have meant little to the Turu, who were never much inclined to fight their neighbors. They did organize to fight off intruders, and the new system was beneficial to them in making defense unnecessary. The friction between Turu and Barabaig is still not completely controlled, but it breaks out only along the border and not as a large-scale combat, so that it is not an important threat.

As a result of elimination of intertribal warfare there was expansion into areas formerly too dangerous to enter, with a resultant rise in population. A reflex of the loss of interlineage combat was the disappearance of the rite of *ifaha*, or "twins" (shown in Plate 7.1), which was disapproved by the government because of the similarity to organized combat. Today young men dress up and paint their faces in *ifaha* style to put on performances at fairs and special nonindigenous events. The loss of the feud was followed by the disappearance of the spear and stick shields, which were offensive devices in the eyes of the government. The stick shield has almost completely disappeared, but spear shields are still used by the husband surrogates in *imaa* rites and by youths seeking wives, for whom they are a standard symbol of the quest (shown in Plate 5.1).

Native authorities were also created to control internal relations. The Germans founded small chiefdoms, apparently Level III lineages, under *jumbes*. Each *jumbe* had a certain number of *anangwa* (*mwanangwa*, sing.) to aid him. In Wahi the British consolidated these chiefdoms into three larger units, giving the two largest clans their own chiefs (called *watemi*; *mtemi*, sing.) but disposing of the smaller clans by either putting them under one of these two large chiefdoms or, as in the Ihanja-Puma region, combining them into another chiefdom. From 1925 to 1939 the chief of the area around Singida town, Chief Mgeni, was also Paramount Chief of all of UnyatUrU, a position he maintained by his charisma; the post vanished a few years after his death, when his son was unable to uphold it. (In 1962 the whole system of chiefs was abolished, to be replaced by a less monarchic structure.)

By 1960 the chiefs had varying numbers of assistants to administer their areas. Called *wakili*, the assistants were further aided by the *wanangwa*, one over each Level III lineage, and their assistants, called *rugaruga*. In addition, each village had an appointed head called *halmashauri*. The chief had no legislative power but was both an administrator and a judge, who had a group of elders to help him consider cases. It is fair to say that the power of a chief to do more than enforce the imposed and traditional laws depended on his ability to lead. Many or most were able to do little more than satisfy the demands of the colonial authorities above them.

This situation existed in part because the colonial authorities tried to turn chieftainship into a hereditary system, so that some inept sons inherited from strong fathers. Opportunities for graft were great, especially since tax collection was one of the chief's main jobs. The further down the hierarchy from the chiefs, the less effectively the authority system related to the ongoing life of the people. In fact, only in recent years was any attempt made to extend authority down to the villages by creation of *halmashauris*, or headmen. It is, then, best to regard the native authority system as an extension of the colonial civil service, meant to be integrated into the life of the people but, in fact, successful to some extent only in the judicial area.

The colonial authorities recognized the ineffectiveness of the system and considered many of the chiefs as little more than tax collectors. It was asserted that chiefs were afraid to antagonize their constituents, who had a tendency, when under pressure, to leave the country to work on plantations in the north and thereby to reduce the tax rolls. The position of village headman was so poorly understood that all the elders of some villages tended to think of themselves as headmen—a retention of the old ideas of village authority.

The ability of some chiefs to actually extend power beyond the structured frame was similar to the way leadership was exercised in the traditional system by local charismatic leaders. When the Germans first came, they tended to turn men into chiefs, but since by the nature of their calling these men were not amenable to such control, they tended to come into conflict with the Germans and to be put down. Despite this fact, the White Fathers explained that the Germans purposely let the Turu run their own affairs unless there was an appeal, although they reserved the right of capital punishment, the use of chains, and flogging.

The instituted legal system judged cases under the traditional English legal categories of criminal and civil, and this distinction in fact proved apt for the Turu system. The chiefdom courts heard all the cases except those of special seriousness, which went to the district court under the district commissioner or a senior magistrate aided by three elders. Local court cases could be appealed to this court. Homicide was judged by a high-court circuit judge. Most of the criminal cases had to do with assault and theft, although murder was also frequent, as can be seen from a random sample of fifty-three cases heard in the district court in 1954. Ten had to do with theft other than livestock; nine with assault of a severe nature; and seven each with theft of goats, sheep, and cattle, and nonpayment of taxes. There were three murder cases (for which the court held preliminary inquiries). The remainder of the cases were of a miscellaneous nature.

Annual reports of both the district and the province have a tendency to attribute a high crime rate to Singida. The 1958 annual report of the judiciary seems to verify this belief; Dodoma, the largest district of the Central Province, had the highest number of criminal cases, at 688; Singida was second, at 336; and Kondoa placed third, at 112. Of course these figures must be judged against the fact that many cases heard in courts at Singida involved, not Turu, but various aliens. Nevertheless, anyone living among the Turu can see the violence that frequently occurs and that makes the district exceptional. Even von Sick commented on the high murder rate among Turu. The 1958 district report for Singida showed that the courts throughout the district handled 2,199 criminal and 579 civil cases. In the 1926 Report of the Provincial Commissioner of the Central Province it is noted that even at that early time the three courts of the district were very busy.

A review of the criminal cases tried in a recent year in the chiefdom court at Ikungi, where few aliens appear, showed them to deal with assault of various kinds, including defamation of character (for example, a woman insulted a sub-chief by accusing him of having only a one-battery flashlight). Civil cases had to do mostly with such important property conflicts as rights in wives, livestock, and marsh pastures.

The conclusion that may be made from data on how these induced courts operated is that, except for prosecution for tax evasion and certain other violations of imposed norms, the courts concerned themselves with the kinds of disputes that are a result of the continued operation of the indigenous social and economic system. These courts even prescribed *njUγUda*. There is no reason to believe that the amount of litigation is a product of changing conditions and every reason to believe that property conflicts are endemic in the system. This new court system seems, therefore, to be functionally equivalent to the indigenous one. Today we find that disputes—other than murder and severe assault, which almost inevitably must be subject to government judgement—are settled in the village unless the defendant denies his guilt.

The Turu did not accept this new governmental system placidly when it was first introduced. Some serious armed conflicts occurred between Germans and Turu, and at least two instances of revolt took place. But after the first decade there seems to have been no further resistance, again suggesting that the new system was not so serious an intrusion on traditional modes as the Turu at first imagined. On the other hand, the loss of interlineage warfare has probably affected the unity of the Level III lineage; one old man was of the opinion that these are now weak as a result.

Other normative changes may be summarized. There is a tendency to shorten the seclusion of the newly menstruating girl, the burial rites have been somewhat affected, and the rite of *njUγUda* of the most violent type is rare, although not when applied to violation of *imaa* and menstrual seclusion. Circumcision for boys has changed slightly in that the rite is held later in the year and earlier in life, so that it does not conflict with the school year; but the essential lack of change in circumcision is illustrated in Plates 8.3 and 8.5. There seems, finally, to be a decline in cooperation within the Level III lineage.

It is instructive to further note what has not changed. The whole system of personal names persists, modified only to the extent that Islamic and Christian names may be added. As far as can be determined, the terminology of kinship remains the same. Although von Sick's account lacks certain key kinship terms, those he gives suggest that kinship terminology has not altered. The use of genealogy to defend rights persists strongly, and the genealogical systems are very much alive. The two largest clans in Wahi in von Sick's time remain the two largest, and while von Sick gives no further help in determining how clans have changed, evidence from the present shows no significant alteration. Clan membership is still used to define exogamy, except among a few permanent exiles on the plantations in northern Tanzania; bridewealth is still required for marriage; and payment must be in livestock. Circumcision rites are as vital as ever, and marriage rites continue to be carried out on the old pattern, taking just as long and being just as complicated as von Sick describes. The ancestral rites are as central as ever (see Plate 3.1), and *imaa* occurs in full force, while the physical form and agnatic composition of villages remains as in the past. Even on the plantations where there are large numbers of Turu, the important rites continue to be observed. The striking aspect of Turu society today is not what has changed but what has not changed, the very weight of retention of traditional forms arguing the functional insignificance of apparently radical changes such as those in the form of government.

STRATEGIES

The day-to-day activities oriented toward acquiring wealth and prestige as traditionally defined have also persisted. This retention is the key to persistence of the normative system.

Certain innovations give a superficial appearance of radical change. The system of taxation, which in the 1950's led to relatively great demands on the resources of the Turu; the growth of livestock markets for beef (Plate 9.2); the presence of foreign traders selling various goods—all suggest that the indigenous Turu economy has been integrated with the larger economy of Tanzania and the world. An examination of yearly expenditures and income refutes this belief.

Yearly expenditures in the external market by the average Turu are made for such important items as clothing, tools, and ornaments. It will be recalled, however, that these expenditures are on the average very small. There are only a small number of trading establishments outside the town of Singida and not a great variety of goods to purchase. The chief expenditure is for taxes, a fact indicated by the continual grumbling about them and the mad scramble that occurs each year at tax time as people try to find the necessary money. From the original tax of about 2 shillings per male adult—(women and children are not taxed), taxes have risen steadily.

By 1960 the tax was in two parts: head tax and the livestock tax. For some years the livestock tax was 1 shilling a head for cattle or 1 shilling for five livestock units (L.S.U.), defined by the government as five goats or sheep, which

PLATE 9.2
Cattle Being Sold in the Government or External Market at Ikungi

the government considered to be the equivalent of one cow of either sex. When the destocking program was abandoned after 1958, the livestock tax was raised to 3 shillings per head of cattle. By 1958 the head tax was 18 shillings per man per year, but this was also raised after 1958 to 30 shillings.

By utilizing reliable available quantitative data, some simple calculations show that the average tax per man paid in 1960 was 51 shillings. This figure is derived from the assumption that the adult male population is about 44,000 and the average number of livestock units (as Turu calculate them) per adult is thirty-four, which is equivalent to almost seven cows or slightly more than eleven steers and bulls. There is little doubt that for most Turu this tax is the biggest expenditure of the year; the amount spent for consumption goods is certainly less and probably far less. In 1959 the Turu generally were urging the government to abandon the prevailing tax system, to be replaced by an across-the-board tax of 42 shillings per man.

The major source of cash income to pay taxes and buy goods in the external market is livestock sales in the beef market established by the colonial government. Other sources of income are principally cash crops, but some people also work in the mines at Geita and on the plantations of the northern provinces.

The produce market, organized under the native authorities, each year buys bulrush millet, maize, onions, castor beans, gum Arabic, honey, and a few other such products. In 1958 groundnuts (peanuts), produced mostly in Unyanganyi, were sold in the amount of 240 tons for a price of 197,200 shillings, and this crop has had a measurable effect on that livestock-poor area. Bulrush millet in the amount of 118 tons brought 45,000 shillings, and other crops brought smaller amounts. Since the produce market is not the only exit for cash crops, the actual amount of sale of such goods is, according to estimates, at least double the above figures. At the most, it might be guessed, sale of such crops over the whole district brings in no more than 300,000 shillings, most of which goes to Unyanganyi because of the value of its groundnuts exports.

While the number of livestock sold over the whole district varies from year to year and has risen gradually from about 7 to 15,000 head of cattle by 1960, in 1958 about 16,500 head were sold, along with 12,500 sheep and goats, for a total of 95,000 L.S.U. The income that year from livestock sales was 2,269,000 shillings. The average prices paid in 1958 for these animals were:

	Shillings
Full-grown cattle (slaughter stock)	152
Young males	73
Heifers	103
Goats	16
Sheep	13

If this income is divided by the number of taxpayers, the average annual income from sale of livestock in 1958 was 51 shillings, to which must be added any income from other sources.

These figures serve to establish that taxes are the largest part of expenditures, since income scarcely exceeds the amount that must be paid out in taxes. Livestock produce most of the income, and expenditures for consumption goods on the external market are commensurate with income—that is, they are small. The annual reports for the district frequently give estimates of average annual income, underlining its smallness. In 1951 it was estimated to be 77 shillings; in 1952, 62 shillings; in 1955, 56 shillings. In 1958 the report stated that people had little money to spend after paying taxes.

It would be a mistake to conclude, however, as the colonial government did, that the average annual expenditure and income of Turu as expressed in the external market are a true reflection of income and expenditures. It is most revealing to compare the situation in the internal market with that in the external market. This comparison is easily made by using the standard conversion rates among grain, livestock, and shillings that were discussed in Chapter 5. In the village of Utatuu, a sample of forty-two homesteads, each with an adult male head, shows that at the time the survey of livestock was made, the average homestead had livestock wealth in the amount of 1,716 shillings, of which 1,467 shillings was cattle and 249 shillings goat and sheep. During the year before the census, the expenditure of livestock, counting deaths as well as exchanges of all types, averaged 468 shillings and the average income from births and other exchanges was 409 shillings (for a net loss). During this same year these home-

steads sold forty-five cattle on the external market for an average income of
107 shillings—only a fraction of the total wealth and less than a quarter of total
income from livestock.

To these figures may be added the income from production of grain in fifty-
two homesteads in Utatuu, where in 1959, 3,914 *debes* were produced, which at
the usual market price of 5 shillings were worth 19,570 shillings, or 356 shillings
per homestead.

From this it may be concluded that in Utatuu the average annual income in
livestock and grain for 1958 per homestead was approximately 800 shillings,
which is equivalent to more than 100 dollars, yet taxes average only 7.14 dollars.
This figure does not take into account other income in the internal system from
the production of honey, tobacco, and other such commodities.

Utatuu is not an atypical community, and 1958 was not an atypical year; it is
therefore clear that income derived from the external market by the sale of cattle
is quite small, as is the amount of wealth diverted from the internal to the external economy. It is the desire to preserve the integrity of the internal economy
while participating in the external economy that explains the paradox of East
Africans, such as the Turu, apparently being reluctant to sell cattle while in
fact willingly selling quite a few. The Turu of today differs little in this respect
from his ancestors, about whom Reche commented that they were reluctant to
sell cattle but did sell some to obtain beads and cloth.

The question remains, however, how Turu can afford even this small annual
take-off—amounting to a maximum of about 7 per cent of all livestock—without
serious effects on the equilibrium of the internal market. The answer seems to
be that intake of meat is reduced. Even von Sick noted that goats and sheep
were more readily slaughtered for food than other animals, but Turu insist that
in precontact times, or before the beef markets became important, it was common for a man to kill a full-grown steer as a gesture to his friends. Today such
an action is almost unheard of. Many goats and sheep—and all cattle not used
for sacrifice, if they do not die first—are sold in the beef market.

Steers are the largest group sold in the beef market (50 per cent), followed
by culled cows and bulls. These animals are least valuable in the internal market.
Heifers consistently do not exceed 1 per cent of sales. Whether this change,
combined with the disappearance of blood eating, has had an adverse effect on
the health of the Turu is not clear.

It is perhaps also indicative of the continued vitality of the internal market
system that during times of famine the sales of both livestock and grain in the
external market drop as the amount of exchange in the internal economy increases and chances for profit rise. Since it is possible to buy grain in significant
amounts only from other Turu, and since the sellers of grain demand livestock,
this alteration is understandable.

The best test of the hypothesis that the traditional economy remains integrated
is to observe what happened when major assults were made on it. The annual
sale of about 7 per cent of the livestock is apparently not destructive of internal

market equilibrium in high-production years. It may be said that the system accommodates this degree of slack. Beginning some years ago the government, working on the assumption that famines are absolutely bad, decided to construct grain silos over the district, and by 1959 there were forty-nine of these. It was the practice to require that each homestead deposit three *debes* of grain a year in these silos as a hedge against famine. The Turu were indifferent to the regulation. On the one hand the assessment was small enough to cause little inconvenience to most people, but on the other hand these storage facilities interfered with the working of the economy by giving people who might otherwise be forced into the market a hedge against selling livestock.

The sharp rise in taxes in recent years shows signs of approaching the limits of what is tolerable to the people. The guess is that this rise takes so much of the income from sale of livestock that there is little left to purchase clothing and other desirable goods. In order to increase income, the only courses open are either to increase the sale of livestock, which was the intent of the tax, or force reduction of the tax, which is what Turu have seemed determined to do.

In the past, forced labor on district projects or pressure to get people to work on the plantations gave rise to reactions that culminated in elimination of force and replacement with voluntary recruiting—which, however, did not produce as many workers as desired. In 1948 the government, again as a hedge against famine, required the planting of cassava and sweet potatoes. The people were very reluctant to cooperate, did so under duress, and finally forced abandonment of the program. The government's face was saved by the discovery that wild pigs will stop at nothing to raid cassava patches.

The chief example of reaction to seriously intrusive pressure on the internal market was the culling or destocking program in the 1950's. It was explained earlier that the Turu began to sell livestock in the external market to a significant degree during the first years of the German occupation. Reche's list of prices paid for various kinds of animals leads to the conclusion that this early trade was of the same type going on in the internal market. That is, the price of cows was 12 to 20 rupees and the price of steers and bulls only 2 to 7 rupees, whereas in present external markets the males are more valued because they are larger. The 1926 provincial report (*Report of the Provincial Commissioners* 1926) shows that, compared to today, comparatively few cattle were sold.

During the second World War pressure was exerted to force the sale of beef cattle, thereby creating better acquaintance among Turu with beef markets. Today Turu almost universally express delight at having these markets because they make it possible to obtain cash to buy imported goods.

There was no real resistance to sales up to 1955, when 14,000 head were sold—the highest number to that date. The district commissioner noted that during 1955 the destocking campaign was on but was having no effect in reducing the number of livestock in the district. The rule that each man had to sell one of every ten cattle was designed to produce a 10 per cent reduction, but since most people own or hold less than ten cattle, the actual reduction was more like 5 per cent, which is less than the annual voluntary sale of 7 per cent. Later, one of the most disruptive effects of destocking was its interference with the loaning system *(Uriha)*, but since people holding loaned livestock are unlikely to have more than ten, this ratio initially did not deeply disturb loaning patterns.

In 1956, the ratio was raised to 1 in 6, and 20,426 cattle were sold—the largest number ever sold by the Turu in one year to that time and a number close to 10 per cent of the total cattle population. As a result there was powerful agitation against native authorities by the people demanding reduction of the ratio, some riots or gross noncooperation occurred, bribery of native authorities to record falsely the sale of cattle became rampant, and the cattle-loaning system was badly disrupted as livestock were sent back to their owners by holders who did not want the responsibility of culling them.

The extent of the agitation can be estimated by the restoration in 1957 of the old ratio of 1 in 10. That year 16,700 cattle were sold, and 16,350 were sold in 1958, after which the destocking program was abandoned. In 1959—the first year since 1954 during which destocking was not in effect—the number of animals sold dropped to 15,500, still a considerable rise over any previous year before destocking, representing a sale of about 7 per cent of the total animals.

Viewed strictly in market terms, the destocking campaign probably affected the internal market as a form of deflation. By making livestock rarer, it inhibited the normal flow of grain from those who had it to those who did not; the consequent drop in the price of grain caused grain holders to refrain from selling. Otherwise, as the Turu saw at the time, the program made the rich richer and the poor poorer, both because it made difficult the conversion of grain to cattle and because it made possible, as was earlier described, the manipulation of livestock entrepeneurs who commanded livestock capital.

Today there are signs of a breakdown in the system of standardized ratios of value of various kinds of livestock. Smaller stock are being devalued in relation to larger, to the extent that one occasionally finds the equation of five goats to a steer and ten to a cow. The reason seems to be a general increase in the number of small stock in relation to the large. In von Sick's time there were about seven cattle to five small animals; a recent census shows the ratio as about eight cattle to eleven small animals.

One interesting effect of linkage with the sterling economy is the growth of one method of money making dependent on the use of sterling coins in the internal market. This is the widespread practice by individual houses of producing beer for sale to other Turu.[1] Beer used to be considered a luxury; it was seen as a sacrifice of grain to entertain and honor friends. Now the rules of reciprocity are temporarily suspended, and beer may be sold in the sitting room of the house of manufacture, with people coming from the village and surrounding villages to buy it, although it is still also made to honor friends. For the day of the sale the house of the woman selling the beer becomes a saloon. In the area around Utatuu five different sales sometimes went on simultaneously, most

1. See Chapter 6 for a discussion of the etiquette of beer drinking in traditional modes.

commonly during the dry season, when the largest amount of grain was available. The government has attempted to control this commerce and to make a profit from it by selling licenses at the rate of 4 shillings per sale. In one area producers were required to bring the beer to the chief's headquarters, to be sold in a special place, thus insuring the collection of the tax. These sales of beer are viewed by most Turu as a way to extend grain supplies and are resorted to mainly by the poor for that purpose, although the wealthy may also sell beer simply to make some money. In former days the poor would have had to sell their labor for the same purpose.

Since the sale of beer is considered a short-range investment for a quick profit, it is usual not to use one's own supplies of grain to make the beer but to buy grain. The method by which the profit is made is theoretically simple, although the manufacture of the beer is not. Usually a whole *debe*—forty pounds of bulrush millet—is processed to make two and a half *debes*, or ten gallons, of liquid. A *debe* of bulrush millet is worth 5 shillings at most times, and it is reckoned that the beer produced can be sold for a total of 20 shillings. It is doled out at 10 cents (.10 shilling) a cup or 1 shilling a gourd. The aim of the seller is to convert the resultant 20 shillings into four *debes* of grain, thus making a profit of three *debes*, not counting the labor of production and sale. If he has to pay the license fee, his profit is reduced to about two *debes*, but commonly people hold illicit sales to avoid this cost.

A survey of the village of Utatuu showed that in the sixty-eight houses investigated, 1,553 shillings were realized in one year from the sale of beer made from 143 *debes*, for an average return of 11 shillings per *debe*. The reason for this comparatively low profit seems to be that the producer is not usually able to hold the line against his own passion for beer and against the rules of etiquette, even though the actual sale is usually run with businesslike efficiency. Nevertheless, for the underproducer of grain, this method is a desirable means of extending grain supplies to the harvest. For many people profits from beer sales make the difference between abject poverty and at least subsistence.

It is difficult to say precisely what happens to the internal economy as a result of beer sales. One has the impression that the beer and money are merely passing around in opposite directions, each man selling beer for a profit at one time and then losing it to buy beer for himself at another. The typical person will not spend more than 1 or 2 shillings on any day (although there are always one or two who spend much more). And in one sense this round is all there is to the practice, although in another sense there is more.

In the course of the redistribution of money and beer—which is like the exchange of grain and livestock or women and livestock—the net gain is a redistribution of grain to the poor when they need it, while the wealthy are paying for the labor put into the manufacture of beer. Each house is equipped to make beer—that is one of the women's prime tasks—but beer is not steadily available, even though in great demand, because it spoils if it is not immediately consumed. The net effect of the introduction of this practice is certainly to give the poor a greater chance to avoid becoming poorer by providing a method of converting female labor to grain. The system of beer sales, therefore, has a leveling effect.

The continued integrity of the traditional Turu economy can be observed in other ways. Initially Turu had no inclination to work outside the area, but over the years the government has encouraged them to do so, and in the census of 1957 about 20,000 Turu were living outside the tribal area. As has been shown, such devices as taxation have encouraged this emigration, which is usually for short-term contracts of about five months. At various times serious famines have encouraged emigration, although the tendency in the case of most famines is rather to create a decline in emigration as the internal economy tightens up.

The figures available show that in 1935, 981 Turu and Iramba went out to work, mostly on the sisal estates in the east. No breakdown is available to show how many of these were Turu, but since by far the greater number of the laborers went to the sisal estates, and since it was specifically stated that the Turu were undesirable for this work, it is fair to conclude that very few were Turu. By 1947 the picture had changed considerably; it was higher, since all who left to work did not contract to do so. During the 1950's there are figures to show that in 1952 there were 2,872 Turu under contract, 4,059 in 1956, 1,807 in 1957, and 2,732 in 1958.

As is clear from the foregoing, going to *manamba* ("my number") or *malu* (for Moshi-Arusha Labour Union) is popular, but there is no sign of a steady increase in emigrants. In fact, there is radical variation, in accordance with fluctuations in the internal economy.

The major portion of recruits are young men, usually unmarried (although in the 1950's an increasing number of wives accompanied their husbands), who have no intention of taking up permanent residence on the plantations but go there to make a stake with which they hope to buy good clothing or invest in marriage and livestock when they return home. A look at the conditions of the Turu at one of the estates in the north that employs a large number showed that they live in filth because they refuse to spend any of their wages on their temporary quarters, saving the money to take home. These Turu attempt to maintain the customs of the homeland. It is significant that in the Turu villages today, among the men who are carrying on the traditional economy and society, there are very few who have not at one time worked on the estates or in the mines. Those that do not come back are viewed as unique.

Among the Turu living and acting in the traditional way, there are differences in attitudes and degrees of involvement in the external market and society. The poor may have poor clothes and great difficulty in paying taxes or feeding their families, while the rich may have fancy clothes and even such luxuries as flashlights, cigarette lighters, folding chairs, and the like. However, these rich are as committed to the traditional system as the poor.

Among the extreme traditionalists, involvement in the external market is scorned. They sell cattle to the beef market only because they must pay taxes, and they are liable to be the ones brought before the court on tax-evasion charges, even though they have plenty of money. They do not wash their clothes, being unconcerned with European habits. The richest man in UnyahatI was described with contempt by some young men because he was dirty and ill-clad by Western standards. Such men believe that they continue to be rich because they do not commit the foolish error of selling more than the minimum number of animals in the external market and because they are uninterested in buying any imported goods other than the bare essentials.

On the other side there is a small, but no doubt growing, segment that includes mostly young men, whose aspirations to change exceed their chances of doing so. Probably one of the most extreme of these is one who has great plans to get rich by expanding agricultural production, both by acquiring more land and by using machines. The hallmark of such progressives is their lack of interest in cattle. Another of these young men has tried to open a store to sell cloth and other goods, in the manner of foreign traders. He has also turned a large area of his land to the growing of castor beans, which many Turu raise to a small extent to sell on the external market. Another has self-consciously built himself a house altogether outside the Turu style and on the European model, plants vegetables in tie-ridged plots as recommended by the agricultural department, and is acting as middleman in the sale of grain by villagers to the foreign traders. He scorns cooperation with his agnates in most matters, even though he lives on the fringes of the village near them, and he is a strong Catholic.

None of these men is successful. Unlike those Turu who have succeeded in abandoning the traditional system, they have not the education or other resources to remove themselves from dependence on the traditional economy, and their efforts, while earnest, are futile. The one large-scale effort at farming with machines, which was begun some years ago by a small number of Turu chiefs, ended in failure. It is easy to see that in all these cases the lack of a cash crop of sufficient potential has prevented the achievement of expanded production and income.

While von Sick was insightful on many matters, his enthusiasm for development programs in the early colonial period blinded him. He predicted that when the railroad edged north into Singida, there would be a blooming of trade as livestock and grain from the "bread basket"—as he described UnyatUrU— moved out. The railroad came to Singida in 1933 and eventually lost any value with the decline of the mines to the north of Singida, so that in 1947 it was removed. Today the abandoned railway embankment stands as a forlorn reminder of the failure of large hopes. Some Turu children literally grew up in the shadows of the smoke of the locomotives without ever having become more integrally involved with the economy they represent than if they had never come.

Has the system been subjected to any inroads that are potentially disruptive in some more significant way than has been discovered? The passion for luxury imports is great, and the impulse to sell livestock to obtain them is strong. The cattle-loaning system, which seemed to have been adequately reconstituted since

1957, did suffer severe disruption, and today many Turu insist that it was so severely damaged that it has not recovered. The new type of witchcraft *(Utambo)* is a sign of widespread use of ad hoc relations of importance with people outside the traditional lineage system. More children are receiving schooling (Plate 9.3), at least to the point of becoming literate. In 1958 there were sixty-one primary schools in all of Singida; three middle schools were proposed to supplement the existing six. There were 7,663 primary pupils; if we calculate these as being for the most part boys and if we estimate the number below sixteen years at 44,000 boys and girls, the number represents a large percentage of eligible boys (about 30 per cent). Cursory observation verifies the large number of children going to school, at least around the urban centers.

In addition to these phenomena, the doubling of population since von Sick's time must be taken into consideration, although it is not as important a factor here as in most places because the Turu had plenty of room for expansion. The lowering of circumcision age for boys and the enforcement of the law against marriage of girls before puberty will have an effect in decreasing the supply of women relative to men of marriageable age, thus decreasing the opportunities for polygyny. The number of livestock sold in the external market has increased steadily over the years, although the number of animals has also increased with new medical techniques and protection against raiding. The inevitable rise in taxes related to increasing governmental needs and services puts great pressure on people to sell more livestock.

All these factors and others suggested in 1960 that the Turu traditional system had reached a critical stage of conflict with the larger economy of Tanzania and with the new aspirations of the people, so that some sort of break had to come. The Turu desired the change and the government demanded it. But the fact was that there was no basis for change, one that would not only increase income, but would also be the basis for an economy as securely adapted to the conditions of Singida as the old. Perhaps this was the message of the schoolboy's painting illustrated in Plate 9.4, in which the subject was altogether traditional, even though it was portrayed in a completely foreign medium.

More recently information from Singida [2] indicates that change is indeed occurring, but at a predictably slow pace. Settlement patterns and production patterns remain traditional, and the literacy campaign has collapsed. On the other hand, the growing of groundnuts, castor beans, and vegetables, in an incipient stage in 1960, has increased appreciably—along with the sale of cattle for meat —partly as a result of government pressure. Agricultural people have been unable to find a major cash crop for the area because of the patchy nature of the soil, which allows one person to grow castor beans or groundnuts while his neighbor cannot.

Perhaps this steady increase in the production of small cash crops and subsistence vegetables, along with the growth in meat marketing, will eventually lead to a quantum jump in the form of the economic system. Time will tell.

2. Personal communication from Marguerite Jellicoe.

PLATE 9.3
Boys and Girls of a Primary-School Band near Ikungi

PLATE 9.4
Watercolor Painting by a Turu Student. The main themes of Turu life are summarized: women as producers, men as guardians of the wealth, represented by cattle.

REFERENCES CITED

BARTH, F.
  1959. "Segmentary Opposition and the Theory of Games: A Study of Pathan Organization." *Journal of the Royal Anthropological Institute*, London, 89: 5–2.
BAUMANN, OSCAR
  1894. *Durch Massailand zur Nilquelle*. Berlin: Dietrich Reimer.
BOHANNAN, PAUL
  1964. *Africa and Africans*. Garden City, New York: Natural History Press.
BURLING, ROBBINS
  1962. "Maximization Theories and the Study of Economic Anthropology." *American Anthropologist*, 64: 810–813.
BURTT, D. M.
  1936. "List of Plant Names in Vernaculars." *Transactions of the Royal Entomological Society*, London, 84: 553–570.
DALTON, GEORGE
  1961. "Economic Theory and Primitive Society." *American Anthropologist*, 63: 1–25.
DESHLER, WALTER
  1963. "Cattle in Africa: Distribution, Types and Problems." *Geographical Review*, 52–58.
EADES, N. W., AND W. H. REEVE
  1938. *Explanation of the Geology of Degree Sheet No. 29 (Singida)*. Dar es Salaam: Government Printers.
EAST AFRICAN STATISTICAL DEPARTMENT
  1958. *Tanganyika Population Census, 1957*. Nairobi: East African Statistical Department.
FIRTH, RAYMOND
  1951. *Elements of Social Organization*. London: Watts & Co.
FORTES, MEYER
  1953. "The Structure of Unilineal Descent Groups." *American Anthropologist*, 55: 17–41.
GRAY, ROBERT F.
  1960. "Sonjo Bride-Price and the Question of African 'Wife Purchase.'" *American Anthropologist*, 62: 32–37.
HERSKOVITS, M. J.
  1948. *Man and His Works*. New York: Alfred A. Knopf.
JONES, W. O.
  1961. *Food and Agricultural Economies of Tropical Africa*. Food Research Institute Studies, 2: 1. Stanford, Cal.

LEACH, E. R.
1965. *Political Systems of Highland Burma*. Boston: Beacon.

MAIR, LUCY
1962. *Primitive Government*. London: Pelican.
1965. "How Small-Scale Societies Change." *Penguin Survey of the Social Sciences 1965*. London: Penguin.

MURDOCK, G. P.
1949. *Social Structure*. New York: Macmillan.
1959. *Africa: Its People and Their Culture History*. New York: McGraw-Hill.
1967. "Ethnographic Atlas: A Summary." *Ethnology*, 6 (2) 109–236.

RADCLIFFE-BROWN, A. R.
1952. *Structure and Function in Primitive Society*. New York: Free Press.

RECHE, OTTO
1914. *Zur Ethnographie des abflusslosen Gebiets*. Hamburg: Hamburg Institute.

REPORT OF THE PROVINCIAL COMMISSIONERS
1926. Dar es Salaam: Government Printers.

RIGBY, PETER
1966. "Gogo Kinship and Concepts of Social Structure." *East African Institute of Social Research Conference Papers*, January, 1–14.

SARGANT, WILLIAM
1957. *Battle for the Mind*. Baltimore: Penguin.

SCHNEIDER, HAROLD K.
1964. "A Model of African Indigenous Economy and Society." *Comparative Studies in Society and History*, 7: 30–55.

STANLEY, HENRY M.
1891. *In Darkest Africa*, Vol. 20 New York: Scribner's.

STUHLMAN, F.
1894. *Mit Emin Pascha ins Herz von Afrika*. Berlin: D. Reimer.

TAEUBER, I. B.
1949. *The Population of Tanganyika*. Lake Success, New York: U.N. Dept. of Social Affairs, Population Division.

TEMPLES, PLACIDE
1959. *Bantu Philosophy*. Paris: Presence Africaine.

VON LUSCHAN, F.
1898. "Beitrage zur Ethnographie des abflusslosen Gebiet in Deutsch-Ost-Afrika." In C. W. Werther, *Die Mittleren Hochlander des Nördlichen Deutsch-Ostfrika*. Berlin: Puetel.

VON SICK, EBERHARD
1916. "Die Waniaturu (Walimi)." *Baessler-Archiv*, Leipzig and Berlin, pp. 1–42.

WEBER, MAX
1947. *The Theory of Social and Economic Organization*. New York: Free Press.

WHITE FATHERS
1915. *The Rimi or Turu*. Unpublished manuscript translated from the French, c. 1915, to be found at the Catholic Mission, Makiungu in Singida and in the library of the author.

WILLIAMS, ROBIN
1960. *American Society*, second edition revised. New York: Alfred A. Knopf.

GLOSSARY

afIkani:	Adherent to indigenous religious system; not a Moslem or Christian.
aramu:	Term of reference by men for the wives of their classificatory brothers.
baisa:	First-born cow; a woman who has had one child.
caro:	Assembly of elders to decide the guilt or innocence of a person accused of a crime.
cwI:	Dry season.
dahwa:	Decorated gourd used to carry ground millet.
daiya:	Mother's sister's son (direct and classificatory).
debe:	Four-imperial-gallon tin.
dIlanda:	Beaded anklets worn by a woman who has had a child.
halmashauri:	Village head man.
ifaha:	Twins; also name of dance in which young men and women act out a feud between lineages.
ifampa:	Bead belt worn by women as a fertility symbol.
ifanda:	Cattle road or path.
igolyo:	Paddle used by circumcision initiates to frighten women.
igwe ra usiera:	Stone platform for grinding grain.
iɣafIŋgo:	Fence between cattle yard and house.
iɣembe:	Hoe.
ihaka:	Forest.
ikiIka:	Ritual cleansing; ritual cleansing rite.
ikita:	Corral fence.
ikumbu:	Men's house.
irika:	Indicates relationship at some genealogical level.
irongo:	Ant-hill mud.
ikuta:	Ghee (clarified butter).
ikuja (ma-):	Pasture.
ilanda:	Preharvest night dance.
imaa:	Uprightness, courage. Rites of *imaa*.

1. Normally only the singular form of any noun is given. In the case of living things, where the singular prefix is *mU-*, the plural is formed by replacing the singular prefix with *a-* (or, in cases where the term is Swahili or Swahiliized, with *wa-*), e.g. *mUɣanga* becomes *aɣanga*.

imaa ra ŋimba: House *imaa*. Ceremony of women's secret society.

imaa ra nyUmba: Lion *imaa*. Ceremony of women's secret society.

iseke: White sandy soil.

isuna: Southernmost Turu settlement, made up of a collection of small clans.

itIma: Cutting; rite of cutting the relationship between a married pair thought to be too closely related and thereby mystically prevented from having children.

itoɣoo: Gray sandy soil.

itUmbi: High place; village.

ianda: Land that has been fertilized and worked.

ixanda: Liver; a fertility rite for girls about to marry, in which they eat ritually prepared beef liver.

ixombi: Cow that no longer bears.

jamaa: Family (from Swahili).

jumbe: Word for chief under German rule.

kanga: Rectangular-print cloth used by women for fancy dress.

kaniki: Rectangular black amerikani cloth used by women for everyday dress.

kanzu: Arab type of gown, used by men for fancy dress.

kIhawa: Threshing place.

kIImla: The Pleiades.

kIIImbIda: Marching dance.

kImaI: One of the bewitching rocks near Ihanja.

kInyamwango: House door.

kInyataUrU: The Turu language.

kIreka: Divorce (leavetaking).

kIrImi: Turu, i.e., Rimi, language.

kIsaywida: Orange stone necklace.

kItikU: Rainy season.

kIu: Grain-storage bin.

kiungU: Avenging ancestral spirit.

kUkU: That class of kin that includes grandparents and their ancestors as well as mother's brothers and their descendants.

laŋilaŋga: Large-seed form of millet.

majemba: Large-seed form of millet.

maɣema: The Thinker, one of the trinity of Turu high gods (see Matunda and Mahanya).

mahaage: Cow peas.

mahanya: The Speaker, one of the trinity of Turu high gods (see Mahanya and Maɣema).

mahukuma: Squash.

majIɣana: A voluntary act of altruism.

malIjanga: Morning meal.

malu:	Moshi-Arusha Labor Union; a term used by Turu to refer to the plantations in northern Tanzania.
mama:	The wife of any kUkU.
mamamai:	Squash.
manamba:	Literally "my number," borrowed from English to refer to work outside the tribal area in the mines or plantations.
masuki:	Gourds.
matuli:	Meat relish eaten with staple porridge.
matumbatU:	Tobacco.
matunda:	The Creator (usually referred to as Mungu-Matunda), one of the trinity of Turu high gods (see also Mahanya and Maγema).
maya:	Skimmed milk.
mkee:	Inner room.
mbojo:	Lion man.
mbUγa:	Marsh.
mbUri:	Goat (generic).
mbUya:	Friend; lover, when used in reference to a person of the opposite sex.
mbeyu:	Clan.
marimbe:	A vegetable relish.
maxanda:	A vegetable relish.
maxoxo:	Dried porridge.
matambi:	Kind of necklace.
mlxoa:	Blessed straps.
moyo:	Heart; the spirit in a living thing.
mpahi:	Castrated goat.
mpembu:	Bewitching rock near Ihanja.
mplγl:	Charm against bewitchment.
mpUma (Puma):	Place in the center of Wahi subtribe containing a collection of small clans; also baboon.
mpUmbUi:	The western area of the NyahatI clan.
mtemi (wa-):	Word for chief under the British.
mtambo:	One who practices Utambo sorcery.
mUfambajo:	Oarlike tool used for planting.
mufanda:	Funeral debate; path.
mUfita:	Corral gate; also used to refer to lineage or clan.
mUfoγoo:	Albizzia (a type of tree).
mUfumbu:	Miombo trees.
mUγanga:	Diviner.
muγosia:	Man.
mUgunda (ml-):	Farm land.
mUgUngusu:	Bewitching rock near Ihanja.
mUhogo:	Cassava.

mUhUi:	Type of tree near which the main rites of Lion *imaa* are held.
mUhUngu:	An initiate of either circumcision or clitoridectomy rites (*ngoi*).
mUhUri:	Man's name; name of the main lineage of Utatuu.
mUjaɣamba:	Young bull.
mUjikU:	Young steer.
mUjUkUU:	Also called *mwifwa*, refers to grandsons and all their descendants as well as sister's sons and all their descendants.
mUkahiU (a-):	A member of the kahiU clan.
mUkUU:	A term for the chief male patrilineal relative, such as the father, the eldest brother, or the chief descendant of the founder of a lineage or clan; the great one.
mUlade:	A semi-domesticated tree.
mUmbll:	Name of the village of the People of NtUnduu which is adjoining to Utatuu.
mUrUngu (a-):	Ancestor, usually contracted to *mUngu*, in which form it is the same as the word used for the Creator.
mUntama:	Maize.
mUnyaa:	Euphorbia tirucalli.
mUnyahatl:	A person of the Nyahati clan.
mUnyambee:	A female initiate in the *Unyambee* menstrual seclution rite.
mUnyampaa:	An elder person; a person of authority; "sir."
mUnyatUrU:	A Turu person
mUnyiŋanyi:	A person of the Nyiŋanyi subtribe.
mUŋlnya:	Precircumcised youth.
mUpanda:	From "paths," the meeting in which members of wife-giving and wife-receiving lineages meet to settle compensation for depreciation on the wife during the term of her marriage.
mUramwane:	Sibling-in-law.
mUrlmi:	A Rimi (i.e., Turu) person.
mUroɣi:	Female witch.
mUrimU:	Secret; specifically the secrets and secret objects of *imaa*.
mUrongacaro:	A legal expert.
mUsae:	Cattle yard or corral.
mUsUngUa:	Albizzia.
mUsUta:	Cowhide bag used as a standard measure.
mUtatuu:	A Tatuu person.
mUtemea:	Male witch.
mUtlnampafo:	The youngest brother.
mUtUfotUfo:	Euphorbia matabeleuse.
mUuna:	Sibling (direct and classificatory, e.g., father's brother's sons and daughters).
mUxai:	A forceful or strong man; a leader.
mUxaikUU:	A female leader.

mUxatI:	Middle; a middle son,—that is, one born between the eldest and the youngest (actually *va mUxatI*, "of the middle").
mUxema:	Woman; wife.
mUxwane:	Parent-in-law.
mUyi:	Arrow; fee.
mungu:	Swahili word for God, now used by Turu with their word for the Creator, Matunda. Hence they speak of Mungu-Matunda.
mwana:	Child; also doll.
mwanangwa:	Assistant to subchief under the British.
mwandU:	Compensation for injury to a person; baobab tree.
mwango:	Sitting room of a house.
mweri:	Moon.
mwifwa:	See *mUjUkUU*, of which *mwifwa* is an alternate term.
mwimiimi:	Spirit that is disembodied; the spiritual equivalent in a dead man to the heart (moyo) of a living man.
mwirUwane:	"My jealous one," a term of address used by one co-wife for another.
mwirwana:	A person of the subtribe of Wilwani.
ndama:	Heifer.
ndUγU:	Relative; general term for all distant members of one's clan.
ngaa:	War helmet made of lion fur or baboon fur.
ngoi:	Puberty rite of passage (clitoridectomy and circumcision).
njaγamba:	Bull.
njikU:	Steer.
njUγUda:	Sanction for affront to authority.
nkambakU	Male sheep.
nkuhl:	Red soil.
nsio:	Grain grindstone.
nsUa:	Wooden trough used as a standard measure.
ntUi:	Beer.
ntusio:	A man born next to another.
ntUnduu:	Man's name; also name of lineage in village of MumbII adjoining Utatuu.
nxama:	Large steer.
nxani:	Words; evil words.
nxomba:	Thick porridge served to sick people and circumcision initiates.
nxoo:	Sheep (generic).
nxwe:	Marriage.
nyonyi:	Vegetable relish served with staple millet porridge.
nyUmba:	Woman's house; *nyUmba nI nkUU* means the senior house or great house; *nyUmba nI nyUUii* means the junior house or houses, or little houses.

ŋangU:	Sanctioning ritual done by women of a village against one of the group who has injured her child.
ŋeŋgo:	An instrument combining the features of an axe and machete.
ŋgUata:	Male goat.
ŋimba:	Lion.
ŋombe:	Generic for cattle.
ŋombe a nduγU:	"Cow of relatedness."
ŋombe a Usale:	"Cow of seriation."
ŋombe a Urii:	"Cow of the bed."
panga:	Machete.
rugaruga:	Assistant to subchief under the British.
sato mUrimU:	Type of secret object used in house *imaa*.
shuka:	White rectangular cloth worn by men over the lower half of the body.
sIIra:	Ground squirrel.
sori a ŋombe:	Type of trough used as standard measure; literally, cattle trough.
sufuria:	Heating utensil.
sunja:	Man's name; also name of village of the People of Munyankonde in the NyahatI clan near Ikungi.
tata:	Father (direct and classificatory, e.g., father's brother).
tita:	Bewitching rocks near Puma.
uγai:	Porridge; the staple food.
unkwama:	Stored grain.
Ufeto:	Lightning.
Uγokie:	Ritual purity.
Ujumya ngoi:	Dance done at circumcision imitating coitus.
UkahiU:	Country of the kahiU clan.
UkUhi:	Finger millet.
UkUU:	Great; large (in a social sense).
UnyahatI:	Country of the NyahatI clan.
Unyambee:	The rite of menstrual seclusion for pubertal girls.
UnyatUrU:	The country of the NyatUrU.
Unyiŋanyi:	The Country of the nyiŋanyi subtribe.
Uriha:	The process of loaning cattle.
UrII:	Bed.
UrImi:	The Country of the Rimi (i.e., Turu).
Uroγoo:	Spear battle.
Usale:	Seriations.
UsUŋgU:	Circumcision dance done by initiates in the healing hut.
Usuke:	Women's hair style.
Utatuu:	The Country of the Tatuu lineage.
Utambo:	Sorcery conducted by a person not of the village against a person in the village.

Uvee:	Bulrush millet or pennisetum.
Uxatl:	"Of the middle"; said of all brothers not the oldest or youngest.
vahi:	The Country of the People of the Wahi subclan.
wahi:	The People of the southern subclan living in Vahi.
waigU:	Father's sister's husband.
waiɣembe:	Loan partners; special friends who have exchanged hoes (*iɣembe*) and other valuables.
wakili:	Subchief under the British.
wilwana:	The Country of the northern subclan.
wijue:	The name of the Level III lineage of the KahiU clan, of which the village of Utatuu is a part.
witU:	Term used by men of the same village to refer to each other; its connotation is that they have a relation of reciprocity.
wlxhul:	Stick battle.
xaya:	Homestead.
yiu:	Mother (direct and classificatory, e.g., mother's sister, father's sister).

INDEX

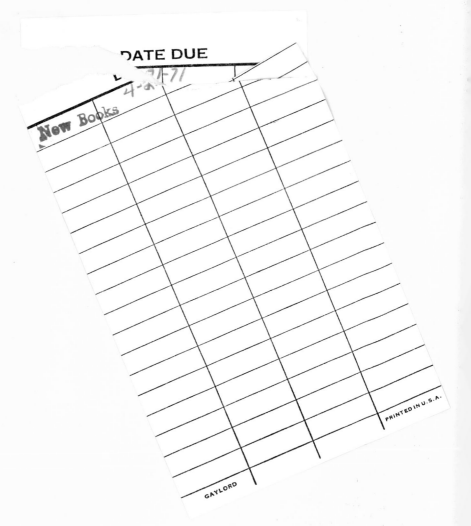